# To Tell the Truth

# To Tell the Truth

## My Life as a Foreign Correspondent

Lewis M. Simons

ROWMAN & LITTLEFIELD
*Lanham • Boulder • New York • London*

Published by Rowman & Littlefield
An imprint of The Rowman & Littlefield Publishing Group, Inc.
4501 Forbes Boulevard, Suite 200, Lanham, Maryland 20706
www.rowman.com

86-90 Paul Street, London EC2A 4NE

British Library Cataloguing in Publication Information Available

**Library of Congress Cataloging-in-Publication Data**

Names: Simons, Lewis M., author.
　Title: To tell the truth : my life as a foreign correspondent /
　　Lewis M. Simons.
　Description: Lanham : Rowman & Littlefield, [2022] | Includes index. |
　　Summary: "At a time when journalism is under attack from Trumpian
　　charges of "lying press," my 50 years as a foreign correspondent in Asia
　　demonstrate that without journalists who risk their lives, American
　　democracy is in danger of shattering"-- Provided by publisher.
　Identifiers: LCCN 2022025841 (print) | LCCN 2022025842 (ebook) | ISBN
　　9781538173169 (cloth) | ISBN 9781538173176 (epub)
　Subjects: LCSH: Simons, Lewis M. | Journalists--United States--Biography. |
　　Foreign correspondents--United States--Biography. | Foreign
　　correspondents--Asia--Biography. | Asia--Press coverage.
　Classification: LCC PN4874.S5163 A3 2022  (print) | LCC PN4874.S5163
　　(ebook) | DDC 070.4/332092 [B]--dc23/eng/20220627
　LC record available at https://lccn.loc.gov/2022025841
　LC ebook record available at https://lccn.loc.gov/2022025842

*For My Grandchildren*
*and*
*For All Who Value the Free Press*

*The first mission of a newspaper is to tell the truth as nearly as the truth may be ascertained.*

—Eugene Meyer, Publisher, *Washington Post*

# Contents

Foreword                                                               xi

Acknowledgments                                                        xiii

Introduction                                                           xv

Chapter One: Murder in Manila                                          1

Chapter Two: The Prince of Paterson                                    37

Chapter Three: A Lost and Found Decade                                 45

Chapter Four: Total Bullshit                                           51

Chapter Five: Tet                                                      75

Chapter Six: Quiet No More in Malaysia                                 95

Chapter Seven: My Favorite Dictator                                    109

Chapter Eight: The Council, the Papers, and the *Post*                 117

Chapter Nine: Molested at Birth                                        129

Chapter Ten: Delhi Wallah                                              141

Chapter Eleven: Excess Baggage                                         159

Chapter Twelve: Stirring up Trouble in India                           177

Chapter Thirteen: Birth and Death in Bangkok                           191

Chapter Fourteen: Knight Rider to the Rescue                           203

Chapter Fifteen: Filling the Dumpling                                  215

Chapter Sixteen: The Other Chinese                                     229

Chapter Seventeen: Time to Go                                          237

Chapter Eighteen: Holding the Line                    247

Chapter Nineteen: Crossing the Line                   253

Index                                                 261

About the Author                                      277

THE DALAI LAMA

## FOREWORD

Journalists have an important role to educate and inform the public, as an observer and in an objective manner. That is what Lew Simons, whom I have had the opportunity to meet several times, has been practicing while covering developments in different parts of the world. His revealing book, To Tell the Truth, is a testament to his application of this approach.

However, journalists too sometimes face a moral dilemma whether to continue remaining an observer or be involved with the subject they are covering. The author details one such experience in the book, which he related to me in one of our meetings, too. While on a reporting trip across Tibet, he found a Buddhist monk, whom he had befriended on an earlier visit, to be gravely ill. His human feelings triumphed over his journalistic need to be not involved and secured treatment that saved the monk's life. From a spiritual perspective too this response is appropriate because of the pure motivation behind it.

5 August 2022

# Acknowledgments

I could not have written this book without Carol, my wife and the love of my life. She kept me going through the isolated covid years. And she caught slips that no one else could.

My gratitude to editor and friend Alan Rinzler. He shaped my scattershot ideas into a coherent story of my half-century of work.

Warmest thanks to my journalist friends: Jonathan Krim generously provided insight and direction. Barry Hillenbrand kept me on the narrow rails of fact. Pete Carey polished our work together on the Philippines investigation for the San Jose *Mercury News*. Jay Branegan and Connie Bond provided over-arching context to the narrative. Photographer and tech maven Alec Dann restored the vintage snapshots included in these pages.

Barbara Meade, co-founder of Washington's iconic Politics & Prose bookshop, was among the first to read the manuscript and her enthusiasm was contagious. Many thanks.

My sincere appreciation to Diane Nine who, finding merit in this book, became my agent and patiently guided it to fruition.

LMS

# Introduction

"You mean you don't *have* to be here?" the baby-faced marine blurted. "Shit, sir, you're fuckin' crazy!"

He had a point.

Unlike him, I did *not* have to be there. A handful of years older than he, I was a civilian. My wife was waiting for me in Saigon, a ninety-minute flight away. Yet, here I was, having just stumbled off the ramp of a rolling US Air Force cargo plane as it disgorged weapons for him and the six thousand or so other marines besieged at Khe Sanh.

As I splashed into his muddy foxhole, I wondered, *Why am I in this god-forsaken place, squatting alongside this rain-drenched kid in South Vietnam's red dirt? Am I in fact crazy?* It was not the first time I'd wondered.

Days earlier, I had walked into the ancient, walled citadel of Hue. It, too, was under siege by North Vietnamese and Viet Cong fighters, initiating the benchmark Tet Offensive of 1968. As I neared the city's gate, thousands of terrified residents, lugging their worldly possessions, streamed past me, headed in the opposite direction. *Why was I there?*

Then there was the day, heart thudding and sweat stinging my eyes, I followed a dozen marines across a mined rice paddy. The man a few feet ahead of me suddenly froze. I heard a soft click seconds before a mine exploded, blowing off both his legs, splattering him with his own blood, flesh, and bone. Brain-fogged, I watched him bleed to death. *Why the hell was I there?*

There would be the Christmas Day, a few years later, when my pregnant wife came down with dengue fever and encephalitis in Malaysia while I was covering a *coup d'état* in Cambodia. And when India expelled me on five hours' notice, forcing me to abandon her and our two little girls to the not-so-tender mercies of the Delhi police. Again, *why was I there?*

I was there because that's what foreign correspondents do. They go places readers and viewers don't. They cover events that often put their lives in

## Chapter One

# Murder in Manila

The skinny kid nearly knocked me over as he darted past the narrow doorway just as I ducked in. He halted, pulled out a bottle of gasoline, touched a lighter to a rag hanging from it, and cranked his arm like a pitcher would.

A rifle shot cracked. The boy crumpled to the road and a crimson rose blossomed on the chest of his yellow T-shirt. The bottle slipped from his hand, jingled across the broken pavement, tapped my shoe, and fizzled out.

This kid, who couldn't have been more than sixteen or seventeen years old, was the first of eleven boys and men I saw shot to death that night. Hundreds were fighting—and losing—a lopsided battle against heavily armed soldiers guarding the palace where Philippines President Ferdinand E. Marcos was hiding.

The protestors had spent the day, August 31, 1983, engulfed in a flood of other furious Filipinos accompanying the corpse of Marcos's chief political rival, Benigno Aquino, Jr., to a suburban Manila cemetery. They believed that Marcos had ordered Aquino murdered as he stepped down from a plane ten days earlier, returning home from exile in the United States. They unleashed their outrage loudly and violently. I had trudged with them all day. I shared their belief, but I didn't say so. I had been trained to withhold my opinions. I was there to cover the story.

It was an extraordinary tale of murder and corruption. I would spend the next three years investigating the Aquino assassination and, with two colleagues at the San Jose *Mercury News*, Marcos's bleeding of the Philippines' national treasury. In the end, Aquino's aggrieved widow overthrew Marcos, and we won a Pulitzer Prize. Here's how it happened.

My wife Carol, my three young kids, and I were in San Jose, on home leave, that summer of 1983. I was chatting with the *Merc*'s managing editor, Jerry Ceppos, in his office when the Associated Press printer clattered to life, bells ringing. Ceppos tore off a slip of paper and handed me the bulletin.

Aquino had been gunned down in Manila.

1

"I'm going," I told Jerry. As I'd done numerous times previously and would do again and again, I left Carol and the children behind and took off for a distant place in turmoil.

Ninoy, as Aquino was known among nickname-obsessed Filipinos, was Marcos's most worrisome enemy. Marcos had held him for eight years in solitary confinement awaiting execution. An inveterately social creature, the isolated Ninoy slipped into depression and, in March 1978, suffered twin heart attacks.

Seizing the opportunity to get rid of Aquino without killing him—which would have been unpopular at home and in the United States—Marcos permitted him to fly to Texas for triple-bypass surgery.

He remained in the States for three years, living with his family in Boston and lecturing at Harvard and MIT. He made influential American friends and was, by his own account, content. Then the bug of political ambition bit again. He told friends back in Manila that he was weighing a run against Marcos in the next presidential election. Alarmed, they urged him not to return; that his life would be in serious danger.

But, after settling to his own satisfaction lingering doubts that unseating Marcos was worth suffering, or even dying, for, Aquino discarded all caution and left for home.

He stopped along the way in several Southeast Asian nations, sounding out leaders on his political plans, seeking their support. On the morning of August 21, 1983, he boarded China Airlines Flight 811 at Taipei's Chiang Kai-shek International Airport. A group of foreign correspondents accompanied him on the sparsely occupied Boeing 767, including American and Japanese TV network crews.

In what would be the last interview of his life, Aquino dispassionately advised the cameramen to be on their toes once the plane landed. "The action can become very fast," he said. "In a matter of three or four minutes, it could be all over you know. I have my bulletproof vest, but if they hit me on the head, there's nothing we can do there."

That was exactly how it played out. It was as insane and brutal a moment as could be seen in a *Die Hard* trailer.

Flight 811 landed at 1:03. p.m. and parked at Bay Eight of Manila International's sleekly curved, concrete-and-tinted-glass terminal building. The captain instructed the nervous passengers to remain seated "until the boarding party is on board." A jetway was rolled into place and three men in snug, tan army uniforms entered the cabin.

On film shot by ABC-TV correspondent Jim Laurie's cameraman, which I viewed many times afterward, a man wearing a name tag that identified him as Sgt. Arnulfo de Mesa approached Aquino. They shook hands.

"Here," de Mesa said politely, "please come with me."

Aquino bent to pick up a carryon bag and, as he did, de Mesa ran a hand along the curve of his back.

*He could feel the bulletproof vest.*

Ninoy stood and another soldier took his bag. A third man approached, and they guided Ninoy toward the front of the plane. The ABC camera caught fleeting shadows of fear and anxiety on his face.

He knew.

Instead of leaving through the jetway, the soldiers, now six of them, led Ninoy to a narrow, steel stairway, normally used by cleaning crews. Dressed in a fresh white safari suit, he was sandwiched front and back between them. Clumsily, they began the steep descent. The soundtrack played back voices screaming in Tagalog:

"Here he comes! I'll do it! I'll do it! I'll do it!"

Then, in the Cebuano dialect, a single word: *Pusila!* Shoot!

A pistol shot clapped. A high-powered .357 magnum bullet slammed into the back of Ninoy's head, tore through the soft tissue within, and burst out of his chin. He was dead when his face slammed into the tarmac.

Pandemonium. Five shots barked in rapid succession. One or more of them killed a man dressed in the blue coverall of an airport maintenance worker who was standing near the foot of the stairway. A pause of seventeen seconds. Then another salvo, perhaps twenty rounds, tore into the inert body of the man in blue. A voice, bellowing in Tagalog: *Tama na! Tama na!* That's enough!

The next evening, President Marcos went on the air and told Filipinos that the dead man in blue was named Rolando Galman. That was true. He also said the man was a small-time hoodlum. That, too, was true. And he had been hired by the Communist New People's Army to assassinate Aquino. That was a lie.

Galman was a stooge, bought off by the army to be present at the airport. Marcos's lie was intended to tamp down rumors already flaring across the Philippines that the army had carried out the killing to protect the ailing president from Aquino's planned challenge. That, I would learn in the course of nearly a year's reporting, was the truth.

I hadn't met Ninoy, but while he was in prison and I was with the AP, I had dinner with his wife, Corazon (Cory) at the mansion of mutual friends in Manila's tony Forbes Park. She was soft-spoken, pleasant, and left no particular impression on me. That would change as I came to know her over the years.

Others at the table that evening told tales of an unraveling relationship between the wealthy and powerful Marcos and Aquino families, from friendship and warmth to friction and bitterness. These stories helped inform my understanding of the murder at the airport.

Chua, whom Marcos called his godfather, was his biological father. The elder Ferdinand supported his namesake progeny, financially, politically, and legally well into adulthood. Chua and the Marcoses helped young Ferdinand hone his competitive, win-at-all-costs nature. He excelled at academics as well as the macho arts of wrestling, boxing, hunting, survival skills, and marksmanship. Achievement and infamy became Marcos's contradictory trademarks. In 1935, when he was eighteen, Marcos shot and killed a political opponent of Mariano's with a .22 caliber target pistol. Chua's influence helped him avoid trial for four years. By then, he'd graduated from law school. He was found guilty of murder and spent six months in jail, during which he wrote his own appeal. Chua bribed the judge handling the case, who dismissed the charge. Marcos returned to court the following day and took the oath making him an attorney.

The Philippines, at the time, was a colony of the United States, which had seized it from Spain in 1898. Ten hours after Japanese aircraft attacked Pearl Harbor on December 7, 1941, they struck the Philippines. Filipino guerrillas joined American troops in a gruesome three-year struggle to recapture the country. Marcos emerged from World War II with a spectacular military record: the most decorated Filipino soldier in the US armed forces. He was the Audie Murphy of the Philippines.

Four decades later, *New York Times* reporters Jeff Gerth and Joel Brinkley reported that University of Wisconsin historian Alfred W. McCoy had unearthed documents proving that all thirty-three of Marcos's decorations, among them the Medal of Honor and the Distinguished Service Cross, were fakes. Marcos had awarded them to himself. The US Army dismissed Marcos's claims to them as "fraudulent" and "absurd."

Coincidentally, years afterward, my younger daughter, Rebecca, became one of McCoy's students in Madison. And, in an ironic twist, "McCoy"—as in "the real McCoy"—was the most commonly used of Marcos's several nicknames.

One prominent American who bought into the Marcos myth was Ronald Reagan who, coincidentally perhaps, nurtured his own daydream of a heroic wartime career. One of his aides told my friend and colleague Stanley Karnow that in Reagan's wide eyes Marcos was "a hero on a bubblegum card he had collected as a kid." That naive self-deception paid handsome dividends to Marcos during the Reagan presidency. Until it didn't.

Marcos used his fake heroism to catapult himself into the presidency of the independent Philippines in 1965. He remained in office for twenty-one years, nine of them under martial law. He had more than 3,200 political opponents murdered or "disappeared." Mutilated bodies were dumped in public places to spread fear. Tens of thousands more opponents were jailed and tortured.

Imelda shared power with her husband in a conjugal dictatorship. She was a real-life rendering of the Dragon Lady, an alluring, avaricious, Asian femme fatale first portrayed in the *Terry and the Pirates* comic strip. During my decades in Asia, other women cast from the same mold took their places alongside strongmen rulers: Qiang Qing, Mao Zedong's vicious third wife; Madame Ngo Dinh Nhu, the manipulative sister-in-law of South Vietnam's bachelor Prime Minister Ngo Dinh Diem; Indonesian President Suharto's wife, Tien (also known as Madame Tien Percent for the minimum cut she demanded in government business deals).

Like the Qing Dynasty Empress Dowager Cixi, who effectively controlled China in the latter half of the nineteenth century, some of these women served principally as buffers against their husbands' critics. Others wielded power from behind the thrones occupied by their menfolk. Imelda Marcos sat proudly on her own throne.

Imelda married Ferdinand in 1954, when she was twenty-six and he a decade older. She was born into the wealthy and devoutly Roman Catholic Romuáldez family. But, by the time she and Ferdinand met, her branch of the family had fallen on hard times, and she was working as a salesgirl in a Manila department store.

Those years of financial deprivation instilled in Imelda an insatiable appetite for extravagance, which she never ceased to feed as First Lady. Her shopping sprees in the fashion centers of Europe and the United States were legendary. She would return home on jetliners chartered at government expense, their holds filled with crates of jewelry, antiques, art works, clothing, and her two greatest indulgences, shoes and black lingerie.

Imelda maintained a sense of humor about her acquisitiveness. Strolling through the homes of wealthy friends, admiring their possessions, one of her frequent hostesses told me, she would joke, "I'm in mining, you know." When these women dutifully pretended surprise, she would respond, "Yes, that's mine, and that's mine, and that's . . . " A onetime local beauty queen, Imelda was slender and, at five-foot-seven, the same height as Marcos. Fair-skinned and with a heart-shaped face, she wore her sleek, jet-black hair in a towering bouffant which, like her husband's pompadour, added height, if not stature. Marcos, in a common-law marriage at the time, was instantly smitten and launched a full-court courtship. His avid pursuit, garnished with flowers, gifts, and hints that one day she could become First Lady of the Philippines, persisted for ten days. On the eleventh, she consented. They were married in secret the next day and two weeks later in church. Marcos paid off his common-law wife, Carmen Ortega, and their three children. They and a fourth child, born shortly after Marcos and Imelda's nuptials, were hidden under the Philippines' huge bundle of smelly political laundry.

Ninoy Aquino, like Ferdinand Marcos, was a child prodigy, though from a far wealthier background. His family owned three vast haciendas in the heart of Luzon. He was Marcos's junior by fifteen years. Both attended the University of the Philippines. As brothers of the elite Upsilon Sigma Phi fraternity, even after their enmity was out in the open, they called each other "brod." Before Marcos swept Imelda off her feet, she and Ninoy briefly were an item. He dumped her and she never forgave him. As a gangly, big-eared kid of seventeen, Ninoy fast-talked his way into a to-kill-for assignment covering the Korean War for the *Manila Times*. He returned home to public acclaim and President Ramon Magsaysay assigned him the extraordinary mission of negotiating a peace treaty with the Communist Hukbalahap. The Huks were a fierce band of guerrillas who'd been staging a bloody rebellion against the Philippines government since World War II. Much as he had talked his way into Korea, the young Ninoy convinced the Huks to surrender. At twenty-two, a hero on two fronts, he was elected mayor of his hometown. "Ambitious" would have been more apt a nickname for Aquino than Ninoy. While others ran toward political goals, he sprinted. By 1972, when Marcos imposed martial law, he had established himself as the president's foremost challenger. Many Filipinos forecast that he soon would replace Marcos.

So, it came as no surprise when Marcos had him arrested. A military kangaroo court found him guilty on trumped-up charges of murder, illegal possession of firearms, and subversion, then sentenced him to death by firing squad. Marcos commuted the sentence but kept him locked up.

The contrast between the two wives, Cory Aquino and Imelda Marcos, was striking. At one of the occasional suppers she hosted at the Manila Hotel for select foreign correspondents (I was not among the chosen), Imelda gaily brushed off tittle-tattle she pretended was circulating, that she was a "hotsie patootsie." I hadn't heard the gossip. Most likely, she cooked it up at the table to draw more attention to herself. Whatever she may have meant (Imelda was a notorious word mangler, in the same league as George W. Bush), she certainly epitomized Filipina glamor. I never saw her in public when she was not expertly made up and coiffed; gowned in a gorgeous, butterfly-sleeved *terno*; fingers bejeweled; long nails lacquered in intricate French designs. When she appeared at rallies for her husband, she dazzled the crowds by serenading them with Tagalog pop tunes. Handing out a few pesos to the poor was another favorite ploy.

Cory, by comparison, defined simplicity. Her hair was bobbed, she wore large schoolmarmish glasses, an inexpensive wristwatch, no other jewelry or makeup, and, apparently, the least fashionable dresses and suits she could find. She referred to herself as "a plain housewife." And that's what she looked like.

But the appearance was deceptive. Cory came from the Cojuangco clan, one of the country's wealthiest lineages. Its great fortune was built on the backs of thousands of peasant laborers who raised sugar and rice at Hacienda Luisita, the family's fifteen-thousand-acre estate in Tarlac, the same province Ninoy came from. She had been a studious girl, valedictorian of her Catholic school class in Manila. When the family moved to the United States in 1946, Cory enrolled in exclusive Catholic girls schools in Philadelphia and New York, then graduated with a major in French and a minor in mathematics from the College of Mount Saint Vincent in the Bronx. She returned to the Philippines in 1953 and studied law before dropping out, as expected of women of her class, to marry Ninoy and raise their five children.

These, then, were the players. Like the Capulets and the Montagues, the Marcoses and the Aquinos were destined to clash. And their conflict, like that of Shakespeare's disputatious families, would climax in death. But the real-life tragedy in Manila, unlike the fictional one in thirteenth-century Verona, would prompt a glorious denouement. And the world, if only for a fleeting moment, would be thrilled.

Housewife and mom though she was, Cory was not a political neophyte. The years with Ninoy had taught her how to play her cards. She was assisted by her large extended family and a coterie of top-tier professionals she hired from around the world. Following the airport assassination, she had Ninoy's body embalmed and displayed in the couple's living room and opened the house to the public. I spent hours there, mingling with mourners, from taxi drivers to wealthy matrons, who streamed through the house, pausing to cross themselves at the glass casket. It went on for days and nights, around the clock. The corpse was dressed in the same white safari suit, stiff and blackened with dried blood, that Ninoy was wearing when he was shot. It brought to my mind images of Jackie Kennedy, stunned but composed, still dressed in her blood-stained pink outfit long after JFK had been slain in Dallas.

On the tenth day after the killing, the Aquinos had the body placed on a large, black, flatbed trailer truck. The bloody clothing was changed, and the battered face coated in pancake makeup. At the family's calculated instruction, a mortician had re-created bruises and the bullet hole in the chin. The makeshift hearse was garlanded with wreaths of yellow blossoms, yellow candles, and handwritten yellow signs expressing love and grief. Many in the horde—police estimated more than a million—wore yellow and waved yellow flags and placards. Yellow ribbons were wrapped around power poles and trees. Filipinos, for half a century torn between love for American culture and hatred for US political intervention, had chosen a 1973 American pop hit, "Tie a Yellow Ribbon Round the Ole Oak Tree," to express their sorrow. As I inched with the cortege past tall buildings, office workers showered us with confetti of shredded telephone Yellow Pages. This was the first time the

panel. At sixty-nine, "Rosie" Agrava enjoyed wearing above-the-knee skirts to display her chorus-girl legs. She insisted the board not spend public funds on room service and the air was growing heavy with the rich smells of adobo cooking in her suite's kitchen. My source, normally an impeccable dresser, had swapped suit and tie for a red polo, khakis, and sockless loafers. He'd stopped shaving and seemed to be suffering from cabin fever. Our steaks arrived and we ordered another round of martinis. He was relaxing. I hadn't expected to learn much. I was wrong. He started out with a bang: The board had concluded that the military was lying. Rolando Galman had not killed Aquino. This, in itself, was major news. But he went on. At the time Ninoy had announced his plans to return home, Marcos, unknown to the public, was gravely ill with lupus. The disease led to kidney failure. He had secretly undergone two transplants and was on regular dialysis treatment in a windowless, hospital-style room in the presidential palace. Those closest to him, especially Imelda and Eduardo Cojuangco, Jr., the president's intimate friend and adviser, believed he was near death. Cojuangco, who had capitalized on his friendship with Marcos to build a huge, largely illicit, fortune, was Cory Aquino's first cousin. He, like Imelda, enjoyed direct access to General Ver and his top commanders. So firm was the bond that they didn't need to order or even ask Ver to have the army assassinate Ninoy. They simply let drop circuitous comments.

As I listened raptly and took notes, my mind flashed on the tale of King Henry II and his nemesis, Thomas à Becket, the archbishop of Canterbury. "Will no one rid me of this turbulent priest!" a frustrated Henry raged at his courtiers. While not expressed as an order, it prompted four knights anxious to prove fealty to their monarch to murder Thomas.

My contact and I stared at each other across the table, and I said he seemed to be telling me that he and his colleagues had determined who had ordered Aquino killed. But he was enjoying himself and didn't want to rush the narrative. Overriding my remark, he said they had determined that Marcos himself was too sick to be directly involved. Rather, the guilty party was, like Henry's knights, someone eager to please the boss. Then he shifted course and turned to personal matters—what it had been like for him and his associates to be subjected to public scrutiny and abuse, how it had affected their families.

"It's been an honest job," he said. "We don't want to embarrass our grandchildren."

"Well," I said, "that really leaves just one question unanswered."

He took a deep breath and exhaled. "It's Ver. Everyone else was responsible to him."

And that was that. I paid the check, and we left the restaurant together. I thanked him for his help. As we shook hands on the deserted street, he said, almost as a postscript, "I think you'd better not single me out." I haven't.

Until now. But my source has since died and any number of my colleagues and interested Filipinos guessed that he was Dante G. Santos, the highly respected president of Philacor, the country's largest maker of refrigerators and freezers. They were right. RIP, Dante. I was uncomfortable relying on a single source, particularly for such an explosive story. And I knew that expecting a second board member to come out of the closet was out of the question. I had dealt with Santos before and found him to be reliable. Besides, he didn't come looking for me, I tracked him down. I believe that once I had presented him with the opportunity, he broke his vow of silence and spoke to me because he worried that Agrava and Marcos would succeed in burying the truth. I decided it was unwise to file from Manila. I flew home to Tokyo and sent the story from our kitchen table. It began:

> The commission investigating the 1983 murder of Philippine opposition leader Benigno S. Aquino Jr. will accuse the chief of the nation's armed forces of ordering the killing, according to a member of the panel.

> In an exhaustive report planned for release within the next two weeks, the commission will charge that armed forces Chief of Staff Gen. Fabian Ver headed a conspiracy to gun down Aquino as he was led off a plane at Manila International Airport, said the panel member, who insisted on anonymity.

I noted that the board's report would not name the "brains" behind the plot—Eduardo Cojuangco, Jr.—but would refer to him as "an ambitious, troublesome individual who had his own plans to become president." The board, I wrote, had concluded that a military security guard, not Rolando Galman, had pulled the trigger. And, to keep the record clear, I added: "The report will in no way implicate Marcos or his wife, Imelda, in the plot to murder Aquino or in the subsequent cover-up, the source emphasized."

The *Mercury News* took the unusual step of copyrighting the story and spread it across the top of the front page on Sunday, August 26, 1984. Other papers in the Knight-Ridder chain, which owned the *Merc*, and subscribers to its news service played it prominently. Wire services relayed it back to Manila, where government-controlled papers withheld it. But the story made a huge splash in the city's influential alternative press. All five board members issued statements denying being my source. Curiously, their denials, absent the story, were carried in the controlled papers, which rebuked the *Merc* and me. The cat was out of the bag. That was where my source wanted it to be. And I was pleased to help put it there. Every reporter loves an exclusive. Nothing quite matches the kick of breaking a story that's yours alone. But there is such a thing as being too exclusive, too alone for too long. My piece had stated that the commission would release its report by mid-September. It didn't. Weeks dragged by and I began to feel in the pit of my stomach cold fear that I'd been used. I had been. But I tried to convince myself that my reporting heightened expectations among Filipinos, virtually all of whom suspected that Ver had ordered the assassination and who would have been maddened if he were not accused. And it helped break a logjam at Philippine Village. An acrimonious struggle broke out in Rosie Agrava's suite. The four men were at her throat and she at theirs. She was unwilling to implicate Ver. Marcos had gotten to her. Dante Santos had told me over our steak-and-martini dinner that Marcos's chief legal adviser, Manuel Lazaro, had secretly brought Agrava to the palace on three separate occasions. Marcos convinced her that accusing the leader of the nation's armed forces of murder would lead to mutiny and tear the country apart.

Midday on Tuesday, October 23, seven weeks after my piece was published and fourteen months after the murder, Agrava appeared on live television alongside Marcos in the ceremonial hall of Malacañang. He wore an elaborately embroidered *barong tagalog*, the translucent shirt crafted from pineapple-leaf fiber that is the national dress for men. She was in a trim, olive-green dress, almost military in appearance. She handed him a 121-page book entitled *Separate Report of the Chairman*. It placed all blame for the murder on the six enlisted men who'd been on the gangway and their boss, Brig. Gen. Luther Custodio. "General Ver was not a plotter," Agrava's report concluded. Marcos thanked her warmly.

Filipinos went to bed that night embittered, believing that the elaborate investigation and hearings had been a cover-up after all; a ruse, as they had anticipated. And that my story had been false. I didn't sleep well either.

But the next morning, the four male board members delivered their own report to the palace. Marcos let them cool their heels for an hour before grudgingly accepting their two weighty volumes. They cited as "indictable for the premeditated murder of Aquino" twenty-six men, all but one military enlistees and officers. General Ver's name was at the top of the list. There was no live TV. A brief clip on the evening news showed Marcos fixing the board members with a cold glare and admonishing them: "I hope you can live with your conscience, with what you have done." What they had done, in fact, was to push Marcos a giant step closer to the cliff's edge. Their findings revived public confidence. It also alarmed a number of mid-ranking military officers. Sensing imminent danger to their institution and themselves, these captains, majors, and colonels banded together. They named themselves the Reform the Armed Forces Movement (RAM).

RAM quickly accumulated 1,500 members and drew vital support from two unlikely father figures. One was Lt. Gen. Fidel Ramos, a cigar-chomping West Point graduate. The other, Juan Ponce Enrile, was a polished Harvard Law School–trained attorney. Though neither knew it then, they eventually would determine the future of the country. Eddie Ramos was the army's second in command and Johnny Enrile was the nation's defense minister. Both were longtime, dyed-in-the-wool Marcos loyalists and beneficiaries, but they had personal axes to grind, too. Ramos was irate that Marcos had bypassed him and promoted the slavishly obedient Ver, who had been a police officer in Marcos's hometown, to the top military job. Enrile had envisaged himself succeeding Marcos. As they watched the president's house of cards begin to shake, they realized they soon would have to make difficult decisions. No one in RAM, not Ramos nor Enrile, had been particularly upset by Ninoy's assassination. The armed forces had benefited enormously from Marcos's patronage. He had imposed martial law, encouraged them to abuse innocent civilians as they saw fit, quintupled their strength, and made the generals rich. Marcos recast the Philippines military, once an apolitical organization based on the US model, into his personal bodyguard. Most soldiers were fine with that, but now, as they saw Ver—and by extension, Marcos—in the crosshairs of justice, they realized the future of the armed forces and the country itself was in jeopardy. Their own reputations and careers were on the line. Fearful, they began meeting and plotting. Joan Orendain, a public relations executive and dear friend, who, like Abby Tan, seemed to know everyone, introduced me to several RAM officers. Joan and Abby once had been rivals for the same boyfriend, which required me to keep my relationships with them separate and distinct. The RAM guys and I began meeting for drinks and meals and they kept me abreast of their thinking. Rumors of a coup were making the rounds.

It was about this time that technology impacted my professional life in a huge way. The *Merc* shipped me my first portable word processor, a Radio Shack TRS-80 Model 100. Known affectionately to enthusiasts as the "Trash-80," it was about the size and weight of a science textbook and ran on four penlight batteries. Its tiny, yellowish screen displayed a half-dozen lines of pixelized letters. Most important to me, it could transmit over phone lines pretty much anywhere. Every once in a while, an event or a thing comes along and proves to be a game changer. The Trash-80 was, for me, a life changer. After writing a story on it, I simply had to attach it to my hotel room's telephone, tap a few keys—*buzz-buzz-screeeeeech*—and off the copy went, straight to the foreign desk at the *Merc*, seven thousand miles away, in almost-real time.

To convey some sense of how remarkable this new technology was for me, it was only a few years since I'd squatted on the dirt floor of a telegraph office in Pondicherry, India, alongside a barefoot Morse code operator, as he dotted-and-dashed my story to the *Washington Post*. Now, I no longer had to bribe and cajole telex operators. I no longer had to run to the nearest AP or Reuters office at ungodly hours. Free at last! Well . . . sort of. The ability to

process before Shah Reza Pahlavi was overthrown. Over $10 billion had been sucked out of the country in recent years, according to Bernardo Villegas, one of the Philippines' leading economists. His colleague, Jesus Estanislao, put the figure at $30 billion. Coincidentally, perhaps, the nation's foreign debt then was nearly $30 billion. I proposed to Krim that I take a serious look at the dollar salting, with a focus on the California properties. He was the most perceptive, most caring editor for whom I ever worked, and he was intrigued. But he also foresaw the difficulties and the practical considerations. I conceded up front that what I'd collected so far was speculation, that I had nothing yet that necessarily would prove out, that there might not be any criminal wrongdoing, that such an in-depth investigation would require a major commitment of time and money, and that the chance of success was slim. Ever since the Aquino murder, the *Merc* had devoted considerably more space to developments in the Philippines than most other US papers had. When I broke the story of General Ver's guilt, members of San Jose's substantial Filipino-American community responded with enthusiasm. Some came forward with new information, fueling more stories. So there was reason to believe the investigation I was proposing would generate major interest and attract additional local help.

Krim discussed the idea with the paper's two top editors, Jerry Ceppos and Bob Ingle. Hesitantly, they gave the project a green light. This dubious beginning would give rise to a journalistic investigation that would help end a corrupt twenty-year-long dictatorship. Like Ida Tarbell's Standard Oil muckraking in 1902, Upton Sinclair's expose of Chicago's meatpacking plants four years later, and Seymour Hersh's 1969 uncovering of the My Lai massacre, it changed history and lives. Stories like these are what makes a free press priceless.

Jonathan and I agreed that he would pass my list to Pete Carey, the paper's chief investigative reporter. "Look into this," Krim said. Pete, ostensibly a laid-back, native Californian, was in reality, a driven obsessive, as a world-class investigator must be. He had been covering Silicon Valley since its pioneering days and was an innovator in the emerging field of computerized data mining at a time when most investigative journalists still relied on shoe leather, door-knocking, and phone calls. Pete went to work with a short-lived, online database being beta-tested by a company called Real Estate Data, Inc. He used it to confirm buyers' identities, prices, and purchase dates of the California properties. Bay Area Filipinos helped him fill in some blanks. Imelda's extensive (and expensive) holdings in New York required more time-proven techniques. Pete flew to Manhattan, where he researched government records, located and questioned sources who didn't want to be found, dug up an obscure lawsuit filed against Imelda in Long Island, and discovered New York Land Co., a small law firm that managed her secret commercial real-estate investments in the city. Owned by Joseph and Ralph Bernstein, American brothers who had grown up in the Philippines, the firm was located on 57th Street off Fifth Avenue, spittin' distance of the Crown Building.

Pete later told me this delightful story: "When I first visited New York Land's office, I noticed one of those velvet boards you put letters in to make words. It was dusty, but there on that board was the name of every shell company I had just looked up at the Recorder's office—40 Wall Street, Herald Center, the Crown Building, Lindemere, etc., along with the names of current and (I suspected correctly) former employees.

"A burly security guard behind the desk eyed me skeptically, and when I proceeded to write down all those names, he said, 'I'm supposed to tell you not to do that.' And I said, cheerfully, 'And I'm supposed to do it.' He grunted 'Okay,' and I continued to scribble in my notebook. Joe Bernstein refused to meet me, though I managed to talk to him on his home phone later. He denied everything, of course."

The Marcoses and their cronies had taken great pains to hide their ownership beneath layers of dummy corporations and false fronts. But Pete's sources led him to believe that the stories could be documented, if one knew where to look. With Pete in the United States and me in the Philippines, we spent six months tapping scores of government officials, politicians, attorneys, real-estate agents, bankers, diplomats, and other knowledgeable people. Once our editors were convinced the investigation stood a strong chance of producing results, they added San Francisco correspondent Katherine Ellison to our little team. Kathy was young, talented, ambitious, and hungry. Armed with ample chutzpah and proven data, she became the project's doorknocker-in-chief, confronting property owners face-to-face with our findings.

Early one Sunday morning, Kathy showed up at the San Francisco residence of Nemesio Yabut, the mayor of Makati, the Manila business district. Hizzoner came to the door in his jammies. Kathy told Yabut we knew he had paid $520,000 for the pink stucco residence in Saint Francis Woods, an exclusive enclave near Golden Gate Park. That was real money in the Bay Area housing market back in the day. Kathy also told Yabut she had learned he owned a $900,000 apartment; at least two condominiums; and a seafood restaurant, The Old Clam House, all in San Francisco.

Presented with these facts, Yabut denied nothing. Rather, he assured Kathy that he unfailingly paid his US taxes.

"I remember the story of Al Capone," he told her, with no apparent sense of irony. "Al Capone was never convicted of anything but tax evasion." Yabut was a piker in comparison with the Marcoses and some of the other cronies. We learned that Imelda paid $51 million for the Crown Building and another $15 million on upgrades, including 1,363 ounces of twenty-three-karat gold leaf. Title was assigned to a Netherlands Antilles shell.

She spent another $46 million to tear down and rebuild a ten-story, glass-encased shopping mall in Manhattan's Herald Square. She named it Herald Center. It quickly deteriorated into a white elephant. Yet another of her landmark Manhattan properties was the green-copper-peaked skyscraper at 40 Wall Street. Donald Trump subsequently bought it and named it after himself. Curious how people like the Trumps and Marcoses so often wind up in bed together. Or, as in this case, the same bed at different times.

In Manila I went through front and back channels, seeking an interview with the Marcoses about their holdings. They ignored me, so I sent them a registered letter: Would they confirm that they owned the above-named properties and that they did business through the Bernstein brothers and several other front men and -women I named? And what were their views on Filipinos salting dollars abroad "at a time when the economy . . . is in such dire straits?" To my astonishment, an aide to the president telephoned me and read out a denial that the couple owned any property in the United States. Incongruously, he then recited, "So long as the acquisitions are legal, nobody can question the owners' right to these properties." When I questioned the disconnect, he said the matter was not addressed in my letter.

Otherwise, while Pete and Kathy were tilling rich soil in the United States, I was scratching dry Philippines sand. As expected, little documentation could be uncovered in the country. Still, tucked away in the *chismis* were sources whom, when I approached them with patience and assurances of anonymity, agreed to talk. Anyone listening in on my phone calls from the Manila Hotel or tracing my tuk-tuk journeys around town would have had a clear idea of what I was up to. I'd seen no sign I was being monitored. But the hotel doorman thought otherwise. Just after sunrise each morning, before the sticky heat grew too oppressive, I would greet him and set off on a run to clear my head and prepare for the day ahead. My route took me atop the broad, stone seawall holding back Manila Bay from the traffic and beggars of tree-lined Roxas Boulevard. After some weeks of this routine, I returned to the hotel one morning, drenched in sweat as usual, and the white-uniformed doorman hissed me aside.

"Mr. Simons, be careful," he whispered as we faced each other behind a corner of the whitewashed building.

"Why?"

"They're watching you."

"Who?" He hoisted his eyebrows, twice in quick succession, then pulled open the heavy, narra-wood door. If I was under surveillance, I (a) hadn't seen any sign of it and (b) didn't have many options. I had to rely on my room phone and travel by tuk-tuk or taxi. I did adjust my morning run, though, and now trotted along the sun-dappled sidewalk, in clear view of traffic and pedestrians, rather than on the shaded, hidden seawall.

In the end, Pete, Kathy, and I were able to confirm much of the *chismis*. We spent several weeks writing, with Jonathan meticulously editing, the complex material. The project had taken us a year. The result was a three-day series of articles that the *Merc* began publishing on June 23, 1985. It was titled, "Hidden Billions: The Draining of the Philippines." It opened with this:

"As the Philippines sinks deeper into a quagmire of poverty, foreign debt, and political unrest, many of its most prominent citizens are systematically draining vast amounts of wealth from their nation and hiding it overseas."

Investigative journalism lives or dies on details. We had plenty. We named ten people. Ferdinand and Imelda Marcos were the principals. The cronies we singled out included cabinet ministers, senior civil servants, politicians, and intimate friends of the first couple. We identified their properties, many of which Pete and Kathy had visited. We unearthed contracts that showed what they had paid for them. We peeled back layers of camouflage to learn how they'd managed to keep deals hidden for years. All had cleverly hidden their investments, often putting them in the hands of seemingly casual acquaintances or small-fry employees with little to recommend their being entrusted with millions of dollars. A commonly used scheme was the use of these people's names in offshore holding companies in Caribbean tax havens. We tracked down these surrogates, questioned them, and reported their responses, mostly denials. Many arrangements were based on *utang na loob*, a traditional Filipino cultural arrangement meaning "blood debt" or "obligation." Under this system, a person is eternally indebted to whoever helped her or him reach a goal. So, when Imelda Marcos promoted Vilma Bautista, a member of her staff in Manila, to a coveted posting at the Philippines' United Nations mission in Manhattan, Bautista understood she would be under the First Lady's thumb for the rest of her life. When Imelda then asked her to sign millions of dollars' worth of checks for real estate deals, she did so unhesitatingly, never admitting that it was the First Lady, not she, who owned the buildings.

Shortly after our series broke and the Marcoses were on the ropes, Bautista, apparently sensing the jig was up, threw in the *utang na loob* towel and poured her blood debt down the drain. She stole four valuable paintings from a Marcos townhouse in Manhattan, then sold one, Claude Monet's famed impressionist *Water-Lily Pond*, for $32 million. Piling audacity upon criminality, she paid no taxes on the sale, as she hadn't on her other income, legitimate and otherwise, for decades. In 2020, New York State found Vilma guilty of evading $14,281,977.75 in taxes—ranking her the second-greatest tax dodger in the state—and jailed her for two years.

*Utang na loob* and numerous other under-the-table arrangements were designed like mazes, to lure trackers down blind alleys and into dead ends. New York Democratic Congressman Stephen Solarz tried and failed to navigate the labyrinth. Even with the assistance of State Department experts, Solarz was unable to solve the puzzle. Our series alarmed the Reagan administration and shook Congress. The heaviest impact was felt, of course, in Manila. Newspapers there dodged official punishment by publishing the articles and then, tongue-in-cheek, belittling them. In these reprints, "hidden billions" evolved into "hidden wealth," which was enshrined in the indigenous lexicon. Saying those two words to a Filipino today evokes much the same reaction as "Watergate" does with an American. Filipinos were electrified. That an American newspaper had presented them with documented facts, where previously there was only *chismis*, added to the story's authenticity. Among the sadder effects of centuries-long Spanish and then American bastardization of their culture was Filipinos' dependence on the United States for back-patting and wrist-slapping. But because the series had originated in the San Jose *Mercury News* and not, say, the *New York Times* or *Washington Post*, Marcos believed he could ride out the storm.

"These are the findings of a small regional newspaper in California," Marcos's loyal labor minister, Blas Ople, snickered to local journalists. "He can overcome this."

Ople wasn't terribly far off in describing the *Merc*. But he was dead wrong about the outcome. Opposition leaders seized on our stories and demanded Marcos be impeached. That didn't happen. But we had let loose a seed on the wind. Opponents circulated a videotape showing the properties we'd exposed. They translated the series into Tagalog and other dialects and distributed copies widely across the archipelago, even dropping them from aircraft. Public outcry was unmatched since the Aquino assassination two years earlier. Marcos was forced onto the defensive. He scorned the series as a "malicious lie" and alleged that those keeping it alive "have done me wrong. They have hurt me."

New York's *Village Voice* followed up with an exposé of the Bernstein brothers. With a hot issue on his home turf, Representative Solarz launched a Congressional investigation into the relationship between the brothers and the Marcoses. Joseph Bernstein confessed that he and Ralph had purchased and managed hundreds of millions of dollars' worth of real estate for President and Mrs. Marcos. As with my report on Ver's guilt in the Aquino murder, another cat was out of the bag. The Marcoses and their loyalists tried to stuff the wriggling creature back in, but, scratching and hissing, it refused to go. As tolerant as Filipinos were to abuse from the rich and powerful, the first couple had gone too far. They had crossed a line no one knew existed until they were exposed stepping over it. For that, they would be punished.

But this being the Philippines, first there had to be a farce. For eleven months, beginning near the end of January 1985, as a follow-up to the Agrava board's dueling reports, a three-judge special appeals court known as the Sandiganbayan conducted what can only be described as a mock trial of General Ver and the coconspirators accused by the Agrava men.

The fix was in from the start.

On the eve of the trial's opening, Marcos summoned the three members of the special court to the palace for a rerun of his secret meeting with Rosie Agrava. With Imelda seated beside him, he received the trio in pajamas and bathrobe. His face was puffy, his voice weak. He lectured them for two hours on the dangers—to him, to the nation, and, most menacing, to themselves—inherent in a guilty verdict.

As Abby Tan reported afterward in the *Washington Post*, another of her strings, the chief prosecutor in the case, Manuel Herrera, testified before the supreme court that Marcos bluntly told him, another prosecutor, and presiding judge Manuel Pamaran to conduct a sham trial, a *moro-moro*. In Tagalog, *moro-moro* means "operetta."

"Put on a show," the president told the men as he wrapped up. "Thank you for your cooperation. I know how to reciprocate."

They got the message. On the morning of December 2, with government TV broadcasting live, the Sandiganbayan trio declared that the Aquino assassination had indeed been a Communist "rub-out job." It was just as President Marcos had told the world the day after the murder. General Ver and his co-accused were not merely acquitted, they were "innocent of the crimes charged." Ver, ringed by bodyguards, strode out of the narrow, high-ceilinged courtroom beaming, his hands clasped above his head like a boxing champion. Within three hours, he was back in uniform, back in command. Justice had been served, Philippines style. General Ramos and Defense Minister Enrile maintained appearances, publicly professing loyalty to Marcos. But they recognized that the government writ large and the armed forces in particular were at a precipice. Ramos slipped into depression. Enrile and his RAM officers began drafting plans for armed rebellion against the Marcos regime.

The across-the-board acquittal was even more outrageous than people had anticipated, but most Filipinos managed to satisfy themselves with the Agrava men's findings. Then Marcos diverted their attention from the courtroom to the campaign trail. He hinted that he would call a "snap election."

Marcos had been toying with the notion of a quickie vote ever since his opponents attempted to impeach him in reaction to our series. President Reagan encouraged him. A hastily called election would catch the squabbling opposition off guard and assure another term for Marcos, America's long-standing friend and ally.

Reagan dispatched Nevada Republican Senator Paul Laxalt, a trusted middleman, to Manila with an urgent message. Laxalt spent five hours with Marcos, though their discussion could be boiled down to two sentences: 1. Hold elections, because Americans believe elections equal democracy and will be suitably impressed. 2. Hire a well-connected Washington lobbyist to clean up your act. Marcos complied immediately with the second command. His son-in-law, Gregorio Araneta (think Jared Kushner), signed a $950,000 (double that for 2021 value) contract with none other than the powerful K Street Republican petitioners, Black, Manafort, Stone and Kelly. The firm went to work, sprucing up Marcos's image in Capitol offices and conference rooms.

Reputation-cleansing is a time-consuming business. Instructions occupy many pages in the propagandist's handbook. And it's expensive. But those who emerge from the steam and scrub to resume business as usual consider it money well spent. And no one does the job better than the cleaning crews of K Street.

Years later, Paul Manafort and Roger Stone were found guilty of federal crimes they committed on President Trump's behalf and were sentenced to prison. Trump pardoned them before leaving office. Similarities between Marcos in 1985 and Trump 35 years later keep crossing my mind as I recall those ugly times in Manila. I recall not only what happened in the Philippines under Marcos but what followed there under the brutish Rodrigo Duterte. Then I think about the violent, Trump-directed climax at the US Capitol on January 6, 2021, and I am certain that it could happen again, and that the next outburst could well rip America's already fractured democracy completely to bits.

A short time after Laxalt returned to Washington, he telephoned Marcos and instructed him to set an election date ASAP. "It would be very dramatic for you to make that announcement on *This Week with David Brinkley*" added Laxault. The ABC-TV program offered a Sunday morning mix of interviews and analyses that was a mainstay among Beltway movers and shakers. "It would be very effective for American consumption," the US legislator impressed upon the skeptical Philippines president. Swallowing whatever shreds remained of his pride, Marcos did as he was told. On November 3, 1985, he promised on the Brinkley show to schedule voting within the next sixty days. Think about that for a moment: At the order of the President of the United States, the President of the Philippines informed the people of the United States that the people of the Philippines would vote for their president a day before he told Filipinos themselves. The humiliating concession laid bare Marcos's servility to Reagan as well as his cavalier disregard of his own people. And it revealed how removed from them he'd become in the tumult following Ninoy Aquino's murder.

As Marcos's health deteriorated, Imelda had had the presidential palace sealed and air-conditioned, its breezy, riverfront porticos glassed in and covered with heavy drapes. Marcos, who seldom left the building anymore, was shuttered, literally, from life on the outside. From the now dim recesses of

Malacañang, he announced that the snap election would take place a month later than he'd promised on American TV—on February 7 (that lucky number again), 1986, following a two-month campaign period. Under pressure from Reagan, he was surrendering a full year of his current term, betting that the old Marcos magic would work one more time.

He could then retire, secure in the knowledge that Imelda would replace him, son Bongbong would succeed her, to be followed by daughter Imee . . . Marcos presidents forever. Had Ferdinand been his old, sure-footed self, he would have foreseen the disaster waiting for him. He would have realized how bitter Filipinos were over Ninoy's killing. He would have anticipated that Cory would run against him as her dead husband's proxy. He would have realized that Cory, despite her inexperience and her mediocre stump speeches, was perfectly situated to defeat him: He epitomized evil. She, all that was good.

But this was not the Marcos that Filipinos had known and feared for two decades. I was shocked when I watched him enter the Fiesta Pavilion of the Manila Hotel to formally accept his party's nomination. I was seated on the aisle of the spacious ballroom, and he passed within inches of me. He was incapable of walking steadily unassisted, so two muscular bodyguards carried him on linked arms. His bloated face, smeared thickly with pancake makeup, looked like a rubber mask of himself. He wore a brimmed golf hat to hide his vanishing hair. Once they reached the front of the room, the bearers bundled him up a few steps and propped him on a chair. A diaper bulged visibly beneath his trousers. He managed to raise his arms in salute to the cheering supporters. A crowd of 1,800 had been bused to the hotel and handed red-white-and-blue T-shirts stamped with the initials in Tagalog of the ruling party, KBL, the New Society Movement. On cue, audience members chanted the president's war cry: "Mar-cos! Mar-cos! Mar-cos *pa rin*!" It's still Marcos! It was the tired mantra of a tired man, one with little new to offer. I had no personal sympathy for Marcos, yet I felt this was pathetic. Among the printed material dished out in the hotel lobby were pamphlets addressing our hidden-wealth stories. The San Jose *Mercury News*, the brochures stated, was "a paper of minor reputation in California."

Cory Aquino perplexed the president. Filipinos who had known the Marcoses and the Aquinos well in the early days told me that the two men were much like each other. What distinguished them was the women: Cory, calm, reserved, sure of who and what she was, had exerted a moderating influence on Ninoy. Imelda, outspoken, insecure, burning with dreams of vast wealth and power, poured fuel on Marcos's ambition. Coming from circumstances in which thousands of plantation workers had treated her with unquestioning deference since birth made Cory completely at ease campaigning among the masses. In an interview I shared with conservative syndicated columnist Robert Novak, she said: "The very fact that I was born privileged carries with it certain obligations. If I were just concerned for myself, I wouldn't even have bothered coming back to the Philippines or to continue to live here after the assassination of my husband, much less be so actively involved." Marcos was too frail to spend much time on the trail, so he waged most of his campaign on television from the seclusion of Malacañang. At first he tried a lofty, superior tack, treating Cory as a mere woman, not to be taken seriously in a macho society. That flopped. He next attacked her for lacking political experience. She hit back with a masterstroke: "I concede that I cannot match Mr. Marcos when it comes to experience. I admit that I have no experience in cheating, stealing, lying, or assassinating political opponents." It was a flawless twist of seventy-three-year-old Ronald Reagan's TV debate rejoinder to fifty-six-year-old Walter Mondale: "I am not going to exploit, for political purposes, my opponent's youth and inexperience."

Yellow, which had dominated Ninoy's huge funeral procession, was now the signature color of Cory's campaign. Traveling in a small, private plane, in a demure yellow dress, she joined low-budget, horn-honking motorcades, bumping along country roads between columns of cheering villagers. They displayed anything yellow they could put their hands on, T-shirts, headbands, bits of cloth, towels, ribbons, underpants, dried banana leaves while chanting, "Co-ry! Co-ry! Co-ry!" and punctuating it with L-for-Laban finger sign—"fight!"

Her stump speeches were dreadful. Her soft, nasal voice and singsong delivery still were those of a schoolgirl. No fury. No fire in the belly. She might as well have been delivering a ninth-grade civics report. Yet it didn't seem to matter. The crowds loved her.

On the southern island of Mindanao, racked for decades by Muslim-Catholic unrest, a nurse who'd slipped out of work to attend a rally told me, "She's so brave to stand up against Marcos. She's the one with real courage. That's why my companions and I are going to vote for her."

Cory concluded her campaign on Tuesday, February 4. Half a million Manilans surged into bayfront Luneta Park and spilled over into surrounding streets, paralyzing much of the city. The government refused to allow her to speak from the concrete bandstand at the front of the park, so she stood on a makeshift platform. The sound system was defective, carrying her wispy voice to just a handful. Yet the throng stayed for six hours, cheering themselves hoarse for her. Characteristically, she invoked her faith, a sensible approach to the devout people of the only Roman Catholic nation in Asia. Her delivery may have been subdued, but she demonstrated once again that in spirit she was attuned to her people. "We have a chance to make history," she said. "Let us pray that we have peaceful and honest elections so that by Christ we can forgive our enemies. Mr. Marcos has committed many sins against the people. . . . Marcos has no respect for the dignity of the people, no conscience, no morals, no soul. . . . Marcos said I don't have the strength to be president. . . . I have accepted all the trials from God. I can accept the challenge of the presidency."

The president closed out the next evening, in the same park. It rained on his parade. What was intended to be a glorious climax, complete with a dazzling laser show and entertainment by some of the biggest celebrities in the country, sputtered into a soggy fiasco. By the time Marcos took the microphone, perhaps ten thousand true believers remained on the mushy Luneta ground. Setting a standard for alternative facts that wouldn't be exceeded until decades later by Donald Trump at his thinly attended inauguration, Marcos delivered an outrageous grand finale. "We have changed the indifferent and uncommitted Filipino soul into a soul that is vibrant and dynamic," he claimed, "as you can see in this almost, perhaps, *one-million* people who squished through the rain in order to attend."

Polls opened at lucky 7:00 a.m. on lucky February 7. Halfway around the world, in another impoverished former colony, Haiti's President-for-Life Jean-Claude Duvalier and his wife fled into the predawn sky aboard a US military plane bound for France. "Baby Doc" and his late father, "Papa Doc," had bled the Caribbean island dry over twenty-eight years. When the news reached the Philippines, the sudden collapse of this cruel, corrupt dynasty gave voters hope for change in their own country. But first they had to vote. And make sure their votes were counted. I had proposed that Knight Ridder form a team of correspondents and that we operate together. This flew in the face of company policy, but editors saw the point. A thousand foreign journalists were in Manila to cover the election. The major American print and broadcast organizations had multiple correspondents on the ground. Why shouldn't we make use of our scale and scope? Reporters from the *Merc*, the *Philadelphia Inquirer*, and the *Miami Herald* assembled at the Manila Hotel, with Jonathan Krim as our editor. On election day, we fanned out across the city and nearby towns. Our core mission was to look for ballot box stuffing, repeat voting, bullying, and other signs of fraud. Senator Richard Lugar, a moderate Republican from Indiana, had brought twenty poll watchers with him to assure the voting was "free and fair." More to the point, the Reagan administration wanted to confirm the appearance of free and fair. A few Filipinos hoped the presence of the Americans would force Marcos to tone down the use of "guns, goons and gold" that trademarked his electioneering. Others were dubious.

"Doesn't your president have a clue about what's been going on in this country?" Jaime Ongpin, the president of a major gold- and copper-mining firm and a committed Cory supporter, challenged me. "They know free and fair elections are damned near impossible here."

Fully aware of the potentially grave consequence of this election, voters took their responsibility with uncommon seriousness. A stunning twenty-six million turned out, more than 95 percent of registered voters. My first stop of the morning was a grammar school in the Manila suburb of Pasay, where I walked along a blocks-long lineup of would-be voters, interviewing them. Many had been there for hours before the sun rose.

A housewife named Vida Balboa summed up her own feelings and those of many of her fellow citizens. "Today could be liberation day," she told me. "Or it could be the start of civil war."

As the sweltering day dragged on, Balboa and millions like her found their progress thwarted by normal confusion intensified by cheating and intimidation. Many were prevented from voting at all. The first sign that something major was wrong occurred as voters found their names missing from registration lists posted on doors at thousands of polling stations. Then there were "flying voters," paid by the Marcos campaign to flit from poll to poll, casting ballots at each.

"There were five of them," Maria Luisa Sison told me at Bayanon School. "They were underage, and they used names that weren't their own." When I asked how could she be so certain, she replied, "One of them was my own brother, Hilario!"

Moments before I arrived at the large Guadalupe Elementary School in Makati, six armed men had burst in, fired their weapons wildly, and smashed chairs over the heads of poll volunteers. Victims were still wandering around, dazed and bleeding. Police officers lounging outside feigned obliviousness.

On the Bataan Peninsula, infamous for the World War II Death March, I watched open trucks loaded with combat-armed Philippine marines roaring up and down streets, raising plumes of red dust, for no apparent reason other than to frighten people. Around midday, I ran into Senator Lugar, who was shuttling among polling stations aboard a gleaming white US Navy helicopter. He was somewhat dismayed. But not much. "The thing is not that far out of kilter," he said. Later in the day, after he'd seen an Aquino worker bloodied and bandaged, he reconsidered, but again, only so much: "It's not all according to Hoyle."

As darkness fell and polling stations closed, journalists and citizens reported many more accounts of violence, abuse, and chicanery. Vote counting was lagging far behind schedule. To tamp down rising concern, Marcos went on TV and announced that the foreign observers were "certainly convinced that the elections have been honest and clean." Like Odysseus, Lugar recognized he was wedged between Scylla and Charybdis. Reagan wanted a Marcos victory, but Lugar's conscience was nagging him. His assessment would have a direct impact on congressional debate over the future of US military and economic aid to the Philippines. At about 10:00 p.m., he met with several of us correspondents at the entrance of the Manila Hotel. His face was grim. He had changed his mind.

"I'm deeply disturbed by the delay in the count," he started. "One of the scenarios we anticipated . . . was if the government was worried by the results, it might try to bring things to a halt. . . . There's a pattern, a very serious pattern, of influence. I plead with whoever is holding up the count to free it, let it go, so we can see what the will of the people is."

Several hours later, both Marcos and Aquino declared themselves winners. The government-controlled papers declared a Marcos victory; the opposition dailies said Aquino had prevailed. Cory summoned reporters to a news conference.

"My victory is irreversible," she told us. "It is evident that I am being cheated out of an election." She demanded that Marcos resign. Marcos, desperate to demonstrate that he controlled the machinery of government, called his own press conference at the palace. He told us he was considering voiding the election. This was a shrewd move. If Cory continued to cry fraud, Marcos could simply acknowledge she was right and, therefore, the election was indeed invalid. Massachusetts Democratic Senator John Kerry, a member of Lugar's observer contingent, warned us that if Marcos went through with the threat, "politically, his credibility with the American people and the Filipino people would be so low, the issue is whether he could govern."

With scores of other correspondents, I settled in for the long haul at the International Convention Center, one of Imelda's glittery edifices, where a bank of giant electronic scoreboards displayed the latest count. Some of the computer operators generating the statistics were growing uneasy. They knew something was wrong. Just not what. At 10:30 Sunday night, nearly sixty hours after voting began, a young woman in a white lab coat told us the computer data weren't simply being tampered with, they were being ignored. She was Linda Kapunan, the senior technician. Her husband, Colonel Eduardo "Red" Kapunan, was a RAM officer. She said votes for Marcos were being tallied while Aquino ballots were not. The computerized data had Aquino ahead, but the boards showed Marcos leading.

Kapunan and her thirty colleagues rose to their feet, pulled off their smocks, and in single file strode briskly out of the hall. People in the galleries began shouting support, *Daya! Daya! Daya!* Cheating! A crowd quickly assembled outside the imposing, concrete building to protect the operators. Some other correspondents and I jumped into taxis and followed the two cars and a panel truck that ferried them to Baclaran Church. They were received by a leading civil rights lawyer with the only-in-the-Philippines name of Joker Arroyo and by Senator Kerry, who applauded them for their courage. Linda Kapunan, obviously frightened, said she and the other operators had walked out because, "We feel that we've been used."

The American observers flew back to Washington, where Lugar reported to the President that Cory had legitimately won "at least" 60 percent of the vote. Reagan listened but didn't want to hear it. To him, and to many US leaders, the sanctity of the military bases was more valuable than democracy in the Philippines. He told a White House news conference, "One cannot minimize the importance of those bases."

In Manila, the controlled press reacted with gleeful programmed headlines that read, "Reagan Expects Marcos To Win."

By going along to get along, Defense Minister Enrile had moved up from abject poverty to become one of the wealthiest and most powerful men in the Philippines. Handsome, intelligent, and cunning, he carried out Marcos's dirty tricks because what was good for McCoy was good for Johnny. In the latest election, he admitted much later, he manipulated the balloting to deliver Marcos an unearned 365,000 votes. General Eddie Ramos was cut from different cloth. With his West Point background, he was a starchy soldier, an exemplary officer who commanded the respect of his troops by actually leading them. I once jogged alongside him at the head of a column of troops on a post-midnight, five-mile run. His cold cigar never left his mouth.

Ramos's ascent was more a product of heartfelt allegiance to flag and country than to one man. Marcos trusted Eddie, but not nearly as much as he did Johnny. Circumstances now threw the general and the defense chief together. With the future of the Philippines and their own survival at stake, they would lead a coup—a bloody one if need be—against the man they'd served for two decades. Their instrument would be RAM, the group of worried officers who had formed in the turbulent wake of the Agrava board's male component accusing General Ver of murdering Ninoy Aquino.

Joan Orendain continued to arrange get-togethers with top RAM officers in her fifth-floor walkup apartment. She invited Sandra Burton of *Time*, one of her favorites, and me. Sandy had accompanied Ninoy on his fateful flight and her reporting dominated the Philippines story from the start. She and I became friends and, since we weren't direct competitors, shared information. We helped each other stay on top of things as the action played out. Once it became apparent to Cory that she and Marcos were locked in a post-election fight to the finish, she called on Filipinos to adopt Gandhian-style civil disobedience. RAM officers let Cory know they supported her, and they took charge of her security. Anticipating that Marcos would respond to their plot with violence, RAM issued an emotional appeal to soldiers and police.

"We implore you to think of your relatives and friends who may be among the millions of Filipinos demanding that their voices be heard," they said. "Be involved in the struggle for democracy and freedom by refusing to use force and violence on innocent and freedom-loving Filipinos."

Enrile contacted Philip Habib, a retired American diplomat and master negotiator who was in Manila at Reagan's behest, and confided that he was going to resign from the cabinet. He calculated that the United States would welcome him as Marcos's replacement since he favored retaining the bases—an issue about which Cory was somewhat wobbly—and was a rock-solid anti-Communist.

Abandoning all secrecy, Enrile confided to Habib that RAM planned to invade the palace, arrest Marcos, and put him on trial. He was convinced, or at least wanted Habib to convince Reagan, that this could be accomplished bloodlessly. Enrile was taking no chances, though. Out of his own pocket, he bought an array of sophisticated weapons from Israel and hired two British mercenaries to train "my boys" to defend important individuals—like himself—and to rescue hostages from hijacked airplanes.

RAM turned its attention to Ramos. He was a slipperier fish to net than Enrile. Jose Almonte, a RAM colonel who was Ramos's closest and most trusted friend, told me that in a long and emotional meeting, he had appealed to Ramos to lead the coup. "We needed him and Enrile," Almonte told me. "He understood that." Ramos, cold cigar in the corner of his mouth, had listened impassively and without interruption. Finally, he cautioned, "Joe, whatever you do, don't make it very bloody." Then everything fell apart. Marcos and Ver learned about the plot. They rushed eight thousand soldiers and marines to Malacañang and mined the Pasig River along the walled palace compound. Enrile was at home, having lunch with his wife, when he received word that the jig was up. He pulled on a pair of dad jeans and canvas shoes and grabbed a newly purchased Uzi from his bedroom closet. He telephoned Ramos, who also was at home, having just finished meeting with a group of church ladies:

"Eddie, we are about to be rounded up. Will you join us?" Ramos warned Enrile not to say anything more over the phone. At last, overcoming the years of waffling and indecision, he drew a deep breath and replied, "I am with you all the way."

The pair met at 6:00 p.m. in Enrile's defense ministry office at Camp Aguinaldo, in Quezon City. Tipped in advance, I was there along with other foreign correspondents and local reporters. Ramos, the old pro, appeared calm. Enrile clearly was out of his element and was a bundle of nerves. But he had the presence of mind to begin placing a round of calls from the bank of phones on a green filing cabinet behind his desk. The first was to US Ambassador Stephen Bosworth, who immediately organized around-the-clock monitoring in the embassy and alerted Foggy Bottom.

One of the most valuable calls Enrile made was to Cardinal Jaime Sin, the head of the Roman Catholic Church in the Philippines. The Church was by far the most influential institution in the country. Enrile appealed to Cardinal

Sin (what a name for a clergyman!) directly, saying, "I will be dead within one hour. I don't want to die. Help us by calling the people to support us."

Ramos got on the line. He was a Protestant, but at that moment, he told Sin, he was clutching a ceramic figurine of the Holy Mother. The smiley, chubby prelate, who had turned against the Marcoses following the Aquino assassination, went on church-backed Radio Veritas and urged listeners to, "support our two good friends at the camp." I realized that Enrile had summoned my colleagues and me to Aguinaldo to bear witness in case of an attack by government forces. Dripping sweat in a tan windbreaker over a heavy bulletproof vest as glaring TV lights baked the overflowing room, he offered us a shaky explanation for having broken with his decades-long friend and benefactor.

"Personally," he said. "I think Marcos did not really win the election. I believe in my whole heart and mind that Aquino was duly elected president of the republic."

Ramos, cool and collected in a short-sleeved sport shirt, provided a somewhat more believable explanation for why he had joined RAM, saying, "It had been building up in my perception that General Ver and the president are bent on perpetuating themselves in power. . . . It is my duty to see that the sovereign will of the people is respected. I am bothered by my conscience."

Both men were skirting the truth. Neither mentioned that they had preplanned a coup and were prepared for it to turn bloody. They wanted us to believe they had been forced to avoid arrest by a power-hungry Marcos. Radio Veritas replayed the news conference throughout the night. Millions began pouring out of their homes and into the dark streets.

This was the grand moment of People Power, the revolution that had been building steam since that murderous day at the airport. It was thrilling to those who participated and no less to those of us who watched and reported. I felt privileged to be there. This was a rare moment in history.

And it was built on a half-truth. Enrile still hoped that, with US assistance, he would emerge as president. But he didn't tell us that.

Guarded by their armed RAM supporters, Ramos and Enrile, an Uzi dangling clumsily on a canvas strap around his neck, scores of journalists from around the world in tow, walked out and crossed Edsa, an eight-lane highway running between the sprawling Camp Aguinaldo and Camp Crame, Ramos's headquarters. More compact, it would be easier to defend if Marcos unleashed the military. I was by then a fairly jaded newsman, blasé and not easily impressed. But what I saw stunned me. An ocean of humanity flooded the broad boulevard. The city's poorest predominated. Middle-class families and the very rich, their Mercedes-Benzes parked helter-skelter on the roadside, had joined them. Everyone wore or waved something yellow. They made the L sign. They cheered for Enrile and Ramos. Then the singular voice of this human wave swelled into a towering tsunami and crashed down thunderously: "Co-ry! Co-ry! Co-ry!"

She wasn't there. The object of their rapture was in hiding, fearing a rash attack by Marcos and the army, uncertain she could trust Enrile not to make a grab for power. But Johnny, overwhelmed by the crowd's adulation of Cory, recognized that she and not he would be the next president. Across town, Marcos was sequestered in Malacañang. Unable to get a call through to Enrile, whom he still believed he could convince to walk away, he dawdled. He was frightened. His forces outnumbered the rebels, but he feared the consequences of ordering them to massacre peaceful civilians. That potential nightmare was wakening on a highway a few blocks from Camp Crame. I hurried there, and as I stood at the front of the throng lining the road, a column of marine tanks thundered past within a few feet of us, toward the broad intersection of Edsa and Ortega Street. For anyone who hasn't had the experience of facing an advancing column of tanks at close range, I can tell you it truly is a terrifying experience to behold the height and bulk, the roar, the shredding tracks.

The football-field-size intersection teemed with Cory supporters. Soft-fleshed humans faced monstrous, steel, killing machines. David glared at Goliath. A lopsided standoff on a Manila street corner.

The marines, anticipating orders to open fire on friends and relatives, were in their own turmoil. The civilians, packed close around me, believed justice was on their side. Arm in arm, determined, they shuffled forward, sweeping me with them, closing the no-man's-land between their unyielding bodies and the mechanical giants. The tanks, engines roaring, belching hot, black diesel exhaust, ground to a halt a few yards short of us. Directly to my left, nuns in blue habits and seminarians in white cassocks walked forward in the front rank. They encircled the tanks and dropped to their knees. Fingering rosary beads with one hand and touching the hot metal with the other, they prayed aloud: "Hail Mary . . . "

Left with the choice of plowing into the wall of humanity—unspeakable—or turning tail—humiliating—a dozen or so tanks angled off; smashed through a low, cement-block wall; and formed up in a vacant lot. The troops clambered out, cradling automatic weapons, bandoliers bridging their chests, and lined up across the road, scowling into the faces of priests, women, and children. A young woman just behind me stepped forward and I gaped in disbelief as she approached a slim marine draped in crisscrossed belts of large-caliber bullets. His fearsome weapon and grim expression failed to mask his boyishness. She held out a bunch of yellow flowers. He stared for a moment, confused and embarrassed, then executed a precise about-face. Another woman, then another and another approached the troops, each offering more flowers. A dirty-faced little boy in shorts and singlet extended a

Thirty-six Marcos-free years would follow. The Philippines' fortunes would rise and fall, but not by much. Cory Aquino would serve, as would her son, Benigno Jr. Eddie Ramos was elected and so was faded movie actor Joseph Estrada. Gloria Macapagal Arroyo, a former college professor, held office for a full decade, and the ruthless Rodrigo Duterte wielded power for four years.

Then, in May 2022, with many of those who'd fueled the People Power uprising against Ferdinand Marcos having died off, the unthinkable turned real. A new generation went to the polls and overwhelmingly voted to install Bongbong Marcos in Malacañang Palace.

How quickly they forget.

Covering the Philippines saga was a matchless experience. Seldom is a journalist granted the opportunity not only to observe a critical shift in history but also to directly affect it. From the assassination of Ninoy through the guilty finding against General Ver to the hidden billions exposé, the People Power uprising, the ascent of Cory and the downfall of Marcos, I had that rare privilege. When we were awarded the 1986 Pulitzer Prize for international reporting, The Pulitzer archive stated: "The investigative stories and exposés of the San Jose *Mercury News* team can be called one of the greatest successes in the history of the internationally oriented Pulitzer Prizes."

Winning the Pulitzer was electrifying for the three of us and for the *Merc*. When the wires broke the awards story, Bob Ingle climbed onto a desk in the newsroom and shouted out the announcement. It was the first Pulitzer the paper had won, and the staff, Kathy told me later, "went nuts." Ingle was generous with his praise. "These three did an extraordinary investigative job," he told the jubilant crowd as champagne corks blew. "At every turn, people said they would never get the story, but they did anyway."

He emphasized that we and Krim proved that "the rumors that had been around for years had been true." Knight Ridder papers around the country won seven Pulitzer Prizes that year, a record in the century-plus history of the award.

Carol and I were asleep on the tatami mats when the phone rang. It was 3:00 a.m. In Tokyo. I'd been told that a win was likely, but there's nothing like getting the official word from your editor.

"You'll want to buy tickets to New York," Ingle teased. I shouted at the top of my lungs. Certainly, I awakened our neighbors on the other side of the paper-thin wall but, being Japanese, they were too polite to yell back for me to shut up.

*Chapter Two*

# The Prince of Paterson

So, how does a kid from Paterson, New Jersey, Turnpike exit 155-A, wind up sleeping on a straw floor in Japan and help overthrow a dictator in the Philippines?

Slowly and painfully.

My journey began with Grampa Yossel and his faded, red, junk wagon. Early each afternoon, after he'd prayed while facing the oak icebox in the kitchen of their little apartment and wolfed down the heavy meal that Gramma had prepared, the old man would stretch out on the bare bedroom floor—shoes on, fully dressed—and fall asleep, snoring contentedly. Gramma wouldn't allow him in bed because he smelled of his rack-ribbed pony, Ferd.

An hour later, he'd clomp back downstairs, and untie Ferd from the sagging fence that separated the vacant lot from their apartment building. He'd remove the pony's feedbag and hook a canvas sling under its tail to catch its droppings. Then he'd climb onto the wagon and Ferd would step daintily into the street, tlit-tlot, tlit-tlot.

Tinkling bells strung above the board seat heralded their gradual progress through Paterson's shabbier streets. Grampa was on the lookout for anything he might be able to retrieve and sell to a dealer—scraps of metal, rubber, wood, cardboard. He was a junkman. How I wished he would take me along, let me sit up there next to him. But Mother wouldn't permit it.

I called him Grampa. He called me Kind, Yiddish for "child," just as he called his horse Ferd, which means "horse." He seldom said anything to me beyond, Oy, mein Kind, mein Kind. And that was more a zifts, a sigh of resignation, than a precursor to conversation. He worried for me as I awaited admission to the grownups' world; a world that had chewed him up and might at any moment spit him out; a world he assumed offered me, like him, little reason for hope.

If I knew what lay behind his melancholy, I might have gained some insight into my own pessimistic instincts. But I was only eight when he died, and I hadn't asked the questions. Perhaps it was that his life in America fell too far short of the hopes and dreams he carried from Europe. Perhaps he lacked the imagination to anticipate that his grandson would have opportunities that didn't exist for him. Or maybe it was simply that, as psychiatrists have determined, Ashkenazi Jewish men are unusually susceptible to depression.

To visit Grampa and Gramma in their one-bedroom apartment, Mother and I would take the gray and red, Public Service No. 30 bus downtown, then walk past rundown two- and three-family houses, most of them occupied by people Mother referred to as "Negroes" or "Colored," the polite terms of the day. Fast music blared through open windows and the smell of frying pork drifted on the air. If Mother grew nervous or felt threatened—I could tell by the moistness of her hand—she might mutter to herself something about *die schwartze*. What was then a Yiddish pejorative, "Black" has become today's term of self-pride.

We passed storefronts with widows smeared with black or green paint for privacy, where women in brilliant, ankle-length skirts and kerchiefs covering their dark hair told fortunes and were presumed to conduct nefarious business. They were Romani or, as we knew them then, Gypsies.

The sounds, the colors, the smells—all were very mysterious for a little Jewish boy clasping the hand of his uneasy mother. Scary, too. These impressions, all negative, stayed with me for many years. Only once I had gone overseas and met people whose ways were even more alien to me, in societies even more fractured and under assault, did I begin to fathom the racial and ethnic divergences that plagued my own country. And that recognition set the direction I took for the rest of my life.

I would watch Grampa wind the black leather straps and mysterious little boxes of the tefillin around his sturdy forearm and yarmulke-covered head every morning when he first woke up. This enigmatic ritual seemed manly to me, like tying on boxing gloves. He flung the fringed, white-and-black wool tallit across his thick shoulders, opened the worn prayer book, and began to daven. Bowing, swaying, dipping his knees, swiveling left and right, he softly recited in Hebrew the midday minhah prayers, "May the words of my mouth and the meditations of my heart be acceptable in thy sight, o eternal, my rock and my redeemer."

Like all observant Jewish men, he also thanked the Almighty for assigning him to the male gender. "Blessed art thou, Lord, our God, ruler of the universe, who has not created me a woman."

Why he performed these sacred rites before the icebox remains an enigma. Maybe he believed that the Western Wall stood in that direction, in Jerusalem, half a world away from the single-bedroom flat. Did he also believe his prayers reached far beyond, to the ears of God himself? If so, how did he reconcile his cheerless life with his faithful obedience? What were the good things God granted him that bound him to Judaism?

None of this crossed my mind until, decades later, as I saw innocent believers suffer horrors no god should visit on his followers, as I witnessed adherents of the world's warring faiths debase and exterminate each other, as I rethought the childhood indoctrination I had absorbed without questioning.

My parents married in 1938. My mother claimed she was twenty-nine, though I discovered later she was thirty-one at the time. "I was no spring chicken," she once confided to me. At her urging, Dad maintained that he was thirty-nine. He was, in fact, forty-two, born in 1896, which I found amazing.

Goldie Fleisher was working as a salesgirl at Quackenbush's Department Store—"Quack's"—when Louis Simons, the father of a butcher named Abe Simons, and Yossel worked out a *shidduch*, an arranged marriage. Goldie and Abe both lived with their parents. Both were socially limited, not particularly desirable catches in Paterson's striving Jewish circle. They were under intense family pressure to marry and likely were each other's last chance.

When I was sixteen, I saw Paddy Chayefsky's classic, *Marty*, at the Fabian Theater, downtown. Marty Piletti, played by Ernest Borgnine, was a stout, middle-aged, Italian American butcher who lived with his mother in the Bronx. He and his best friend, Angie, were inept and bored with their lives and with each other and utterly at wits' end.

Angie: "What do you feel like doing tonight?"

Marty: "I don't know, Ange. What do you feel like doing?"

In Marty, I recognized my father. Angie was a ringer for Dad's friend, a newsstand operator named Irving Frankel. Clara, a schoolteacher, with whom Marty eventually formed a pragmatic bond, approximated Mother. Their story of loneliness and eventual accommodation moved me deeply.

After finishing eighth grade, Dad went to work with his older brother, Morris, in their father's butcher shop. The store provided the brothers and their parents with a basic living; enough to get by but never enough to relieve their worries.

When Woodrow Wilson broke his neutrality pledge in 1917 and sent American boys "over there" to fight in the Great War, dad enlisted in the navy. He was scrawny and had to gorge on bananas and malted milk to make the minimum weight requirement. Rated an Electrician's Mate, he saw the war through at the Brooklyn Navy Yard.

Deeply patriotic all his life, Dad volunteered as a civilian air-raid warden during World War II. On nights when the warning sirens went off, he'd pop on a silver-painted, surplus doughboy's helmet and rush out to make sure our neighbors pulled down their window shades and that the top halves of car headlights were blacked out.

I was proud of him.

Of the handful of life lessons my father taught me, one that stuck was, "You can't judge the other fella until you've walked in his shoes." I put it to

As for national pride, after reporting from scores of countries, I've come to recognize that my own, for all that is good about it, is darkened by hypocrisy, loaded with shortcomings and stained with misdeeds. Many Americans have advanced humanity in extraordinary ways. Others have inflicted violence, destruction, and death. I take neither pride nor shame in being an American. I simply wish that my country, which I know to be well-intended overall, populated mostly by decent people, was better.

Certainly, I am grateful for the numerous and extraordinary opportunities afforded me as an American. Then I consider that my country maintains by far the world's greatest, deadliest killing machinery, which it deploys offensively at least as often as in self-defense. My country has been at war at home and abroad almost without cessation since before it was founded.

Early Americans abused their natural gifts—the wealth, power, and lofty intentions of its White settlers—to suppress the Red people whose land they took. They used brute strength to enslave and control the Black people they imported, bought, and sold. These abominations have been part of my country since before it gained its independence—in a war—and they are still. When I hear members of the political class rationalize our transgressions with the assurance that "we're better than this," I stiffen because we're not. Perhaps we can be. But we're not.

I reject pride in nationality, religion, and race. What have I done that entitles me to such superiority? What has any of us done? True, some actively make a choice by naturalizing, some convert, some cross other boundaries. But overwhelmingly, our associations with these artificial divisions result from one or another of life's arbitrary dice rolls.

My East European, Jewish grandparents emigrated to America and were naturalized. Their children were born here as American citizens. So was I. I was circumcised at a bris eight days later, became a bar mitzvah thirteen years after that, went to shul on occasion. I was a devoted Boy Scout. I enlisted in the Marine Corps Reserve. I vote and willingly pay my taxes. I am Jewish. I am American. These are two pieces of who I am. No more, no less. No shame. No pride.

I am proud I've spent five decades as a journalist. I consider it noble work and I have done it to the best of my ability. Informing people is the journalist's great contribution to society and I am happy to have paid my share.

One summer morning in 1950, when I was eleven and perusing the comics in the *Paterson Evening News* at the kitchen table while Mother scrubbed laundry on a ridged galvanized board in the sink, a large slab of plaster crashed from the ceiling, missing us by inches. That did it! Applying a full-court press, Mother played off the incident to hector Dad into fulfilling her lifelong dream and make an offer on a two-bedroom, one-bath, half-brick bungalow in the adjacent suburb of Fair Lawn. Committing to a mortgage of $13,000 caused Dad sleepless nights and days of heartburn. Then he bit the bullet.

Overnight, my life changed dramatically. How could such a trifling move, a ten-minute drive in my father's thirty-year-old Packard, be so transformative? It was just a hop across the narrow Passaic River, from a fading industrial city to an emerging suburb, from a cramped apartment to a slightly less cramped house on a treeless cul-de-sac.

Yet this short step turned out to be the first of many in what would become a peripatetic life, one that until then had been utterly snug and predictable. Having crossed the Passaic, I one day would cross the Pacific. I would live as far from Paterson and Fair Lawn as is possible on Planet Earth.

But first, Fair Lawn would leave its mark on me. Sterile and tidy, the town that was selling off its last truck farms to tract developers, implausibly and unpredictably became what Emma Lazarus called the "golden door." That door had swung inward to allow my grandparents entry to America. Half a century later, I pushed, and it swung out. I walked through and kept going into a world of wonder.

There was no shortage of Jews in Fair Lawn, but it was not a shtetl either. More of our dozen neighbors on the Madelyne Place cul-de-sac were Christians than Jews, blue-collar and white-collar, plumbers and electricians, office workers and machine operators, linked by economic status rather than religion. Everyone, of course, was White.

For me, the greatest change was that in Fair Lawn High School (I was entering seventh grade and the building also housed the junior high), a place where academic excellence counted for less than it had in my life until then. At least that's the way I chose to see it.

Our move had nothing to do with my parents seeking a better school for me. I was a strong pupil at P. S. 21 and had I, like other neighborhood kids, gone on to Paterson's Eastside High, with its stringent academic competitiveness, I likely would have continued to do well. Mother had no reason to worry about my schoolwork in Fair Lawn; she simply wanted to elevate our status and moving from an apartment to a "home" achieved that.

We had a grassy yard, and I had my own room. Ironically, in this newfound luxury, I rejected my parents' plan for my success and broke with the past. I discovered new heroes, not the best scholars, but the jocks, the older, bigger, high-school athletes who strode the corridors with puny kids like me trailing worshipfully in their shadows. I wanted to be one of them, no textbooks beneath their arms; cool and cocky; the prettiest girls at their sides, knitting intricate argyle socks as symbols of their devotion. Mother and Dad dismissed such boys as mere ball spielers. Wastrels. They were not Nice Jewish Boys.

At the top of my list of new idols was an upperclassman named David Sime. He was a track star of such extraordinary ability—as well as a professional-caliber football and baseball player—who would one day hold six world sprinting records simultaneously. In 1960, *Sports Illustrated* named him the "World's Fastest Human." A tall, rangy redhead, Sime was born in Paterson to parents of limited education. The first three letters of his name were the same as mine. And that's where our similarity began and ended.

What I didn't realize was that Sime also was a superior scholar. He went on to Duke University and its medical school, graduating near the top of his class. As an ophthalmologist, he pioneered lens transplants. He compiled a dazzling roster of celebrity patients, among them Ted Williams, Mickey Mantle, Sugar Ray Leonard, and Richard Nixon, whose winter getaway was down the block from Sime's home in Florida's Key Biscayne.

I knew I was seriously short of athletic talent, but I had decided I could remake myself, turn away from my natural abilities and instincts, become different. Different than what my parents wanted of me. Different than what I myself long imagined. I proceeded to misdirect effort and false hubris, striving to succeed in track, wrestling, and, most absurd at 118 pounds, football.

My grades crashed and burned. I graduated from Fair Lawn High in 1956 with a C-plus average. The only college that would accept me was Rutgers, which, as the New Jersey state university, was obligated because I slipped under its cutoff.

I continued to screw up.

# Chapter Three

# A Lost and Found Decade

I drank and played my way through two foggy years at Rutgers. My parents paid the tuition, and I took unchallenging part-time jobs to fund my extra-curricular activities.

One was testing Band-Aids for Johnson & Johnson at its headquarters in New Brunswick. Squares of experimental adhesive tapes were stuck to my back in neat ranks. A week later, I'd return, and a white-coated lab tech peeled them off, examined my skin for rashes and other undesirable outcomes, and applied new patches. I also repaired vacuum cleaners in a downtown shop and peddled snacks at a drive-in movie, pushing a cart up and down the lanes of cars as couples made out in the dark. My parents, appalled by my abysmal academic performance and betrayal of their trust, finally adopted a tough-love tactic, and cut me off financially. I dropped out of Rutgers and returned, head bowed, to Madelyne Place. After a dispiriting year of working as an assistant cabinetmaker and an apprentice butcher for my father, which humiliated both of us, I realized I was rushing headlong toward a destination I had no desire to reach. Somehow, I was able to clear my mind of the haze through which I'd been wandering and make a plan. I moved to New York, where, for $35 a month, I rented a one-room apartment on the Lower East Side. The bathtub was in the kitchen. When I covered it with a sheet of plywood, it became the dining table. My new home was not far from where my grandparents had come ashore all those years before. It also was walking distance to the New York University (NYU) campus, at Washington Square, in Greenwich Village. I enrolled in night classes in English literature and took courses in filmmaking, which I enjoyed enormously.

NYU was for decades a huge academic sausage grinder, which drew in tens of thousands of mainly Jewish and Catholic kids from blue- and no-collar families and churned them out equipped for white-collar professions and business. By the time I got there, though, with New York City reeling from years of rising crime and falling finances, enrollments at "NY Jew" were down. No doubt that helped explain why I was accepted.

45

I had deceived my parents and myself into believing was my goal and for which I possessed neither the talent nor the will. But what?

A week or so after I'd completed Advanced Infantry Training at Camp Lejeune in North Carolina and returned to New York, I spotted in the *New York Times* classified section an opening in the mailroom of ABC-TV. I took the subway to the network's offices, on West Sixty-Sixth Street, and was hired on the spot. It was the quintessential starter job, sorting letters and delivering them throughout the building, but it provided an opportunity to meet people. Some of them were writers.

A favorite stop on my rounds was the office of Adolph "Al" Seton, a crew-cut former Navy commander, then in his mid-forties. Al ruled the On-Air Promotions Department and ran a team of creative people. He was gregarious, and I enjoyed schmoozing with him. One day I asked if he would read a sample of my writing. He agreed, so I typed up a mock promo for ABC's popular police drama, the one that began with the intro, "There are Eight Million Stories in the 'Naked City.'" I left the single page on his desk. When I returned a few hours later, I found Seton in his chair, my copy before him, eyes shut, chin on chest, snoring. I slunk away and returned with trepidation the next day. My promo was awful, Seton told me. The prose was purple, the delivery repetitive, utterly lacking in the excitement needed to entice a viewer to tune in. As he rained down blow upon blow, I felt as though he was hammering me into the floor. Any moment, I would slip between the boards and disappear.

"But," he said at last, "you should try again."

Thus began a trial by one-man jury, with me writing and Seton critiquing. A few weeks later, he called me into his office and offered me a job, writing promos. Thrilled, I crept back up from between the floorboards. No longer was I a mail boy. I was a writer! I had my own gray, metal desk and a battered manual Royal typewriter. On my twenty-first birthday, Seton invited me to join he and his wife, Stella, who'd come into town by ferry from their home on Staten Island, for a celebratory drink at Café des Artistes, across the street from the office. It was a favored ABC watering hole, lined in dark wood and leather and renowned for its pastel murals of nude wood nymphs by Howard Chandler Christy. I'd never seen such decadent opulence. For my first legal drink, I ordered Al's standby, "Beefeater martini, straight up, very dry, very cold, with a twist." Stella gasped in mock maternal horror. "Goodness, Lew, what will you have to look forward to?"

As the evening wore on and martini glasses were refilled (I vaguely recall three), Al spun tales of his navy adventures, including surviving the attack on Pearl Harbor aboard the USS *St. Louis*. He also mentioned that he had been a reporter at the *Providence Journal* in Rhode Island, after attending the Graduate School of Journalism at Columbia University. That last part caught my attention. Al became my mentor. He encouraged me to apply to Columbia. Acknowledged to be the best in the country, the J School was highly selective. Given my sketchy academic history and years of aimlessness, acceptance came as a surprise. With full credit to Al, I enrolled in the class of 1964.

I fell in love on my first day at Columbia. Leafing through the class's black, loose-leaf "face book" (yes, Virginia, those were the originals), my eyes settled on a postage-stamp-sized photo and thumbnail bio of one Carol Seiderman. She was stunning. But something more showed through the grainy, black-and-white photo. Reflected in the large, bright eyes, I saw intelligence and gentle awareness. I had to meet her, without delay. I lurked near the registration table at the front of the school's newsroom until she walked in. Those eyes were green. She was tall and willowy with wavy, auburn hair. I introduced myself and tossed one of the lamest pitches in the history of boy-meets-girl: "I've got an hour to kill. How about a cup of coffee?"

Perhaps having an hour of her own to kill and, what the hell, a cup of coffee is a cup of coffee, she accepted. We strolled from the campus across Broadway to Chock Full o'Nuts. She dazzled me. While I'd been directionless, she was focused. While I had wasted years, she had worked hard and achieved goals. She told me she'd known since third grade that she wanted to be a journalist. She'd been the editor of her high-school paper and the first woman to run the *Tufts Daily*.

She was cheerful and optimistic. Having grown up in a family shrouded in pessimism, speaking with someone who could find promise and joy in almost anything was a revelation. Where I saw black or gray, she saw white; where I saw half-empty and dropping, she saw full and spilling over. I knew with absolute certainty that we were a perfect fit. How I knew that after a single cup of coffee remains a mystery. But, more than half a century later, I can safely conclude that I was right; I had met the girl I was going to marry. Carol didn't buy it. A few days later, as we were climbing the stairs in the journalism building, I told her my plans for us. She was horrified. She was having the time of her life. She was enjoying New York and her dating calendar was packed. My declaration was not what she wanted to hear. We continued through Columbia as friends with no benefits. We graduated in June and went to work the next day at jobs for which we'd been recruited at the school: me with the Associated Press (AP), she with *Newsweek*. Back then, representatives of leading print and broadcast companies around the country came to Columbia toward the end of each academic year in search of promising talent. Nearly all of our eighty classmates were employed by graduation day. That's the way things were in the news business back then. At a class reunion, twenty years later, I joined a table of half a dozen graduates of the class of 1984. None had a real job. One had an unpaid internship.

A few were developing something they called "podcasts" and other "online" phenomena I'd barely heard of. That's the way things are in the news business today. I had decided toward the end of the school year that I wanted to become a foreign correspondent. It was the most exciting journalism work I could think of, and the AP fielded more people abroad than any other news organization. I used my dream to entice Carol, telling her about all the fascinating places we'd visit. Carol was one of three classmates who went to work at *Newsweek*. She had the good fortune of being hired as a researcher, replacing a woman who quit on short notice. She gathered material for a man who wrote a weekly column called "Newsmakers," made phone calls to sources, checked facts, and ran errands for her boss. The second *Newsweek* classmate was Margie Lindauer. She became a "clipper," a standard beginning position for women. Each morning, Margie, who also had a degree from the University of Michigan, pulled on a pair of white cotton gloves and spent the next eight hours wielding scissors and a straight edge, clipping articles out of newspapers to be perused by reporters and editors. By the end of the day, she was smeared in black ink. The third member of our class to join *Newsweek* was a witty fellow named Paul Zimmerman. He was hired as a reporter, at a substantially higher salary than "the girls." That, too, was the way things were in America's newsrooms in 1964.

While Carol was researching in the *Newsweek* building on Lexington Avenue, I was editing copy on the AP news desk at Rockefeller Center, a few blocks away. On Friday nights, after *Newsweek*'s 11:00 p.m. closing, we'd meet at Tad's, in Times Square, where a gristly steak and baked potato cost $1.99. Persistence served me well throughout my career, and I persisted for a year to convince Carol that a two-journalist household could be a happy one. I sweetened the pot with promises that we would lead a glamorous life abroad. We were married on February 7, 1965. She was twenty-three and I was twenty-six. The wedding was at the Doral Country Club in Miami. Forty-seven years later, Donald Trump bought the Doral in a bankruptcy sale.

## Chapter Four

# Total Bullshit

The morning after our wedding, we set out for Denver, where I was assigned to the Associated Press (AP) bureau. We had answered a want ad in the *Miami Herald* seeking a driver to deliver a repossessed Plymouth to a used-car dealer in Boulder. Carol's cat, Haiku, nestled in her lap.

As we drove across the country, terra incognita to both of us, the orange-and-cream Plymouth sedan, distinguished by a faux "continental wheel" on the trunk, fell apart. By the time we reached Alabama, a chrome door strip had dropped off and rattled between us from dashboard to rear window. Tires blew in Mississippi and Louisiana. The fan belt ruptured somewhere in East Texas. The battery expired. So did the heater, causing us to bundle up in coats and hats for the last several days of the journey across the plains toward the Rockies.

We loved every minute, every mile.

Approaching Denver from the south just after sunset, we suddenly were drenched in a shower of golden light cast by the Mile High City, silhouetting a black stretch of jagged foothills.

AP, with uncharacteristic generosity, had booked us into the historic Brown Palace Hotel. All polished brass and sparkling cut-glass, it was the sort of place where moneyed visitors to the Old West had put up. We checked in, feeling like minor royalty.

I went to work the next morning. As would become the pattern in our travels over the decades, Carol began the stressful process of finding work. After several weeks, she wangled an interview with *Denver Post* editor and publisher Palmer Hoyt, one of the day's leading reform-minded journalists. He hired her as a reporter. For the women's pages, of course.

For the next fifteen months, she reported for the *Post* from 9:00 a.m. to 5:00 p.m. while I worked overnight, from 11:00 p.m. to 7:00 a.m. The AP bureau was in the *Post* building and we'd leave notes on each other's type-writers. I'd return home and down a bedtime Coors while she sipped her

imagined an office would have its own elegant dining-room, a fully staffed kitchen, and uniformed waiters.

One by one, the dark-suited executives interrogated us: What did we want to be doing now? In five years? In ten? At the culmination of our careers? One wanted to have his own column; the other said he wanted to occupy Gallagher's position. I wanted to go overseas to Africa, because, I proclaimed with certainty born of ignorance, "the future of the world is there."

We left Manhattan the next morning, scattering across the country to our home bureaus. A month later, I was back in Rockefeller Center. My parents, who garnered timeless wisdom through their lifelong subscription to *Reader's Digest*, had imparted that "the wheel that squeaks loudest gets the grease." I had squeaked, loudly, and the grease was a six-month trial period on the foreign desk in New York, editing incoming raw copy from AP correspondents around the world. It was the overnight shift, but still . . .

Mornings, after work, I would ride the elevator down to the Berlitz language school on the ground floor, where I took intensive lessons in French, the lingua franca of western and central Africa. Some days, I walked over to the United Nations building, to meet with African diplomats. Then I'd head home to our tiny apartment on West Fifty-Seventh Street. It was just a block from the CBS-TV studios, where Carol had landed a job with Walter Cronkite, everyone's favorite uncle, on *The 21st Century*, his speculative program on how humans might be living in the not-too-distant future.

One morning, moments after I'd dozed off, the phone rang. On the other end, a resonant voice; the conversation, brief and, for me, so memorable that I can replay it in my mind verbatim.

"Lew, Keith Fuller."

"Yes, Mr. Fuller."

"Sorry to wake you, but we need a warm body in Saigon. Interested?"

Vietnam! Truth to tell, I had no interest in covering the war. I'd had just enough military experience to have a pretty good idea of what I'd be in for. But I very much wanted to go overseas and understood that declining this offer would diminish chances of a future posting. Dodging, I responded after what seemed to me like a very long, very pregnant pause.

"You know, I'm preparing for Africa."

"Yes," he replied, "but we don't need you in Africa now. We need you in Vietnam."

"Okay, Mr. Fuller, pencil me in as interested," I said. "But I've got to discuss this with my wife before I can give you a definite answer."

I hung up and phoned Carol at work. She responded with one word, "Yes." So Carol. So up for anything.

What I didn't tell Fuller was that I also felt obliged to speak with my parents. I was an adult, I was married, but I also was their only child. Guilt was an integral part of my package.

The scene unreeled in my imagination: We'd drive to Fair Lawn in our blue Corvair, have supper around the wood-tone Formica table in my parents' dinette, and then I'd break the news.

"Mother, Dad, Carol and I are going to Vietnam."

"Ha, ha."

"No, really, I've been offered an assignment covering the war."

(Parents would turn pale.)

(Silence would come from Carol and me.)

"Lewis, Carol, please don't do this. We beg you. It will be the end of us."

(Long pause.)

"Okay, Mother and Dad, if you feel so strongly, I will tell them no."

The real conversation went pretty much as I'd imagined. Carol and I drove back along Route 4 and across the Washington Bridge to Manhattan in pained silence, utterly dejected.

The next morning, as I was about to call Fuller and say I wouldn't take the Saigon assignment, the phone rang. It was Mother.

"Lewis, Dad and I couldn't sleep all night," she said. "We don't want you to go. But if you feel it's that important, we're not going to stand in your way."

Astonished and impressed by my parents' forbearance, and knowing how wretched their night must have been, I ended the call by thanking Mother and assuring her that everything would be fine. Then I hung up and dialed.

"Mr. Fuller, I'm your warm body."

The AP is a nonprofit cooperative, established in 1846 as a kind of telegraphic pony express to carry news of the Mexican American War northward. The five founding New York City newspapers have since ballooned to 1,900 outlets worldwide. AP today delivers the news by state-of-the-art electronics, but it's still known as a "wire service," a holdover from when it moved signals on copper strands strung on overhead poles.

Those that rely most heavily on the service are small and mid-sized papers and broadcasters. Major dailies and networks subscribe but also field their own correspondents, to whom they grant pride of place.

During the Vietnam War, before CNN and other twenty-four-hour news outlets, AP, its chief American rival, United Press International (UPI), and the British-owned Reuters were the world's leading news wholesalers. Even the big print and broadcast organizations, with their own staffers on the ground, relied on the wires and their deadline-a-minute culture for backup and tips.

The smaller papers and stations tended to be more politically conservative and more hawkish on the war than their big-city cousins. Many complained that the AP Saigon bureau, in particular standout reporter Peter Arnett, consistently delivered what they considered an anti-war, anti-American message: the US military effort in Vietnam wasn't going well. This line of reporting was similar in tone to that of the giants—the *New York Times*, the *Washington Post*, *Los Angeles Times*, ABC, CBS, and NBC. And it irked folks in places like Wichita and Tuscaloosa, Lubbock and Missoula.

My Marine Reserve enlistment had been peaceful, brief, and utterly without distinction, but it turned out to be a key factor in my being offered the assignment. AP management viewed my military service as the answer to their Saigon bureau problem. A recent grunt, hair still clipped short, was unlikely to be critical of the US war effort. He'd be a hawk, or at least hawkish.

They were right.

"Just report what you see and hear," Gallagher told me in a bon voyage pep talk. "No analysis, no interpreting. Just the facts." Unspoken but understood was that such unevaluated reporting would be read as pro-war.

That, I assured Gallagher in all honesty, would not be a stretch for me. I believed President Lyndon Johnson and General William Westmoreland were doing the right thing and that the United States soon would prevail over the ragtag Vietnamese Communists.

As for those Vietnamese, I was mystified by what sustained their seemingly suicidal drive against the world's mightiest power. What enabled them to hold on so stubbornly while suffering devastating losses? What could they hope to achieve? But these were not questions to which I or many other Americans, including the troops on the ground and our leaders in the White House, Congress, and the Pentagon, devoted much thought in those early years of the war.

What we were sure of was that those little, brown peasants intended to seize the southern, democratic half of their divided country, then plot with the Soviet Union and China to make it part of a worldwide Communist dictatorship. Their cause was futile, we would prove, by next Christmas . . . next year . . . soon . . .

Gallagher, whose rumpled face competed for attention with a salt-and-pepper crew cut and twin awnings of luxuriant eyebrows, had led AP's World War II combat coverage. He once posed, smiling, for an AP photo wearing a white bullet-proof vest over his bare chest, gripping a Luger in one hand and examining other captured German weapons with the other.

During World War II correspondents were subject to military censorship. Their patriotism ran high, and their criticism of the war effort was limited. Some of this unquestioning acceptance—support, really—carried over to Korea and then to Vietnam, particularly during the early days. Correspondents relayed the command's claims of success and approaching victory with minimal dissent.

There was no censorship in Vietnam. As the fighting wore on and journalists began to detect daylight spreading between what they were told and what they saw, their reporting grew more discerning, even disparaging. This frustrated senior commanders and government officials, and they began urging reporters to "get on the team." Not to do so, they argued, was un-American.

I bought in. If the people we'd elected determined we must go to war, then we must. The war was just. Only over time did I come to realize that determining who was patriotic wasn't up to the government. All governments make wrong decisions. All lie, more so while at war than any other time. If any institution has the right—the responsibility, constitutionally guaranteed—to question government actions and relay the answers to the public, it is the press.

In his later years at the helm, Gallagher recognized that in Vietnam, AP's responsibility had moved on toward providing something deeper, grayer, more nuanced and analytical than what it had provided historically.

"The man in the street has become more cynical," he summed up in 1976, a year after the last shot was fired in Vietnam. The man—and woman—in the street wanted more interpretation and perspective. But Gallagher hadn't gained that insight until well after I departed for Saigon. Neither had I. The months I'd spent working on the foreign desk in New York, editing war copy, only added to my determination to be the team player Gallagher needed.

While honing my gung ho persona, I also began accumulating trepidation for what our lives would be like in Vietnam. I edited stories of deadly Viet Cong attacks in Saigon, on a floating restaurant frequented by Americans and on the Brinks Bachelor Officers Quarters, near the AP bureau; hair-raising tales of Americans being stabbed on the streets with poisoned umbrella tips and, of course, the ebb and flow of daily warfare.

Despite the scary stories, Carol and I were more eager than afraid. We shared the excitement and anticipation of a new experience. She had managed to keep her job with CBS and would be a researcher in its Saigon bureau.

Like most young Americans crossing the Pacific to Southeast Asia in July 1967, I had never before left the United States. Carol had traveled in Europe the summer after college. I'd flown on an airplane once to New Orleans, to visit family friends, a high school graduation gift from my parents. Now, we were on a very different trip. To a war. A war that would change America, change Vietnam, change Asia, change the world.

Change us.

As our Pan Am flight from Honolulu descended, I was dumbstruck by the delicate beauty coming into focus beneath white wings of our plane. Precise rows of emerald-green rice in sparkling paddy fields; palm-fringed, sandy beaches; the chocolate waters of the Mekong snaking crazily across a table-top floodplain to join the Saigon River, coil the city, then flow into the fertile Mekong Delta, all came into view. We admired the pretty little houses of white stucco with red-tile roofs, many with circular swimming pools, and imagined that we might live in one. Then we learned that the pools were bomb craters, filled with rainwater reflecting the brilliant, blue sky.

I half expected that when our plane touched down at Tan Son Nhut Airport we'd have to dash to a bomb shelter. We had discussed this in considerable detail. Who would go first? Should we hold hands? Who would carry the cat?

Instead, we filed in orderly fashion through customs and immigration formalities. A few dollars quietly changed hands and our crisp new passports were stamped. We claimed the two suitcases we'd packed for the thirteen months ahead and entered the fray.

The small reception hall was crammed with sweating, chaotic humanity, a Babel of shouting in melodic Vietnamese scrambled with English and French echoing off the walls. We spotted Bob Tuckman, the AP bureau chief. Florid, graying, and smiling broadly, he was accompanied by a placid Vietnamese, Anton, the bureau's driver, who took our bags. We climbed into the office sedan and headed for town.

A beguiling new world unspooled before our eyes, like a Technicolor travelogue, during the half-hour drive:

Flocks of deceptively delicate-looking women in conical straw hats, black trousers, white blouses, and plastic flip-flops, shuffling along the dust-blown roadside like ducks in a row, balancing across their shoulders split bamboo poles bowed by overflowing baskets of tropical fruits and vegetables.

Entire families perched on motor scooters, some hauling a brace of trussed, live chickens or a squealing, suckling pig. Schoolgirls in white gowns, *ao dai*, satiny trousers flashing through waist-high slits, wove their bicycles through unruly traffic. Clusters of solemn Buddhist bonzes, heads shaved, swathed in ankle-length, saffron-colored robes clutched begging bowls to their waists. Wiry men in black shirts and shorts were bent parallel to the ground, knee-deep in watery paddies while other men, in Western clothes, strolled in pairs, linking their long-nailed pinkies, a sign that they did not perform manual labor.

Snarling, canvas-topped US Army trucks belched black fumes, fouling the air. The spinning rotors of American helicopters overhead beat the signature tattoo of the war as machine-gun-armed cowboys hung recklessly out of the open sides, scanning for possible threats and targets of opportunity.

The fears that had accompanied me across the ocean drifted out the open car windows, swept away by sheer fascination, and evaporated on the sticky, hot breeze. From that moment on, I was simultaneously hypnotized and flummoxed, yet immediately comfortable in this incomprehensible place.

Over a career of fifty years, this paradox would replay itself in country after country. Like Dorothy in Oz—"Toto, I've a feeling we're not in Kansas anymore"—nothing was familiar. Yet I felt at home.

Tuckman and Anton delivered us to the Hotel Continental. The celebrated French-colonial relic, which once provided respite for up-country planters, now bustled with visiting correspondents who met for drinks and gossip on its open porch, which they called the "Continental Shelf." More than a decade earlier, Graham Greene had written his Indochina masterpiece, *The Quiet American*, in room 214. Coated in mildew-stained whitewash, the building still evoked a faded Belle Époque sensibility.

In a small plaza fronting the hotel stood the flamboyantly arched Saigon Opera House, another hubristic expression of imperial France's certainty that its dominance in Indochina—like Britain's in India and Holland's in Indonesia—would last forever. But history buries its passage in layers and now, with the United States running the show, South Vietnam's National Assembly performed its rubber-stamp role in the auditorium.

A bellboy in a frayed white tunic and pillbox hat lugged our bags up the stairs to our second-floor room. With a fourteen-foot ceiling that loomed over a mosquito-netted bed, the room was spacious enough for us to host a large party. We didn't, but a uniformed attendant, who sat full-time in the hall, was ready to spring into action at our command if we did.

The bellboy yanked up tall, creaky windows and pushed open dusty-white, wood-slat shutters. We glanced across Rue Tu Do at the sooty Eden Building, where AP and other news organizations maintained offices. Tu Do, which the French had boasted of as the Champs-Elysées of Saigon, retained a veneer of elegance, although military truck exhaust was choking the life out of its ancient shade trees. If we shut our eyes to the thousands of refugees sleeping on the sidewalks, it was almost possible to imagine why the French colonials, with exaggerated Gallic pride, once described Saigon as *le Paris d'Orient*.

A sickly sweet stench drifted in through our windows on amber shafts of scorching sunlight: open drains; stale urine; rotting garbage; sugarcane husks squeezed dry of their juice; sizzling cooking oil; and, most potent, putrefying, fermenting anchovies, the basis of nuoc mam, the essential sauce of Vietnamese cuisine.

Repulsive yet intoxicating, the stink was, for me, the first of many of the most powerful and most memorable sensory identifiers. To this day, I know by whatever is in the air which Asian country I'm in.

I handed the bellboy a wad of multicolored Vietnamese piastres. Not until the next day, when I realized that, discombobulated and jet-lagged, I'd tipped him the equivalent of $100, did I understand why he had appeared faint as he backed out, bowing and murmuring, *merci beaucoup, Monsieur, merci beaucoup, merci*.

While enjoying a few recuperative days at the Continental, we located an apartment, on the second floor of what Southeast Asians know as a shop-house: a store on the ground floor and living quarters above. It was in the center of a narrow, one-block street named Rue Nguyen Thiep, less than five minutes' walk to our bureaus. On our limited budget, we got two rooms linked by an unlit hallway. We designated the smaller room, which had no windows, our bedroom. The larger one became the everything-else room. Each contained a shower, toilet, and, *naturellement*, a bidet.

We created a kitchen in one of the showers with a gas hot plate on a metal folding table. We bought a little fridge at the American-operated post exchange and installed it alongside a wicker sofa, two chairs, and a table we found at a street market. Our favorite spot quickly became the balcony over-looking the street off the everything-else room. We cooked hamburgers on a small charcoal hibachi while Haiku relaxed on the wall.

Sharing our home were swarms of glistening brown cockroaches and chir-ruping geckos that skittered across ceilings on suction-cupped feet. Haiku never stopped chasing, though never capturing, one of the little lizards. Carol, a lifelong herpetophobe, remained petrified that one would land in her hair.

Our landlord, Monsieur Nguyen, operated a tailor shop on the ground floor with his two daughters. Wisps of pungent smoke from the back room informed us that he was an opium addict. He may have been fifty, but looked seventy, with sharply protruding cheekbones and a single, long, meticu-lously cultivated, white hair flourishing from a mole on his left cheek. He insisted that we deposit our monthly rent, in US dollars, directly into his Swiss account.

We spent most of our time working. The CBS office was housed in several rooms at the Caravelle Hotel, a contemporary egg crate with a rooftop bar that offered splendid nighttime son et lumière displays of artillery fire and rockets exploding on the edge of town. To get to the AP office, in the Eden Building, one could climb the stairs, as I usually did for the exercise, or ride a wheezing elevator. The lift bore a brass plaque engraved with a warning in French that *boys et boyesses*—Vietnamese service workers of both genders—were not permitted aboard. It was a small, tarnished reminder of the role that racism had played in igniting the revolt against French colonialism.

The AP bureau comprised a newsroom with half a dozen desks and type-writers. Clipboards on a varnished wood counter held the day's wire reports from around the world, a magnet for visiting journalists in those pre-Internet days. They congregated around the printouts, shared gossip, and caught up on the progress of the world and the war.

There was a cramped teletype room and a darkroom where photo chief Horst Faas held sway. An instinctive news photographer and brilliant orga-nizer, Faas was legendary. He was burly but agile and spoke English fluently in a basso profundo with a broad Teutonic overlay. He was accompanied by his wife, Ursula, and the four of us occasionally dined together. Horst was particularly fond of the blood sausages at the Aterbea, a nearby restaurant run by a Corsican. Like any number of long-term expats in Indochina, the restaurateur was addicted to opium and joked with us about his *chaser le dragon*.

One morning, shortly after we arrived, Horst invited me to an alfresco breakfast. We sat on kindergarten-sized bamboo stools at the curb while the cook, a toothless woman in a straw hat, served us generous bowls of pho, thin noodles in beef broth. Although soup for breakfast seemed odd, I loved the tangy mixture. Nowadays, I seldom go more than a week without a pho infusion.

For our second course, Faas ordered *nem chua*, chunks of fermented pork wrapped in banana leaves and tied with straw into cigarette-pack-size parcels. I knew he was testing me, and I was damned if I'd fail. Doing my best to ignore the powerful odor and the off-putting idea of consuming uncooked pork, I chewed and swallowed. And smiled. I didn't love it, but it wasn't awful either.

Food trials like this, I would learn, were standard practice across Asia, used by old hands to take the measure of new arrivals. There was potentially deadly fugu sashimi in Japan; fried crickets in Thailand; cold, rubbery jelly-fish in mustard sauce and toasted scorpion perched on potato chips in China. I passed the tests and discovered that having been raised on overcooked meat and potatoes, I'd become an adventurous diner.

In addition to managing his staff of Western and Vietnamese photographers, Horst encouraged young freelancers to bring him their work in return for a few dollars and a crack at recognition. He and Arnett, both of whom won Pulitzer Prizes for their remarkable war coverage, helped make the AP bureau a matchless powerhouse.

I still cringe when I recall a heated discussion I got into with Arnett over dinner at the Aterba soon after we arrived. I had noticed that he and other staff members, when mentioning US forces, used "the Americans," just as they used "the NVA" or "the Viet Cong." I took that as excessively dispassionate, if not unpatriotic, and said I believed we should be writing "us" and "our side."

A broader debate ensued. Arnett, whose Vietnamese wife, Nina, sat beside him, smiling tranquilly, argued that the Americans failed to understand the Vietnamese and therefore were losing the war. I insisted with baseless certainty that "our side" was right, that "our cause" was just, and that inevitably "we" would win. All this after being "in country" less than a month. Talk about chutzpah.

Several other superb AP correspondents and photographers had been covering the war for years. Eddie Adams and Nick Ut won Pulitzers for iconic photos that branded themselves on the world's memory. Henri Huet, son of a French father and a Vietnamese mother, had been a paratrooper with the French army before joining AP. He was killed in 1971, when a helicopter in which he was riding with three other photojournalists was shot down over Laos.

These men and others—women were few and far between—gave AP a depth of knowledge and experience that few other, if any, Saigon news bureaus enjoyed. In some, especially the TV networks, correspondents commonly competed with each other as rivals. The AP people worked together, some lived together. They shared meals and what little free time they had. They helped each other, took care of each other. And they quickly made me, the virginal, wide-eyed newcomer, their brother.

For my maiden voyage into the field, days after arriving in Saigon, Bob Tuckman arranged for me to travel with General Westmoreland, the commander of US forces. AP was under intense pressure from its conservative newspaper members and by the Johnson administration to hew closer to the official position on the war. I was there to help make that happen or, at least, to give that impression.

My marching orders, echoing Wes Gallagher's bon voyage speech, were to report what I saw and heard. Nothing more. I was the newest kid on the block and the assumption was that, as a Marine Private First Class, I wouldn't be inclined—or know enough—to ask awkward questions of America's top general. The assumption was correct. I looked on the great man with esteem.

Westmoreland had been the top graduate of the West Point class of 1936 and amassed a distinguished combat record during World War II and Korea. Unlike in those campaigns, though, there were no clear front lines in Vietnam, no great corps-on-corps confrontations, no game-changing victories and defeats. Just relentless, erratic, shifting, hit-and-run attacks and counterattacks. Day in and day out. Death by a thousand cuts. So Westmoreland chose a strategy of attrition. Capitalizing on overwhelming US troop strength, advanced weaponry and backing by the Army of the Republic of Vietnam (ARVN), he believed he could grind the North Vietnamese Army (NVA) and its allied Viet Cong (VC) guerrilla force into submission.

Westy, as he liked being called, wasted no opportunity claiming battlefield success upon success. But he wasn't winning the hearts and minds of ordinary Vietnamese. Nor was he convincing a progressively more skeptical American press corps that the war was going his way.

Arithmetic illustrated his problem.

When he took command, in 1963, some sixteen thousand US troops were stationed in country. When he departed in 1968, the number was in excess of half a million. Over those five years, the number of Americans killed in action soared to 16,899. (By war's end, in 1975, that figure had more than tripled.)

Yet, day after day, Westmoreland claimed minimal American losses and staggering enemy body counts. True, the enemy death count was enormous. But the foe was relentless. Regardless of how many they lost, the NVA and the Viet Cong never seemed to run out of fresh manpower, never seemed to tire. Meanwhile, Americans at home and on the ground were growing weary and dispirited.

I met up with Westmoreland and a young aide early in the morning at Tan Son Nhut and we climbed aboard the general's light plane. To deny that Westy was a Hollywood studio's dream, the very model of a modern four-star general, would be like arguing that George C. Scott wasn't Patton or John Wayne didn't slog across the sands of Iwo Jima.

Westy portrayed a classic, central casting image: silvery sideburns peeping from beneath an olive-drab ball cap; dark, piercing eyes; granite jaw; arrow-straight posture; fatigues meticulously starched and pressed; jungle boots with black leather toes spit-shined to a glassy sheen. The aide carried the general's brown leather attaché case, from which he dispensed lemon-scented, moist towelettes to the boss as temperature and humidity rose through the day.

We flew north from Saigon to the narrow waist of the dragon-shaped country, an area the US military designated II Corps. Our first stop was at a First Cavalry Division firebase. After the little plane skidded to a halt on the dirt landing strip, a boyish lieutenant with rosy cheeks and a toothy smile stepped forward and introduced himself.

"Hi, Mr. Simons, I'm Don Graham, the information officer here. How can I help?"

I thanked him and said I was there to shadow Westmoreland, which he knew.

We would meet again, four years later, in the composing room of the *Washington Post*, where we both were going through the newspaper's introductory program for new journalists.

"Hi, Lew," he shouted over the metallic racket of linotype machines. "We met in Vietnam, remember?"

A lightbulb flashed on. Don was the son and heir apparent to Katherine Graham, the *Post*'s owner.

Officers snapped to attention, exchanged crisp salutes with Westy, then escorted him into the command bunker, a sandbagged hole in the ground furnished with a few folding chairs. With red grease pencils, the officers traced their recent operations on a plasticized map of the immediate area. Their message was undeviatingly upbeat—enemy KIA high; "friendly" losses low. I sat in the rear and jotted notes.

Following repeat performances at two more locations, we boarded the plane for the hop back to Saigon. Westmoreland wiped the sheen from his forehead and I, unable to restrain my curiosity, screwed up my nerve.

"General," I began tentatively, "this may seem arrogant for a reporter who's been in country barely a week." He grinned accommodatingly. "It seems to me that what's going on here is something like a district sales manager back home calling on his staff and being told business has never been better. Do you take it with a grain of salt or is this what you report back to Washington?"

He smiled again, reached across the narrow space between our facing seats, and tapped my knee with a neatly trimmed index fingernail.

"Son," he said in the paternalistic tone that senior military officers and football coaches use to remind their young charges who's in charge, "I take it with a large grain of salt. I know that these officers, like those salesmen, are trying to impress the boss. So, of course, I take that into consideration in my reporting."

But he didn't.

His optimistic body-count assessments to Washington reflected precisely the kind of briefings I heard and saw that day. Eventually, they raised an inescapable question on the home front. If that many bad guys have been killed, how come they're still fighting?

My report for AP, which I filed that evening, ignored that unpleasantness. It included Westy's grain-of-salt disclaimer, without comment, and cast no doubt on his positive assessment of how the war was going. It was a straight-forward account of what Westmoreland had seen, heard, and told me. That's what AP wanted. And that was fine with me.

But a tiny grain, not of salt but of unanticipated skepticism, had lodged in my mind.

One of the little secrets that correspondents keep from their editors is that life in a war zone, while often risky and at times deadly, can also be privileged, comfortable, exciting, even fun.

The war became my life. I didn't just do the job and go home to watch TV. The war was everything. I lived it, breathed it, ate and drank it. Wherever I went, whatever I was doing, the war was always on my mind. But, unlike the soldiers I covered, who were permitted only scant moments away from the fight, I could leave the battlefield whenever one encounter ended and before the next one began; whenever I chose to, in fact.

While the troops only rarely enjoyed hot showers and meals, I had plenty of both. There was excellent French, Vietnamese, and Chinese cuisine at local restaurants; steaks and burgers broiled to order at American-run clubs. Good wine, hard liquor, and cold beer flowed. Like my colleagues, I stretched the purchasing power of my dollars by swapping the green for South Vietnamese piastres at "The Bank of India," a shady money-laundering operation run by a band of expat Indians.

Our first visit to the Saigon PX was an eye-opener, a surreal journey back to the United States. Along with imported American food and beverages, cosmetics and smokes, it offered the latest TV sets and other electronics, refrigerators and air-conditioners, all at reduced, government-subsidized prices. Soldiers from some allied countries, Filipinos and Thais especially, exploited their PX privileges, reselling their purchases on South Vietnam's thriving black market or shipping them home to their families.

Elbowing our way through shouting street vendors in the narrow alleyway leading to the PX, Carol and I found ourselves pushing a cart behind a broad-beamed senior NCO in Air Force blue. "No martini olives," he groused to a uniformed companion. "Jesus!"

"War is hell!" I stage-whispered.

To this day, when something less than serious goes sideways in our lives, one of us will remind the other, "No martini olives!"

I learned the twists and turns of developing news sources. A few days after filing a detailed, up-close piece on an ARVN-VC skirmish I'd covered, I received a phone call from a man with an American accent.

"Hi, Lew, this is _____ at the embassy. Could you stop by for a chat?"

Sure. We discussed my story. He was interested in what I'd written about the South Vietnamese soldiers' fighting spirit. (It was lacking.) I answered several of his questions. He replied to some of mine, but mostly he waltzed gracefully off topic. It dawned on me that he was a spook. He wanted me as a source, just as I wanted him as one. But at what cost?

"Remember," he said, "information is a two-way street. If you want to get, you have to give."

That was the price. I'd have to spy for a spy. Some correspondents did. I decided I wouldn't. After half an hour or so, I thanked him and he said, "Let's stay in touch." I never saw him again.

The experience planted a sapling that grew to maturity over the years. I came to recognize that close personal relationships with spies, diplomats, politicians, and others in positions of power, while appealing, carried a major downside. Insiders could provide otherwise-unavailable information, but they often required compromise.

That, I decided, was a line I was unwilling to step across.

I was so naive. Corruption fueled by a massive influx of US taxpayers' dollars was rampant among military and civilian Americans and South Vietnamese. GIs were smuggling narcotics back home. South Vietnamese generals and government officials were hoarding gold and stashing dollars in Hong Kong or Swiss banks. In time, I caught on.

I also became aware of a journalistic caste system. With both Carol and I low on the career ladder, our shophouse living quarters were, to put it gently, simple. On the other side of the journalistic tracks, correspondents of the upper echelons led very different lives.

R. W. (known to all as Johnny) Apple was a talented and courageous correspondent who ran the *New York Times* bureau. After we'd been in town for a few weeks, he invited us to dinner at his home to meet various press and diplomatic luminaries.

Apple and his wife, Edie, lived in a beautiful colonial villa, decorated with artwork and furniture shipped over from the States. The long dining table was set with starched, white linen; fine china; crystal; and silver. Barefoot Vietnamese servants in white uniforms glided softly across polished teak floors, offering drinks and hors d'oeuvres. It was a glamourous evening.

We were immediately impressed, then envious, then realized how pointless it was. Apple was nothing less than the ambassador of the *New York Times* to the Republic of Vietnam. His home met the diplomatic standard of "representational dwelling," suited to receiving the power elite. It reflected his and his paper's stature.

I did have a few small advantages open to me, particularly in the field. I wore my out-of-date USMC utilities with my name and the AP logo newly embroidered over the breast pockets. The faded uniform made clear to the grunts that I'd once been one of them, which went down well. For old time's sake, I spent more time with the Marines than with the other services.

On one outing, I linked up with a marine patrol on a search-and-destroy mission near Dong Ha, in South Vietnam's far north. We tramped for a couple of hours through spotty jungle and across open fields without making contact. When we reached a dry rice paddy, the sergeant called a break. He anticipated that the paddy had been mined and he wanted his marines alert before beginning to cross. Like the others, I slumped onto my rucksack and relaxed.

After fifteen minutes or so, the sergeant ordered us back onto our feet.

"Saddle up!" He barked a final warning, "Step *only* on the footprints of the man in front of you!"

We stripped our smokes, tipped a last swallow of tepid water from our canteens, and fell in at the edge of the paddy. The sergeant placed me near the rear of the single file.

"Safer," he said, for a civilian, a reporter. I was the thirteenth man.

We began the crossing. At the head of the column, a marine waved a mine detector, which resembled a Brobdingnagian dental tool, slowly back and forth, back and forth, before taking each hesitant step. I was terrified. Stubby rice stalks from the last harvest crunched beneath my boots. My eyes drilled into the faint bootmarks left in the dust by the marine treading warily two yards ahead of me.

Click.

He'd stepped on a mine.

A sharp crack. Red dust, clods of earth, bits of rice stalks. His arms flew over his head. His M-16 clattered to the ground. He collapsed backward onto his ruck, legs shredded to pulp, screaming in shock and agony. I was paralyzed in body and mind.

As my fogged-over thinking returned to reporting mode, a ghostly figure floated into view and sank to his knees at the wounded man's side. Cradling his comrade's head to his chest, he whispered something I couldn't hear. He and another phantom lifted the limp marine and carried him across the remaining few yards of paddy and up a dirt berm. I followed them, taking each step in dread.

They propped his back against a banana tree and gently lifted off his cockeyed helmet. His face was spattered with dirt, blood, bits of pink flesh and white bone. A corpsman tied a tourniquet tightly around the more grievously wounded leg, the left, now a ragged stump severed above the knee, and stabbed a morphine syringe through the man's trousers into his thigh. He wrapped a thick bandage around the right ankle, its booted foot dangling from a strip of blackened skin.

The radio operator called frantically for a medevac helicopter, reciting our site coordinates over and over. The rest of the squad hung back, mute, staring into the sapphire sky, at the ground, left and right, anywhere but *there*.

I looked *only* there. I was transfixed by the suffering young man. He may have been twenty. He was sturdily built, his sandy-brown hair razored high and tight, his eyes pale and blue. *Did those eyes still see anything? Was he thinking? About what? Who was he? What road had brought him to this awful place?* I never found out. By the time the Dustoff chopper arrived, he was dead.

On an army excursion, I joined half a dozen soldiers of the First Cavalry Division who were reconnoitering scrubland and dense jungle in Quang Ngai province. They were volunteers for the exceptionally dangerous job of "tunnel rat." Four of the men were Hispanic; all were short and slim. At five-foot-nine and 150 pounds, I was considerably larger.

Among the specialized fighters in Vietnam, tunnel rats were in a class of their own. Whether they were slightly mad or incredibly courageous is debatable. In *The Tunnels of Cu Chi*, BBC correspondents Tom Mangold and John Pencayte wrote, "There never were more than 100 tunnel rats, and most were killed in the tunnels. [After the war, the authors] spent three years scouring the U.S. for them and could find only 12. [We] suspect there's another 10 left. The attrition rate was appalling."

On one day, I was a few hours into the day's march with the tunnel rats when the man leading our little column halted and raised a hand. He pointed silently to a small, irregular patch of twigs and leaves to his left. A closer look revealed that the scrub covered a hole, no more than two feet square. I certainly wouldn't have spotted it on my own. It was the entry to a larger, blacker hole.

Three rats inserted cigarette filters into their ears. One held out a couple to me and, without a thought, I pressed them into place. Why I didn't say, "No, thanks," escapes me. I suppose I was too consumed in the moment to register the danger. They checked their handguns in underarm holsters and flashlights clipped to web belts. Others quietly pulled away the expertly arranged camouflage material and, grasping our hands, lowered us one by one, feetfirst into the tight opening. I was slotted between the second and third rats.

Imitating the man ahead of me, I knelt on the damp soil, breathing shallowly for a minute or so as my eyes adjusted to the dark. The hole was airless, sweltering, and deathly still. The men drew their .38 caliber revolvers. Fitted with noise suppressors, the smaller weapons were better suited to confined spaces than the standard-issue, heavy-duty .45, with its eardrum-busting muzzle blast. Rats were instructed to fire no more than three rounds at a time; six would let the enemy know the weapons were empty.

Their flashlight beams flicked along the dirt walls of a banana-curved excavation. It was perhaps fifteen feet long, so narrow that my shoulders brushed both sides, and so low that we were forced to duckwalk. Carved into the left wall was a narrow shelf that served as sleeping quarters, kitchen, and dining area for three or four Viet Cong. A few white grains of rice scattered on the red dirt were the only sign they'd been there recently.

Having missed the opportunity to kill them, what remained for the rats was to destroy the tunnel. We backed out, which was easier than turning around, and were hoisted to the surface. We moved off a few yards and lay facedown on the ground. A rat approached the opening, pulled the pin on a grenade, and rolled it in. Seconds later, it went off, the explosion muffled by our cigarette filters. The earth around the entry humped and then settled back. One small tunnel gone. Hundreds more hidden in the moist, red earth of South Vietnam.

Before my experience with the tunnel rats, I had wondered how I would perform in moments of high danger. Would I seize up, unable to do my job? I learned that day and from future encounters that intimate involvement in warfare's violence can be so overwhelming that all else—not just fear but even awareness of time passing—can cease to exist.

That evening I returned to the AP bureau from the day with the rats and was writing my piece when Peter Arnett passed by my desk. Glancing over my shoulder at the paper slowly curling from the typewriter, he blanched.

"Don't ever do that again!" he snapped in his froggy New Zealand twang. "Stay the hell out of the tunnels!"

I followed his advice for the rest of that tour, but, I would have one more go. In 1985, the tenth anniversary of what the American side called the fall of Saigon and the North Vietnamese termed Reunification Day, I returned to Vietnam. At Cu Chi, twenty miles from Saigon, by then officially renamed

Ho Chi Minh City, I underwent one of the more harrowing trials of my reporting career.

Beginning in the late 1940s, the Viet Cong had excavated complex tunnel networks totaling more than 150 miles, between Cu Chi and the Cambodian border. My government guide led me on a short walk through dense jungle. Then, in a gesture reminiscent of what the lead tunnel rat had done that day years before, he held up his hand. I stopped.

"Can you find the entrance to the tunnel?" he asked, knowing full well I couldn't. I turned this way and that, kicking at dead leaves and twigs. I saw nothing but dead leaves and twigs. With the toe of his flip-flop, the guide nudged some aside and exposed a two-foot, plywood square. He removed it and levered himself into the black opening. I followed, and for the next hour, duckwalked and crawled behind him. I clenched a pocket flashlight in my teeth, which strained my jaw but did little to relieve the blackness or my claustrophobia.

I went on this little guided tour before the tourism ministry supersized some of the passages to accommodate Western travelers. My hips and neck ached as I crept through the unending maze. Temporary relief came when we entered caverns that had served as hospitals, schools, and kitchens. Here, soldiers and their families had lived, worked, and plotted attacks throughout the struggle against the French and then the Americans.

With dirt and sweat stinging my eyes, my imagination raced wildly between logic and panic. I was in a grave. I was buried alive. What must it have been like with tanks rumbling overhead and planes dropping bombs? The Americans and South Vietnamese operated vast military bases directly on top of some of the Cu Chi tunnels.

When at last I clambered out, gulping for air, heart pounding, I confessed to my guide, "Now I understand why your side won."

To the skeptics who distrust journalists' veracity, who doubt their motives, I ask this: Who in his or her right mind would do these things, would cross a minefield or creep through a claustrophobic, dirt tunnel and then perpetrate a lie? Not that a correspondent's willingness to take risks assures honest reporting, but you must make that kind of effort to get closer to the truth. You can't do it from a distance or from the convenience of the press gallery.

Some afternoons when I wasn't in the field, I'd walk across Rue Nguyen Hue from the bureau to an auditorium in the Rex Hotel to attend a matinee of the Five o' Clock Follies.

This daily briefing by JUSPAO, the Joint US Public Affairs Office, earned its term of faux endearment from correspondents who mocked it as a vaudevillian dog-and-pony show. The follies were orchestrated to accentuate US victories and play down defeats in an effort to influence the reporters and keep the home fires burning.

## Chapter Five

# Tet

I was alone in the AP bureau at around seven o'clock on the morning of January 30, 1968, when the phone rang. An AVRN public relations officer was inviting a reporter to fly to Ban Me Thuot, the largest town in the coffee-growing Central Highlands.

"We have just won a great victory," he said. I told him I'd go. The call signaled the climax of my tour in Vietnam and, in a very real way, the beginning of the end for the American war.

As I hung up, Peter Arnett walked in and offered to drive me to the airport. At thirty-four, Arnett had been reporting from Southeast Asia for eight years and, as I've already written, was celebrated and highly respected among the war's journalists. Short, wiry, and pugnacious, with a nose bent as an amateur boxer, he wrote with the punch of a young Hemingway.

With Peter at the wheel of the bureau's white Mini Moke, a British-built, open-topped cross between a Jeep and a Beach Buggy, we threaded our way through unusually quiet streets. People should have been out in throngs, shopping for Tet, the approaching lunar new year.

"Something's off," Peter muttered. "Doesn't feel right."

We sped unimpeded to the airport, where I joined half a dozen colleagues, among them Kate Webb, my UPI rival. A New Zealand–born Australian, Kate was one of the few women then covering the war full-time. In 1971, she would be captured by North Vietnamese forces in Cambodia and held prisoner for twenty-three harrowing days. She was one of the most daring, most admired journalists to serve in Indochina.

Because of the short notice and an assurance that we'd be back in Saigon by dinner, none of us was equipped for war. Kate wore a floral, sleeveless dress and rubber flip-flops while the men were in sport shirts. We had no protective gear, no rations, nothing but the basics needed to cover a show-and-tell—pen, notebook, tape recorder, camera.

A slim, young ARVN lieutenant led us aboard a beat-up Douglas C-47 Skytrain, a flying jalopy that entered US service in World War II. This

Some correspondents regularly carried weapons, although it made service-men accompanying them uneasy, not convinced they could rely on journalists to be as skilled at pulling a trigger as pecking at typewriter keys. I had thought the matter through before arriving in Vietnam and opted against carrying a gun. My thinking was that if I was captured with a weapon, I couldn't possi-bly claim that I was a noncombatant. I declined the captain's offer with thanks and did what I was paid to do: bear witness.

As daylight faded to dusk over Ban Me Thuot, I watched the soldiers, listened to rifle shots rattling in both directions, and jotted notes. A Green Beret, on a knee alongside me and scanning the ground beyond the log rail-ing through his rifle sight, tipped his chin toward a spot on the soccer field's concrete wall.

The wall was shaking.

A thin crack appeared then widened and chunks of concrete tumbled to the ground. Two ARVN armored personnel carriers shoved their way through and rumbled to the center of the field. The lumbering machines engaged in a clumsy pas de deux for a few minutes, the crewmen evidently confused about their mission. Then they turned and left through the opening they'd made.

With the wall now shattered, North Vietnamese soldiers intensified their fire on the hunting lodge. Bullets whined and cracked, splintering logs. My hosts returned fire. The two-way fusillade was intense but, on our side any-way, largely ineffectual. No one was hit.

I heard the captain summon a helicopter gunship over the walkie-talkie. Time for me to call the bureau. I had all the ingredients of a dramatic story: US Special Forces fighters holed up in the emperor's hunting lodge; under attack by North Vietnamese regulars; secret records burned; gunship support on the way. I was thankful to hear the soothing voice of Ed White at the other end of the staticky phone line. He was an expert editor and rewrite man who was dependably calm under the most trying circumstances. We called him "The Unflappable." I summed up what was going on while Ed typed.

"Call again when the situation changes," he said, and we rang off.

About an hour later, a helicopter clattered into view and opened up with its Gatling gun behind the broken wall. But the assault on the lodge only intensi-fied. NVA riflemen, greatly outnumbering the Green Berets and hidden from our view, fired round after round, pinning us down. The Americans were in a defensible position, but time was working against them.

By now, we were shrouded in inky darkness, the only light an occasional white spray from illumination flares that the Americans fired into the sky. They soared, erupted, and then, dangling from small parachutes, settled slowly to the ground. The brilliant pyrotechnics cast long, ghostly shadows, while red tracer rounds stitched dotted lines over the field.

A second gunship emerged from the black and swooped toward the far-right end of the playing field. The chopper hovered for a few seconds above a grove of tall bamboo. Then, the whoosh of a rocket and a series of thundering explosions as a North Vietnamese ammunition dump cooked off beneath the slender trees.

Deprived of their stockpile, the northern soldiers gradually withdrew, and the battle petered out. It was about 3:00 a.m. My little picnic in the countryside had been going on for eight hours or so. I placed another call to the bureau. It didn't go through. I tried again and again. At last, The Unflappable Ed White picked up.

"Ed," I began, "we've just had a helluva fight here. A gunship blew up an ammo . . . "

He cut me off. "Make it quick, Lew! What's happening there is happening everywhere. The whole country is under attack. Saigon, too."

And that's how I first learned of what became known as the Tet Offensive, the massive communist onslaught that changed everything.

In Saigon, Carol was in our apartment, writing to her parents. Her intuition outpaced the best intelligence of top American and South Vietnamese commanders. "Everyone here has been hanging long strings of firecrackers on their houses and shops to celebrate the lunar new year. The racket is so overwhelming that we could be in the middle of a Viet Cong invasion and we'd never know it."

I remained at the lodge until dawn, then caught a Jeep ride into Ban Me Thuot and found Colonel Henry Barber, the senior Green Beret officer.

"It looks like he is determined to die on the field of battle," Barber said of the North Vietnamese enemy. "He is not retreating, and he is taking at least ten dead to every one of ours."

The NVA forces did retreat shortly afterward, only to return two weeks later. They struck the town again, and this time overwhelmed its ARVN defenders. The defeat forced the southern forces to evacuate the entire Central Highlands area. The end was beginning.

I hitched a flight back to Saigon and went directly to the bureau. Bubbling over with adrenaline, I began writing the story of the attack on the hunting lodge when Bob Tuckman walked over and sheepishly handed me a strip of paper torn off a teletype machine. It bore an all-caps message that already had been read in AP bureaus around the world, LEWIS SIMONS CALL YOUR MOTHER SHE'S WORRIED.

I left Saigon again, three days later, to help cover one of the most critical battles in the ongoing Tet Offensive, another turn of the North's screw on badly shaken South Vietnamese and Americans. The city of Hue was under attack by NVA and Viet Cong. AP, like other news organizations, was shuttling reporters and photographers in and out as those on the ground were worn out by the around-the-clock fighting.

Hue, pronounced "whay," is located on the South China Sea coast at the country's narrowest point. Vietnam's third-largest city, it was a popular prewar tourist destination, famed for its spectacular, walled citadel. The seventeenth-century emperor, Gia Long, had ordered his geomancers to choose a propitious site for what he intended to be Vietnam's answer to China's imperial bastion in Beijing, the Forbidden City.

Thousands of laborers had built the stronghold, encircled it with towering, orange-tile-topped walls, and dug a broad moat, more than six miles long. The original earthen walls later were reinforced and faced with brick and stone to a thickness of six feet. Over time, a second moat was excavated, and numerous ornate courtyards, gardens, pavilions, and palaces added.

By the time of the American war, Hue had sprawled outward from the citadel. The modern town was separated from the historic core by the inaptly named Perfume River. The city lay astride Highway One, which dispirited French troops, after suffering a terrible drubbing there in the summer of 1953, named *La Rue Sans Joie*, The Street without Joy.

For the US and ARVN forces, Highway One was a vital link between coastal Danang and the demilitarized zone. And Hue, with a railroad and a port for US Navy supply boats, was a critical communications hub. But, despite its vital logistics, the city was poorly defended when the communist forces struck.

South Vietnamese and American commanders had anticipated a nation-wide ceasefire respite, as had occurred on previous Tet holidays. They were mistaken. The invaders quickly overran Hue, making it the first major South Vietnamese city to fall under their control. Now US Marines were struggling to recapture it.

I hopped a troop transport plane in Saigon, and it landed at the edge of town. Also aboard was Jack Foisie, an experienced and deceptively mild-mannered correspondent for the *Los Angeles Times*. Jack was in his mid-forties, fifteen or so years older than I. He was short and slight, with a pink, pixyish face, a feathery-white tonsure, and wore rimless glasses. In the debilitating heat and humidity, he'd already sweated through his khaki shirt and was puffing with exertion. *How does he do it?* I wondered. *Would I be able to do it at his age? Would I want to?*

As we trudged a mile or so along the riverbank, a flood of Vietnamese civilians, hundreds at least, swarmed past us, loaded down with bundles of clothing, sleeping mats, pots and pans, sacks of rice. The men, many wearing no more than pajama bottoms or boxer shorts, looked terrified. Women carrying heavily laden bamboo shoulder poles wept as they dragged shrieking children.

They were headed in the opposite direction than us, away from the city.

An alarming thought dawned on me. *These people are running away from the place I'm going to.* Jack read the look on my face and laughed.

"That's why they pay us the big bucks," he cracked.

If there had been a class at Columbia Journalism School on what a reporter should do at a moment like this, I must have slept in that day. In fact, there was no choice at all. I was there to cover the agony of a city facing death, and I had to expose myself to that same threat. I recalled the inescapable advice of Robert Capa, probably the greatest war photographer of all time: "If your pictures aren't good enough, you're not close enough."

Then and there, I adopted the lesson and lived by it throughout my career. Whatever the threat or danger, I had to be there. I had to see, hear, smell, and touch. I had to get closer. I was hardly the only reporter who did.

Approaching a narrow roadway leading up to the citadel's main gateway, Jack and I bade each other adieu and went our separate ways. To get inside the citadel safely warranted some reconnoitering. So I headed to a small concrete structure, possibly a pump house, set in a grassy drainage ditch alongside the road. There, I'd figure out my next move.

Moments later, David Greenway joined me. He was an engaging Boston brahmin of pre-Revolution lineage, then writing for *Time* magazine and, I would learn as we periodically reconnected over the years, good company. At that moment, I was absent-mindedly standing on one foot, pondering what to do.

"Your pose reminds me of a Maasai tribesman," Greenway said.

We laughed. He seemed cool and calm. I pretended to be. We traded thoughts on how to get into the citadel. The entry arch was maybe two football fields' distance from the little pump house. Sporadic gunfire echoed from inside the walls. For reasons that now escape me, I decided to cross the road and move up a parallel ditch on the opposite side. In retrospect, my crossing made much the same sense as the proverbial chicken's.

Wishing Greenway good luck, I scrambled out of the recess and darted to the road. Automatic gunfire rattled. Bullets thudded into the hard-packed dirt surface a few feet to my left. I dropped and pressed my body flat, willing to be invisible, and frantically scissored elbows and knees the rest of the way, as I'd been trained to do at Parris Island.

Flopping into the second ditch, I yelled furiously in the general direction of the citadel wall one of the very few Vietnamese words I'd memorized, "*Bao chi, bao chi*—I'm a journalist, you asshole!" This, of course, was lunacy. I was wearing military fatigues and helmet, and though I was unarmed, the shooter, presumably on the distant wall, would have no way of knowing that, couldn't hear my protest, and wouldn't have understood or cared if he had.

vicious. One rationalization is that Hue involved the most dreaded form of modern warfare, building-to-building, house-to-house, room-to-room, hand-to-hand, face-to-face.

Military high commands typically avoid admitting they were caught flat-footed. The Marines were not prepared for Hue. In training for Vietnam, US forces had focused on jungle warfare and counter-guerrilla tactics, investing minimal effort practicing in urban battles.

The Hue nightmare led to a policy reversal. The Pentagon learned it had to prepare for every form of warfare waged simultaneously. But whether the Defense Department and its civilian overlords ever realized that starting a fight without a clear picture of how it will end is a recipe for disaster is another matter. A succession of wars in the Middle East and South Asia suggests not.

US military and political leaders frequently misunderstand not only the motivation and the patience of the enemy but also of the American people. In a post-conscription era, in which active-duty military personnel comprise less than one half of one percent of the US population, getting into a war is easy. Getting out isn't.

After I'd filed a series of stories and it was evident that the battle would rage on indefinitely without significant change, I called the bureau and said I was ready for a break. My replacement was already on his way.

I walked out the same way I had walked in a week earlier, through the citadel gate and back along the riverside road, where I overtook a group of Vietnamese women in long, navy-blue dresses and head coverings. They were Roman Catholic nuns. A French-speaking sister told me they were expecting to board a riverboat and leave the city. I tagged along. We reached a small pier, where a dented metal landing craft was tied up. A barefoot man in grease-stained singlet and shorts waved us aboard.

Moments later, a Westerner wearing fatigues and an oversized helmet hopped onto the boat. This was Gene Roberts, then with the *New York Times*. Roberts had made his bones covering the civil rights struggle in his native South. After Vietnam, he would become executive editor of the *Philadelphia Inquirer*, a position he held for eighteen years, during which members of his staff were awarded an extraordinary seventeen Pulitzer Prizes. Accompanied by the nuns, we motored out of Hue, exchanging war stories.

As poorly prepared as the Marines were for the urban warfare of Hue, they were not much better suited for the siege of Khe Sanh. Here, the US Marines, whose traditional mission was to act as a fast-moving, amphibious strike force, were utterly out of their element. They were pinned down and surrounded in a classic blockade which, but for lack of a crenellated stone castle, could just as well have been set in medieval Europe, with catapults in place of artillery pieces and longbows for rifles.

Like Hue, Khe Sanh reflected extraordinary advance planning by North Vietnam's military chief, General Vo Nguyen Giap. This wasn't Giap's first go-round. In 1954 he defeated the vaunted French army, forcing it to surrender in a merciless battle in the northern city of Dien Bien Phu.

Giap was a brilliant strategist, tactician, and logistician. In Hue, his forces were prepared and in position well before the arrival of the inappropriately trained Americans. At Khe Sanh, a full six years before firing their first shot, North Vietnamese units began installing artillery in the surrounding mountains, from where they could rain death on the vulnerable US combat base below.

Khe Sanh was a village of 1,500 inhabitants situated amid coffee plantations six miles east of the border of Laos and fourteen miles south of the western end of the DMZ. Years before the Tet Offensive, US planners recognized Khe Sanh's strategic value and set up a small, lightly defended camp. It made an ideal setting for American forces tracking the northern movements across the DMZ. It also was well-located for monitoring their activity along the multiple legs of the so-called Ho Chi Minh Trail, inside Laos.

In the fall of 1967, Giap began adding strength in the mountains, eventually installing twenty thousand well-armed troops. US commanders anticipated that this massive force soon would target Khe Sanh and began their own buildup. By 1968, six thousand marines were in position to answer the expected onslaught.

Westmoreland believed that Giap intended to use Khe Sanh as a jumping-off point from which he could move south and seize control of a broad swath of territory. Westy ordered the Marines to expand their garrison of sandbagged bunkers and foxholes.

Nevertheless, whenever Giap determined the time was right to strike, the Marines—greatly outnumbered, pinned down, and surrounded—would be at his mercy. His plan essentially was a rerun of Dien Bien Phu. If the NVA succeeded, they would gain virtually unobstructed control of northwestern South Vietnam. Giap drove his forces mercilessly to maneuver additional mortars and rocket launchers into shielded emplacements. Some armaments were disassembled and trundled on bicycles to caves as far as fifteen miles inside Laos, well within range of the Americans at Khe Sanh.

Giap unleashed his assault on January 21, 1968. He intended it to be the keystone of the Tet Offensive. Giap gambled that Westmoreland would defend Khe Sanh at all costs, shift troops from other bases in South Vietnam, and thus expose them to North Vietnam's invading forces. That, at least, did not happen.

The attack began with a thunderous artillery barrage from the mountain redoubts. For the next seventy-seven days, marines and NVA soldiers fought another of the longest and most savage battles of the war. Each placing huge bets on the fate of Khe Sanh, the two sides struggled ferociously.

While a second Dien Bien Phu was Giap's fondest dream, it was Westmoreland's worst nightmare. France had committed some of its most elite forces to the defense of Dien Bien Phu, including paratroopers and Foreign Legionnaires. Their defeat marked the end of France as a colonial power.

Khe Sanh, too, was held by elite troops, and the Johnson administration knew the US public would not tolerate their being overrun by Third World soldiers. Losing Khe Sanh, the president feared, would do incalculable damage to America's reputation as the world's leading military power.

Such weight did the United States place on the future of Khe Sanh that Westmoreland quietly drew up an astonishing contingency plan. Named "Fracture Jaw," it called for moving tactical nuclear weapons into Vietnam to defend the base in an at-all-cost, last-ditch effort. When word leaked in Washington, a furious Johnson was forced to order Westmoreland to scuttle the nuclear option.

In the end, Khe Sanh held. But the cost to both sides was huge. By the time the siege was broken, on April 6, some ten thousand North Vietnamese soldiers and nearly five hundred marines had been killed.

While the Marines battled valiantly on the ground, the outcome would have been much different had it not been for massive US Air Force support. Americans owned the sky and that shifted the equation. Planes bombed NVA artillery positions; delivered ammunition, rations, medical supplies, and other matériel; ferried in fresh fighters; and carried out the dead and grievously wounded.

Fighter aircraft averaged three hundred attacks a day. Trios of high-altitude Air Force B-52s traversed the sky in V-formations, invisible and silent from the ground, dropping seventy-five tons of five-hundred-pound bombs.

The air assaults were crucial in the day-to-day fighting. But, with NVA gunners dominating the ground, it was the air delivery of fresh men and supplies that enabled the Marines to hold out.

Because aircraft coming and going on the Khe Sanh landing strip were vulnerable to intense NVA groundfire, cargo crews polished their techniques until they could land, offload, taxi, and take off in less than three minutes. It was on one of those fast-turnabout deliveries that I arrived at Khe Sanh in the beginning of February, two weeks after the siege began. I was there to replace John Wheeler, a battle-hardened AP correspondent, who had been living with the marines almost since the first shots were fired. Wheeler was reluctant to surrender his identification with this key battle in a war he'd been covering for years, but he was exhausted.

As the pilot put the plane into a stomach-flipping dive, the loadmaster instructed me to place my flak jacket on the C-130's floor and to sit on it. Scant protection against a direct hit, it was marginally better than nothing. Seconds before the plane's wheels slammed onto the runway, a crewman opened the rear ramp and began releasing the straps holding huge wooden crates of arms and equipment in place.

The plane kept rolling toward the far end of the landing strip as the boxes tumbled off in a long row. When the last one cleared, the loadmaster shouted, "Go!" and I ran down the juddering ramp. I made a sharp right and continued running, gummy red mud sucking at my boots, until I reached a foxhole. It was raining hard and as I stumbled into the shallow dugout I splashed mud over a poncho-wrapped marine sheltering there. The C-130 roared back into the air, automatic-weapons fire cracking around it.

"Welcome to my humble home," the young marine said with a puzzled grin. After giving me a once-over, he asked why I was there. I explained.

"You mean you don't *have* to be here?" he responded, adding the observation that had caused me to question myself. "Shit, sir, you're fuckin' crazy!"

We chatted for a few moments. He was twenty years old, a lance corporal, from Tennessee, and had been in-country seven months; Khe Sanh for one. I asked him what life was like there.

"Shootin' and prayin' mostly."

"Praying for what?

"To get the hell out of here in one piece and get back to the world."

After a few more minutes of small talk, I wished him well and left his foxhole.

Wheeler had recommended I visit Charlie Med, the base's subterranean field hospital. The expanded bunker had much to recommend it to a journalist. Not only was it the scene of some of the most dramatic life-and-death stories at Khe Sanh, it also was comparatively safe, made of heavy timbers and multiple layers of sandbags. And, incredibly, it was air-conditioned.

An amputation was underway as I entered. In a pool of brilliant light, a short, slender man in green surgical gown, cap, and mask was removing most of a marine's left arm, shattered at the elbow. Once he finished, the surgeon backed away from the operating table, removed the mask, and wiped it across his sweaty face, dark with stubble. I introduced myself, asked if he could spare a few minutes, and was pleased to find him accommodating and patient.

He was Dr. Edward Feldman, a Navy lieutenant and a Khe Sanh celebrity. As he told me his story, it became obvious that we had some background in common. Feldman was two years younger than I, had been born in Manhattan, moved with his parents to suburban Forest Hills shortly after his bar mitzvah, was a middling student and so-so athlete. His mother was a schoolteacher and his father, who worked for a textile firm, volunteered as a World War II air-raid warden. Father and son were ardent patriots.

Feldman succumbed to parental pressure and attended pharmacy school at Columbia University, squeaked through, then declared that he dreaded the prospect of working behind a drugstore counter. He wanted to become a physician.

With considerable finagling, he won probationary acceptance to an osteopathy college in Kansas City. He viewed it as the best alternative to medical school, to which he was unable to gain admission. He excelled. In 1967, having completed his internship, he volunteered for the Navy with an eye on a Marine Corps commission, a lifelong dream. A few months later, he shipped out to Vietnam.

"I got here less than two weeks before the siege began," he told me. "On the day the battle started, with the base under heavy mortar and rocket attack, a seriously wounded marine was brought in. He had a live mortar round protruding from his abdomen."

"Jesus!" I said.

"I ordered a sandbag barricade erected around the patient, took off my helmet and flak vest, and began operating under flashlight illumination."

"But how did you know if . . . " I began.

"I was well aware," he interrupted, "that the round could explode in my face without warning, so I cut around the wound and removed the shell very, very carefully. Then I ordered it taken outside for disposal. The guy made it. He survived."

For this remarkable feat, Feldman was awarded a Silver Star and a Bronze Star. Further heroic action earned him a second Bronze Star, and he became the first osteopath ever nominated for the Congressional Medal of Honor. That ultimate acclaim, however, eluded him.

Though Feldman and I shared some history, we parted over America's purpose in Vietnam. He retained his youthful patriotism while I was losing faith, if not in my country, then certainly in its leaders' conduct of this war. The siege of Khe Sanh was the latest example of America's failure to comprehend what drove the North Vietnamese and their Viet Cong comrades. As my career progressed over the years, covering US military and diplomatic involvement in a score of countries, I reported on such failures again and again.

I usually was criticized by readers whose view of warfare and diplomacy effectively boiled down to, "My country, right or wrong." Unfortunately, most of those who followed this credo of the German-American statesman and reformer Carl Schurz failed to recall its second half: "If right, to be kept right; and if wrong, to be set right."

The US political and military establishments, lopsidedly confident in the nation's massive armed power, had neglected the most essential requirement of warfare, as espoused by the ancient Chinese strategist, Sun Tzu: "If you know the enemy and know yourself, you need not fear the result of a hundred battles. If you know yourself but not the enemy, for every victory gained you will also suffer a defeat. If you know neither the enemy nor yourself, you will succumb in every battle."

Certainly, we did not know this enemy. How much of ourselves we understood remained debatable.

After the war ended, American veterans, tourists, and journalists traveling to the northern part of a unified Vietnam, myself among them, were shocked by how well we were received, even by those who suffered unspeakably under B-52 bombings and Agent Orange chemical attacks. But from a Vietnamese perspective, the American war was just a two-decade blip in a two-millennium history. The real enemy always had been, and remains, China, which occupied and threatened Vietnam for two thousand years. Even the country's name, originally Nam Viet, meaning "beyond the southern boundary," was imposed by China.

A strong case can be made that the United States missed the boat—a lifeboat—when, at the end of World War II, President Harry Truman sided with France as it struggled to regain Vietnam and its other two former Indochinese colonies. Had Truman listened to appeals for cooperation from the anti-colonial, independence-minded revolutionary leader Ho Chi Minh, millions of Vietnamese and tens of thousands of American lives may have been spared.

Though a committed communist, Ho first and foremost was a Vietnamese nationalist. And he sincerely admired the United States and its people. He had worked for a few years in his twenties as a baker, cook, and dishwasher in Boston and New York. During World War II, he cooperated with the US Office of Strategic Services in fighting against Japan, whose forces occupied Vietnam and were starving its people.

On September 2, 1945, Ho stood before a massive crowd in Hanoi and, declaring Vietnam's independence from France, spoke these words, familiar to all Americans, translated into Vietnamese: "All men are created equal. They are endowed by their creator with certain inalienable rights, among them life, liberty, and the pursuit of happiness."

Lest there be any doubt among his listeners of the words' Jeffersonian origins, Ho explained, "This immortal statement was made in the Declaration of Independence of the United States of America in 1776. In a broader sense, this means: All the peoples on the Earth are equal from birth, all the peoples have a right to live, to be happy and free."

And yet. . . . And yet. . . . Rejecting Ho's heartfelt words and his people's two thousand years of hatred for China, the United States blindly anticipated that if Vietnam became independent and communist, it would join its millennial enemy and the Soviet Union and set about crushing the United States. In an attempt to rally congressional support for the French colonial war in Indochina, President Dwight D. Eisenhower in 1954 forecast a "domino" effect in Southeast Asia. It proved to be one of the most vivid and lasting—though ultimately wrong—descriptions of American Cold War beliefs.

As the war dragged on and we eyewitnesses reported its horrors, some Americans, especially the young and better-educated, demanded it be ended. These were the Americans whom, as Sun Tzu wrote, the leaders failed to understand.

In 2005, following a reporting trip I made to Iraq for *National Geographic*, I wrote an op-ed for the *Washington Post*, in which I compared American attitudes about the war going on there with the one I had covered in Vietnam.

"Most didn't understand the enemy, its objectives, or the lengths to which it was prepared to go to attain them," I wrote. "We had a fuzzy notion of Communist 'world domination,' and the 'domino theory' and no realization that what the Vietnamese wanted, South and North, was independence. They didn't want to take over Southeast Asia. They didn't want to invade Los Angeles. They wanted to run their own country. They wanted us out."

Americans see other nations through American eyes. That is understandable. It also is myopic. We assume if you're not with us you're against us. We assume everyone wants to be like us. Therefore, who better to instruct them than we?

In reality, all the world's people, most of whom belong to cultures and countries centuries, millennia even, older than ours, want to choose their own path. Whether that path parallels or intersects or completely departs from ours means little to them. Meshing the two is a complex if not impossible task. And yet, we plow ahead, repeating mistakes and remaining oblivious to others' reality.

During two weeks at Khe Sanh, I spent as much time as possible with everyday marines. I shared their bunkers and foxholes, their rations and latrines, their braggadocio and terror. I attempted to absorb their attitudes and emotions and to convey them in my stories. I wanted to give readers back home honest portrayals of what their sons, husbands, and fathers were doing, for better and for worse, in their name.

Overwhelmingly, I reported, the marines at Khe Sanh, grossly outnumbered, exhausted, dirty, sweaty, sometimes hungry and thirsty, always frightened, performed as they were trained to. They fought until they fell.

Between bombardments, I slogged across the sticky red ground, trying to avoid tumbling into artillery-shell pits. And rats' nests. Khe Sanh was plagued with fat, ferocious rats, and no amount of traps or poison reduced their number.

One night, as I was making my way to a bunker for a few hours' sleep, I heard a rapid burst of gunfire coming from somewhere in the black distance, probably in the vicinity of the heavily fortified perimeter. I tripped and fell into a shell hole. Poking my head up, I saw nothing. Then I heard shouting, first faintly and then much louder:

"The wire! They're coming through the wire!"

More rifle fire.

Closer.

Then: "Gas! Gas! Gas! Gas!"

Fumbling at my hip, I yanked a black rubber gas mask out of its canvas bag and pulled it over my face just as I caught the first stinging whiff and tart taste of tear gas. I had come to hate the claustrophobic masks during boot camp and advanced infantry training. But I also learned their value when ordered to remove them as gas was pumped into a sealed room. Now I lay on my back, hands clasped on my chest, sucking air through the filter, and staring through dirt-spattered plastic lenses into the void.

Penetrating the Khe Sanh perimeter wasn't a cakewalk for enemy soldiers. The entire boundary was fenced in barbed wire and German-manufactured razor tape. The marines dug six-foot-deep trenches in the most vulnerable places. But General Giap was persistent. His sappers dug their own zigzag trenches to within touching distance of the wire and blew breaches with pipe bombs and satchel charges. This night was one of those occasions.

In the darkness, pierced by brilliant bursts of illumination flares, I heard chattering rifle fire, grenade blasts, the whump-whump-whump of mortars exiting their tubes. And screaming, lots of screaming.

"Fuck, where's my mask! Shit, my fuckin' mask! Watch where you're goin,' Marine! Get your fuckin' ass down!"

Finally, after twenty minutes or so, I heard, "Stop firing! Stop firing!"

I stayed put for another few minutes, then tore off the mask and groped my way to the bunker I'd been heading for, where I'd holed up the previous two nights and had stashed my portable typewriter. I joined three grunts sprawled inside.

"Like a fuckin' John Wayne flick, wasn't it?" one said in a dense drawl. It was the kind of remark I'd heard before and would hear again—experiencing real terror but recalling it as make-believe. Psychological transference? Maybe just a small way to stay sane.

The marines lit up and exchanged tales of what they'd just been through. I sat cross-legged on the dirt floor with the pale green Olivetti propped between my knees, hunting and pecking my rendition of the night's events. The next morning I learned the marines had recovered two dead NVA soldiers just inside the wire. Another one or two had escaped. One marine had been wounded. This infiltration attempt, like most, failed. Still, it enhanced the effect Giap intended, rattling the marines and shaking their confidence.

I called the story in to Saigon.

One afternoon, hearing engine-roar overhead, I looked up to watch a C-130 cargo flight begin its steep descent under fire. As the plane banked toward the landing strip, it shuddered, like a huge goose grazed by a hunter's birdshot. A fiery, orange flower bloomed at the front of the aircraft as it dropped to the ground and crashed, a wing snapping off. Flames raced along the length of the fuselage, black plumes billowed, and sixteen thousand pounds of fuel exploded with a mighty roar. All six crew members were killed instantly. It was the worst catastrophe I witnessed at Khe Sanh.

A week later, my rotation ended and I departed for the serenity of Saigon and Carol.

On Friday, April 5, 1968, in Vietnam, Thursday in Memphis, Tennessee, the Reverend Martin Luther King, Jr. was gunned down on the balcony of his room at the Lorraine Motel. Among those of us who were White, there was little sense that day of how King's assassination would impact the thousands of Black marines, soldiers, airmen, and sailors who had offered their lives in the latest war of a country that scorned them. Few, I imagine, foresaw our country again tearing itself apart along the perforated line of color. US relief forces broke the siege of Khe Sanh the next day. That was our big news.

Months earlier, Muhammad Ali, the greatest boxer of his era, had refused to be drafted into the Army. Speaking to reporters in his hometown, Ali demanded, "Why should they ask me to put on a uniform and go ten thousand miles from home and drop bombs and bullets on Brown people in Vietnam after so-called Negro people in Louisville are treated like dogs and denied simple human rights?"

And so we Americans now were at war not only with Vietnamese but with each other as well. Again.

I returned to Khe Sanh for the final time on June 19. With the siege broken, the US command had decided to evacuate the base and destroy it. Lying spread-eagled atop a sandbagged bunker, I peered through field glasses at a three-pronged formation of marines and soldiers, ant-sized in the distance, inching toward us. Above the dust-stirring columns of troops, trucks, and tanks darted flocks of helicopters, firing rockets and machine guns at the last few enemy holdouts.

I passed the binoculars to some marines lolling nearby They had little interest. I don't think I've ever seen men so spent, so utterly exhausted, bodies limp, deadened eyes staring from dirt-crusted faces. Their battle was over.

The war continued.

Among the true believers in America's Vietnam war effort, then and still, the Tet offensive ended in a US victory. As viewed from the firing line, they're right. The two most crucial battles went to the American side: Hue was taken back from the combined communist forces, and the Northern army was forced to retreat from Khe Sanh. Giap's expectation that vast numbers of South Vietnamese would revolt against their corrupt leaders and rally to the communist side turned out to be a pipe dream. Many Southerners despised their own government, but many more, particularly the large Catholic population, harbored far deeper hatred and fear of godless communism.

But, while a US military victory, Tet proved most significant for its enormous symbolic and psychological impact. After being assured for years that our boys were overwhelming the communists, Americans suddenly realized that US forces were vulnerable.

This was devastating. It stamped an indelible mark of defeatism on much of the public. To them, the war now seemed never-ending, with no attainable objective. Each evening, millions of American families were horrified by scenes of slaughter and devastation flickering across their television screens, the first time a war America was fighting was broadcast almost live every day. Much of what they saw and read made little sense to them: communist spies working as waiters in the US embassy; our boys slicing ears off their boys; our boys incinerating families in their straw hootches, our boys raping women, murdering babies.

Hard-core hawks blamed the messenger—the press—for delivering this unpalatable information. Doves praised us. Whatever one's attitude, the direct result was that thousands of Americans, led by anti-war and draft-dodging college students, took to the streets of Washington and other cities, chanting, "Hey, hey, LBJ, how many kids did you kill today?"

Hoping to dampen the unrest, Johnson initiated what would evolve into an extended period of "Vietnamization." This new policy sharply reduced US troop presence on the ground while boosting funding to the corrupt Saigon government. It proved futile.

Johnson succumbed. On the evening of March 31, 1968, he announced that his decades in public office were over. Tet and the King murder had worn his famously dogged will to a raw nub. It was April Fools' morning in Vietnam, and I had stopped by an Army command tent in the Central Highlands to ask about an impending operation. The tent was empty, hot, and silent but for a portable radio tuned to the Armed Forces Network. Through the stuttering reception, I made out Johnson's unmistakable Texas inflection, delivering his version of Union Army General William Tecumsah Sherman's oft-quoted refusal to seek the presidency in 1884, "I will not accept if nominated and will not serve if elected."

Johnson's version went like this:

"With American sons in the field far away, with the American future under challenge right here at home, with our hopes and the world's hopes for peace in the balance every day, I shall not seek, and I will not accept the nomination of my party as your president."

I wandered out into the brilliant sunshine, blinking, stunned. Vietnam had exhausted the indefatigable LBJ. Now he was just one more casualty of America's latest ill-considered war.

## Chapter Six

# Quiet No More in Malaysia

Thirteen months had disappeared in a moment, and I was leaving the war behind. I had anticipated that AP might send me back to New York or to a domestic bureau, neither of which appealed, but, the correspondent for Malaysia and Singapore, Myron Belkind, was being transferred to New Delhi, and the foreign desk assigned me to replace him in Kuala Lumpur, the capital of Malaysia.

I knew next to nothing about this Southeast Asian backwater. I would have to learn quickly because the assignment gave me sole responsibility for an entire country. Unlike in Vietnam, where my duties focused narrowly on bits and pieces of war, in Malaysia I covered political, economic, business, social, human-interest and all other manner of what constituted news. And I would run a bureau.

Because of its small size and limited significance on the world stage, Malaysia was an ideal fit for me at that stage in my career, though I needed some time to recognize the wisdom of the appointment. At first, I felt as though, after a year as a chronic insomniac, I'd developed a case of sleeping sickness. From the biggest story in the world to one about which few had heard and fewer cared. From front pages to space fillers.

For a budding foreign correspondent, the transfer was, to put it mildly, a letdown. It was as though my first car had been a shiny Cadillac Eldorado and now I was driving a Ford jalopy. Still, the timing wasn't bad, as we were soon to be first-time parents. As Carol put it, "I've heard that KL is a great place to have a baby." Living costs, including household help, were low. People were friendly, gentle, kind, and spoke English.

A decade after winning *merdeka*, independence, from the British Empire; putting down an internal communist uprising; and emerging relatively unscathed from armed *konfrontasi* with neighboring Indonesia, Malaysia was at peace with itself and its neighbors. Nagging ethnic strife among the Malay majority and Chinese and Indian minorities had receded to a low ebb. This being well before "Islamic" and "terrorist" became synonymous around the globe, the communities lived side by side, in restrained tension, more or less calmly.

Malaysia was just rich enough to keep its people well fed and content. Overwhelmingly rural, it lacked ambition to raise its global profile. The nation's mood was personified by Prime Minister Tunku Abdul Rahman. A member of the Johore State royal family, the Cambridge-educated *tunku,* or prince, was an easygoing bon vivant who enjoyed the company of women, playing poker, betting on the horses, and sipping a tall gin and tonic. Throughout his long public life, he promoted the notion of Malaysia as a multiracial, secular state wrapped loosely in the Islamic fold.

The country's name was adopted in 1963, only five years earlier. Formerly, it had been Malaya. The indigenous occupants, Malays, were known as Bumiputera, sons of the soil, and the national constitution required all of them to be Muslim. Malays dominated politics. A figurehead king, the *yang di-pertuan agong*, was a Malay, chosen every five years in a rotation among the sultans of nine states. Ethnic Chinese controlled business and the economy. Indians, whom the British shipped from one colony to another across Asia and Africa, did the hard, dirty work of rubber tapping and tin mining.

In 1968, Kuala Lumpur, known casually to all since British days as KL, had a population that was creeping toward half a million. Its name, cheerlessly meaning "muddy confluence," derived from its location at the fork of two sluggish rivers. It was ringed by dense jungle and well-ordered rubber plantations.

A showplace it wasn't. Notable architecture was limited to an onion-domed railway terminal, which resembled a classic arabesque mosque, and an ultra-modern, glass-and-steel mosque, which resembled a railway terminal. The tallest building in town, the sixteen-story Federal Hotel, was topped by a revolving restaurant that spun just a bit too bumpily and speedily for our stomachs. We abandoned our first and only meal there between courses.

We found a small, bright, modern apartment on Pantai Hill, overlooking the leafy campus of the University of Malaya. Our daughter, Justine, was born October 26, 1968, at Assunta Hospital. The genial Chinese obstetrician wore a flowered sport shirt and white rubber galoshes for the delivery, which he granted me permission to photograph. The full price for one brand-new baby girl was $25.

Justine rode home with us in the red 1952 MG-TD I'd bought from a departing Brit. This being well before seat belts and baby seats, we tucked her into a wicker basket we wedged behind us. In time, we would meander, top down, through quiet city streets and, on weekends, to pleasure spots like Port Klang, for chili crab dinners, and Fraser's Hill, for cooler air.

We placed an ad in the *Straits Times* for an amah. The thought of employing a live-in servant unsettled us at first, but every middle-class family, local and expatriate, seemed to have at least one, and we quickly grew accustomed to this luxury. A soft-spoken, young woman by the name of Catherine Leong Sow Yong answered our ad. Over the fourteen years that she would remain in our lives, Catherine became a beloved member of our growing family. She helped raise Justine, Rebecca, who was born in KL a year later, and Adam, born in Bangkok in 1977. She roamed the world with us, sharing our homes in KL, Manhattan, Washington, DC, New Delhi, Bangkok, and, finally, back to Washington. Inveterately frugal, Catherine invested in Wall Street and bought two houses when she returned to KL years later.

I was determined not to repeat what I regretted most about our time in Vietnam—failing to make friends among local people and learning their culture. This self-appointed mission required little effort because Malaysians readily opened themselves and their homes to us.

The resident foreign press corps comprised just me and the Reuters correspondent, a zealously competitive New Zealander by the name of Colin Bickler. The other journalists were locals, working for domestic newspapers and broadcasters or as stringers for foreign outlets. In no time, I was eating and drinking with them at an astonishing assortment of restaurants and food stalls around town.

Inevitably, we made contact with the diplomatic set, an essential part of life for foreign correspondents everywhere. Journalists and diplomats do pretty much the same work, gathering information about the country where they're based and writing what they learn for an audience back home. So, swapping observations and interpretations of the host government is important to both sides, and social exchanges are commonplace. But the correspondent must always be on guard against manipulation by the officials carrying out their home government's agenda.

One of the first envoys we came to know was the British high commissioner, as London's ambassadors to Commonwealth nations like Malaysia are known. This knighted gentleman, with an eagle beak and impeccable Oxbridge elocution, and his wife invited us to lunch at Carcosa, their official, colonial-era mansion.

Uniformed staff served a dozen well- dressed Malaysian and foreign guests at circular tables in a lush, tropical garden. Conversation dwelled on gossip about Tunku Abdul Rahman and his government, the current state of Chinese-Malay relations, the war in Vietnam, and so on.

I found the vast array of silverware and crystal intimidating but, by copying other guests, manageable. Until dessert. It was elegant but simple enough—bunches of chilled grapes, which a servant passed around on a silver platter. I would have torn off a few but, fortuitously, noticed that the perfectly coiffed English woman to my right had used dainty silver scissors to snip off her modest serving. I followed suit.

About to pop a grape into my mouth, I glanced rightward again and observed my neighbor applying a miniature fork and knife to one of hers. I'd never witnessed this before and couldn't imagine the point. Gentility, it seemed, required elevating the basic act of eating to the very pinnacle of absurdity.

Pinioning the little, round fruit to her plate with the mini fork, she daintily drew the little knife blade across the surface vertically, incising its thin, purple skin ever so superficially. Then she meticulously peeled the skin from the flesh with knife and fork. Next, she sliced the flayed fruit into two halves. Holding one half in place with the fork, she used the tip of her knife to remove two offending pips. Only then did she raise the fork-impaled morsel and insert it between her lips.

I made two attempts to replicate this feat of botanical surgery. On the first try, a grape skidded off my plate and dropped to the grass. The second time, I succeeded in impaling one, but was unable to keep it on the fork. Conceding that the effort was beyond my digital dexterity, I carefully lay the tiny utensils at an exact, forty-five-degree angle across the upper right edge of my plate, picked up an unmolested grape with my fingers, popped it into my mouth, chewed it up without obviously moving my jaw, and swallowed, skin and pips included.

A handful of colonial-era Brits had stayed on in KL. One, the manager of a large tin mine, invited us to dinner. Dress was "semiformal," the beautifully hand-inscribed invitation advised, meaning black tie for Western gents, "national dress" for Malaysians, and "Red Sea rig," (bow tie and cummerbund but no tunic), which regulations permitted British military officers in the heat east of Suez.

About thirty guests were in attendance at the tin man's rambling, tree-shaded bungalow, a style of house that the raj had exported throughout the tropics from Bengal, in India, where it originated. After dinner, the hostess invited the ladies to adjourn to the library. We gentlemen, after postprandial brandy and cigars, followed our host out to the garden. There, with everyone but me seeming to know why, we formed a large circle, facing inward, unzipped, and casually peed onto the manicured lawn. Conversation continued unabated. We zipped up and returned to the house, to rejoin the ladies.

Rule Britannia!

The AP bureau occupied a suite of small rooms on the top floor of the China Insurance Building. This five-story structure poked above the shophouses of Batu Road, the city's main commercial thoroughfare, lined with covered sidewalks known as "five-foot ways." Very practical in a climate that swung between broiling sun and pounding rain.

The bureau staff reflected KL's cosmopolitan population: Brian Gomez, of Indo-Portuguese extraction, who was my assistant; two teletype operators, a

Malay and a Chinese; a Chinese photographer/darkroom technician; and an office manager, also Chinese. The latter, Tan Boo Thien, had been with AP for decades, in Singapore and KL. He knew everything there was to know about how the organization functioned in that part of the world. Hair slicked back with pomade and a foul, black cigar dangling from his mouth, Mr. Tan ran the show. He had firmly but genially guided generations of upstart correspondents as they launched their careers. I was his latest project.

Brian handily managed the daily fare—local politics, the domestic stock market and prices of palm oil, tin and rubber, the basis of Malaysia's wealth. This freed me to expand my knowledge, roaming from Burma in the west to the Philippines in the east. I wandered peninsular Malaysia and the East Malaysian states of Sabah and Sarawak, on the island of Borneo. There, I visited Iban tribal longhouses, in which a hundred or so families lived under one long, thatched roof. In some of these stilt-elevated structures, human heads shrunken to the size of baseballs hung by hanks of hair from bamboo eaves. A few old men proudly told me they had killed their tribe's enemies and processed their heads into these trophies.

On the northern coast of Borneo, I attended the coronation of Hassanal Bolkiah as sultan of Brunei. He was twenty-two years old and the world's wealthiest royal, with an oil-sourced fortune estimated at $28 billion. (The sultan later slipped behind the king of Thailand, whose wealth exceeded $30 billion.) The spectacular investiture featured the goateed new ruler, awash in gold regalia, aboard a golden chariot hauled by a team of a dozen men. The crowd in the throne room, a traditional wooden structure built on pillars, included gorgeously dressed grandees as well as tribal notables just arrived from the bush, many barefoot.

I repeatedly explored the vast sprawl of the Indonesian archipelago—17,504 islands stretched 3,200 miles from one end to the other, about the same distance as the United States from Atlantic to Pacific. Comprising the world's largest Muslim population, it was a land of unending fascination. I felt fortunate to be able to watch and write about it, particularly on someone else's dime.

In Indonesia, I became familiar with poverty and human misery of a breadth and depth beyond my prior comprehension. President Suharto gripped the country in his iron fist—a fist that required continuous lubricating. Suharto, his family, and the top military officers he controlled had grown very rich on "donations" extracted from domestic and foreign companies that required government permission to function in Indonesia. The vast majority of people existed in misery.

Like other cosseted American kids, I'd been pestered to eat my spinach and broccoli because, somewhere, children were starving. I had observed poor people from a distance in Paterson's Black neighborhoods. And I'd witnessed poverty in Vietnam. But in Indonesia, a nation that was home to almost twice as many people as Russia, rich in natural resources, and beginning to rise from Third World to developing world status, I met people suffering night-marish deprivation.

Musa Sayed Ajiman was one of them. He, his wife, and their two small daughters lived crammed into a ten-foot-wide strip between a black-scum-coated canal and a busy railroad track in central Jakarta, the nation's capital. They and several hundred neighbors did without fresh water, toilets, or electricity. In fact, they had no houses. Cardboard cartons were their only shelter. Some managed to scrounge plastic sheets to deploy against the monsoon deluges that otherwise dissolved the cardboard into paste.

Their clothing was the absolute minimum needed to provide a shred of dignity—a sun-bleached tissue of cloth tied around the neck into a sarong for a woman, underpants for a man. Perhaps a T-shirt for the bare-bottomed children who squatted anywhere the urge struck. Hardly a day passed without someone, most often a child, being crushed beneath the squealing wheels of a freight train.

*Surely*, I thought, *human beings were not meant to live like this*. I spent nights between my visits with them luxuriating at a five-star hotel. Each morning, I returned to them refreshed and well-nourished. They were weak, hungry, and scourged by diseases I'd never heard of. So incomprehensible were these discrepancies that I could cope only by shutting them out of my mind once I departed.

I knew correspondents who opted out of this kind of coverage, preferring to concentrate on macroeconomic and political stories. I didn't blame them. But I was determined to tell my comfortable readers halfway around the world what I was learning: that, whatever their discontents, here were millions whose pain lay beyond their worst nightmares. I wanted Americans to know, as I now did, how much of the world lived.

I began to form what would become my long-term approach to reporting. A journalist can take one of two broad approaches to covering a story: top down or bottom up. Most take the first. They focus their attention on leaders, be they in politics, economics, business, academia, science, the arts, whatever enterprise they choose to cover. This is rational. Those at the top make the decisions that affect the others. The journalist and the reader want to know what makes the power brokers tick and what their plans for us may be.

And, of course, life on this road is more comfortable. Reporters interview well-dressed people in tastefully furnished, air-conditioned offices, hobnob at A-list cocktail receptions, and lunch at fine restaurants. Urban slums and subsistence-level villages are less pleasant.

As I spent more of my time among those who paid the price for decisions made for them by others, I realized they were voiceless and invisible. My interest piqued, I wanted to know why. I wanted to know more about them. I vaguely counted myself among them, even though I most certainly did not endure anything even remotely like the suffering and deprivation they did. I wanted to cover them, to let them speak through me.

By "them," I meant not only Third World peasants, like Musa and his family, but also victims of biased economic and social policies in my own country, my hometown, which happened to be the capital of the United States of America, and the soldiers who lay their lives on the line in foreign wars not of their making.

There are others who make similar commitments in other, very personal ways: helping the sick obtain health care, the illiterate to be schooled, or the homeless to be housed. That wasn't me, but, as a journalist, a foreign correspondent, I was in a position to listen and to tell the stories.

This was a momentous decision for me. It changed my life completely and forever.

Early one steamy morning, Musa and I spoke about his life between the tracks and the canal. Not a pinch of spare flesh clung to his skeletal frame; his belly sank toward his spine; cheekbones and ribs protruded beneath sun-darkened skin. The few rupiah he earned came from foraging and recycling discarded bottles, cans, and plastic bags. He was a junkman, like my Grampa.

When I asked to see the interior of his box-home, Musa recoiled.

"That would be beneath the dignity of a White gentleman like you," he said.

I pressed and, finally, he agreed, but only after ignoring my protestations and dispatching his older daughter to buy a bottle of warm orange soda for me.

Shedding my shoes, I crawled in on hands and knees. Standing was impossible. The interior of the box, which originally might have contained a stove or a washing machine, was suffocating. Musa and I sat facing each other on the cardboard floor, he compactly folded on his haunches, occupying minimal space, I sprawled clumsily. My interpreter squatted halfway in and halfway out of the box. Tucked into a corner were rolled straw sleeping mats. I saw no other possessions. Cooking was done outside in a blackened aluminum pot on a tiny charcoal fire.

Musa began his story. He and his wife had migrated to Jakarta three years earlier from their village, a few hundred miles away, in the interior of Java, Indonesia's largest island.

Why?

"We were newly married, and we thought we would have more opportunities in the city."

Were they disappointed?

"No. We do better here than we could have back home."

But life is hard here, too . . .

"Yes, of course."

Across the canal, in clear view from Musa's box, the glass-and-steel tower of Pertamina, the national oil company, glittered in the brilliant sun. Many of the people who worked in the building's air-conditioned comfort came and went by car, some chauffeur driven. Some lived in Jakarta's first few high-rise condominium buildings, others in gated mansions, attended by underpaid servants. The appliance that originally was packed in Musa's carton probably was installed in one of those houses.

That was the story of Indonesia from the 1960s through most of the 1990s. It was a story of extremes—extreme poverty and extreme wealth; extreme corruption and extreme suffering; extreme hatred between the Malay and ethnic Chinese populations.

In 1965 and '66, Indonesian soldiers had slaughtered an estimated half a million of their countrymen, mainly Chinese and kindred political leftists. The governments of the United States, Britain, and Australia, fully aware of the bloodbath but desperate to keep Indonesia anti-communist, made no attempt to intercede. The slaughter formed the backdrop for *The Year of Living Dangerously*," an Academy Award–winning film about a determined, young foreign correspondent, frustrated in his efforts to make a difference.

Indonesia's middle class had yet to be born. That would occur only with the approach of the millennium. In 1998, after thirty years in absolute power, President Suharto and members of his family would be arrested on charges of massive corruption. Democracy would take tenuous root. For a time, Indonesia and its long-censored press would be among the freest in all of Asia.

That, too, would change.

During my first few visits to Jakarta, I got to know a handful of bright, youngish men whom Suharto had charged with restructuring the failed economy. He'd sent them to the University of California at Berkeley to study for advanced degrees. They became known as the "Berkeley Mafia." Among them were Widjojo Nitisastro and Emil Salim, who together administered national development policy. They were knowledgeable, pleased to answer my questions, and made me feel welcome whenever I dropped by their offices.

Then I wrote a story in which I quoted an economics professor at the University of Indonesia who had criticized the Suharto family for its rampant *korupsi*.

On my next visit, Salim took me to task.

"Indonesia is a developing country," he said, staring coldly into my eyes as we sat opposite each other in his compact office. "Criticizing the government in the press, either at home or abroad, works against the common interest. It runs counter to national needs. Journalists must be on the team with all the rest of us."

I was no longer welcomed by the Berkeley Mafia.

Salim's scolding, versions of which I'd been subjected to by US officials in Vietnam, reawakened me. I wasn't cut out to play on any country's team, my own or anyone else's.

Since little in the way of hard news from Malaysia was of interest to editors and readers around the world, I searched out colorful features. Malaysia, as it happens, was and remains a treasure trove of bizarre events.

Every so often there'd be an outbreak of Koro Syndrome, in which frantic young men, terrified that their penises were retracting into their bodies, flocked to doctors' offices and shamans, called *bomohs*. Some were so panicked that they would tie a string to their genitals, clutching it as they ran for help.

Women working in large industrial settings, like some of the American-owned semiconductor plants I toured outside the northwestern coastal city of Penang, were subject to mass panic attacks of a different variety. For no apparent reason, a woman would begin screaming hysterically, then swoon and faint, setting off a ripple effect up and down the assembly line.

Durian, a pineapple-sized fruit with a hard, spiky hull and creamy white segments within, was another source of news oddities. The fruit emits a smell so putrid that regional airlines and hotels ban it. The Brits used to say that consuming durian was like eating strawberries and cream in a public loo. I couldn't stomach it. Aficionados, though, consider the taste nothing less than sublime. Enhancing the attraction, durian is credited with aphrodisiac powers.

"When durians fall, sarongs rise," goes a droll Malay adage.

Owning a durian tree in Malaysia is akin to owning an oasis in the desert. Every summer brings tales of neighbors fighting, even killing each other, over whose durian has dropped into whose yard.

I covered extraordinary religious festivals, such as Thaipusam, in which a million Malaysian Tamil Indians, faces and bodies grotesquely painted and pierced with spikes and hooks, flocked in mass procession to a sacred cave north of KL.

One Malay cultural phenomenon is anything but entertaining. *Amok*, the lone Malay-language word commonly used in English, translates roughly as "murderous frenzy" or "berserk." An *amok* (in Malay, the word is used as noun and adjective), loses all sense of logic. Slow to anger, Malays tend to bottle up rage and resentment until, without warning, they erupt in unrestrained fury. A lone amok, running wild, is frightening. An amok mob is terrifying.

On Saturday, May 13, 1969, in the streets of Kuala Lumpur, I witnessed great mobs of Malays running amok. They slaughtered more than a thousand people, most of them ethnic Chinese. Bodies lay where they fell. Blood ran in open sewers. Sleepy KL turned into an abattoir.

The madness was provoked by a national election three days earlier. When ballot counting was completed, the governing Alliance Party, which was moderate and pan-ethnic but Malay-dominated, had won less than half of the votes it had projected. The largely Chinese opposition, despite finishing in second place, rashly proclaimed victory. Chinese partisans took to the streets to mock the Malays, igniting rumors that raged through Malay kampongs like forest fires:

Chinese had thrown pieces of pork at Malay homes, an archetypal insult to Muslims. Chinese youths had exposed themselves to Malay girls.

KL's Malays quickly organized a counterprotest. Thousands more, armed with spears, knives, and parangs—a kind of machete—were bused and trucked from the countryside into the city. On the afternoon of May 13, they stormed Chinese neighborhoods, setting fire to houses, shops, and cars. Looting and murder followed.

Because Malaysia, like Britain and other of its former colonies, retains rigid firearms laws, the Chinese initially retaliated with butcher knives and cleavers. Eventually, though, both sides brought out illegal guns. Shooting victims joined those stabbed, slashed, and hacked. Chinese armed with steel construction rods invaded movie theaters, one a few blocks from the AP office, and battered Malay patrons to death.

I phoned Carol to tell her what I saw happening downtown, to remain indoors, and not to expect me home that night. For the first time since coming to Malaysia, I had a big story.

Brian and I had covered the election as a routine regional event. There had been only limited interest in parts of Southeast Asia and virtually none anywhere else. That changed dramatically. We had a mini Tet Offensive on our hands. Correspondents poured in. For the next four days and nights, Brian and I spelled each other, patrolling the streets, hiding in doorways and behind buildings, shocked by the brutality, visiting hospitals to interview survivors and gather death counts from doctors and nurses.

With no phone booths in the streets, we banged on locked doors and steel shopfront shutters, pleading with owners to use their phones to call the office and dictate to each other. We punched stories into the teletype machine ourselves because our two operators were, reasonably, afraid to leave home.

The predominantly Malay police and army announced shoot-to-kill orders. Chinese contacts phoned us to report that soldiers were firing indiscriminately at them whenever they peeked out of a window or door.

I was at my desk taking notes from Brian when I heard gunfire from the street corner below. Grabbing a camera from the darkroom, I dashed out onto the terrace and began snapping photos of black-uniformed special police shooting into a bolting crowd.

One gunman spotted me. Without warning, he pointed his assault rifle in my direction and squeezed the trigger. Whether he was a poor shot or intended only to frighten me, two rounds passed over my head and pierced a large steel water tank on the roof. I ran back inside. A torrent of water gushed through the plaster ceiling and flooded the office.

Over the next three days and nights, between 1,300 and 1,500 people were killed, according to our Chinese, Malay, and Indian sources. Most were Chinese. The government, having lost control of the situation and desperately hostile to any criticism, claimed the toll was two hundred. Hundreds of shops and dwellings were trashed or burned to the ground. Thousands of suddenly homeless Chinese were moved into a government-run camp in one of the city's two major stadiums. Malays were placed in the other. Everyone was exhausted, drained, terrified.

Brian and I, too, were spent, neither of us having eaten or slept for seventy-two hours. During a break in the curfew, I encouraged him to go home and get some rest. I was slumped at my typewriter, staring at a blank sheet of paper, incapable of tapping out a coherent sentence, when the office door banged open. A large, bearded figure bounded in, bellowing in an inexplicably jovial, Anglo-Australian accent, "You look a wreck, mate!"

It was Harvey Stockwin, a freelance journalist and dear friend whose knowledge of Asia was encyclopedic. He pulled from his pockets two baby-food-size jars of Brand's Essence of Chicken. A salty, smelly, soupy concoction, it is alleged to contain the "essence" of an entire chicken, miraculously compressed into one miniature glass container with a green and yellow label. George IV's chief cook is said to have created the stuff in 1820 as a tonic to perk up the dissolute monarch. It became a popular energy booster across Southeast Asia long before a Thai entrepreneur created Red Bull. Harvey swore by it.

I gulped down both jars. Damned if it didn't work! I leapt to my feet, fully recharged, ready to take on the world. Then I sat back down and wrote another story.

Covering the Malay-Chinese riots opened my mind as never before to the hatred that religion breeds. I had sensed this at a childish level on the school playground in Paterson. But the brutality I witnessed in the streets of KL sickened me. Over the years ahead, I would see it replayed in country after country, among Muslims, Christians, Jews, Hindus, and Buddhists. In KL, I began questioning all faiths, including the one in which I'd grown up. In time, as my skepticism grew deeper and broader, I turned away.

Violence resurfaced periodically in parts of Malaysia for months after the riots and briefly spilled over into Singapore. Its most notable victim was

Tunku Abdul Rahman. A year after the 1969 outbreak, dispirited and with his popularity plummeting, he was forced to resign as prime minister.

His successor, Tun Abdul Razak, a titled Malay who had been his deputy, appointed him ambassador to Saudi Arabia, essentially putting him out to pasture. He was sixty-seven. The Tunku griped to friends back home about the difficulty of finding a decent gin and tonic in Riyadh.

The most lasting harm was done to the Tunku's dream of a multiracial, multireligious, multiethnic society. The riots stamped an indelible watermark, visible to this day, on the nation. May 13 is to Malaysians what 9/11 is to Americans. With the fragile social fabric frayed, educated Chinese and Indians fled, moving to Australia, Britain, Canada, and Singapore, creating a brain-drain that Malaysia couldn't afford. Among those who left was my assistant, Brian, who wound up in Australia, never to return.

Malaysia's economy rebounded, though, and thrived. Today, KL's ultra-modern center spills into ever-spreading suburban sprawl. Where strolling pedestrians once found a touch of relief from heat and rain in old-fashioned sidewalk arcades, office workers now bustle through air-conditioned skyways linking sky-high glass and steel towers. Commuters shuttle from the city to outlying technology and administrative centers on a super-efficient, high-speed rail line. Dusty little shops and charcoal-burning satay stalls have given way to glittering department stores, boutiques and restaurants offering the best of what the world has to offer. KL is comparable to Singapore, Hong Kong, and Jakarta—tomorrow's metropolises in the tropics today.

This extraordinary progress must be credited to the efforts of one controversial man and his revolutionary ideas, Prime Minister Tun Dr. (Malays love titles) Mahathir bin Mohamad. A champion of Malay advancement through affirmative action, Mahathir was elected in 1981, and quickly instituted a series of socioeconomic policies that granted special privileges to the majority community.

Educated as a physician, he had for years contemplated the need to elevate Malays' well-being. In *The Malay Dilemma*, an inflammatory book he wrote while we still lived in KL, he shocked the nation by openly acknowledging indolence among the Bumiputera, the "sons of the soil."

In early Malaya, no great exertion or ingenuity was required to obtain food. . . . Even the weakest and least diligent were able to live in comparative comfort, to marry, to procreate. . . . The hot humid climate is not conducive to either vigorous work or even to mental activity. The British, recognizing the problem, brought in huge numbers of Chinese immigrants to run the colonial economy. Suddenly, Malays were second-class citizens of their own homeland. . . . Whatever the Malays could do, the Chinese could do better. . . . Before long the industrious and determined immigrants had displaced Malays in petty trading and all branches of skilled work.

His fellow Malays were infuriated by this self-denigrating assessment. But once in power, Mahathir boldly overrode their complaints and launched a sweeping program to reverse, or at least reduce, communal economic imbalance. He opened doors of universities, the civil service, and government-owned companies to Malays, easing admission and hiring standards to boost their numbers. Another Mahathir strategy put new emphasis on the Malay language, making it compulsory in schools while cutting back on Chinese and English. This left minority citizens with no choice other than to swallow their bitterness or leave their homeland.

On the international stage, Mahathir tightened Malaysia's links to Arab states and Iran. He accused the United States of being a "state sponsor of terror." He baited Israeli and American Jews, singling out financier George Soros for special opprobrium, in return for Arab investment in Malaysia.

Although Mahathir's anti-Semitism provoked a succession of American leaders during his twenty-two years in power, it didn't interfere with economic relations. The United States is Malaysia's third largest trading partner (after China and Singapore). Military and intelligence ties are strong as well.

By focusing attention on Malay rights, Mahathir was attempting a tricky juggling act, trying to hold back Islamic extremists while acceding to a less threatening set of demands for economic advancement. How well the strategy has worked—for Malaysia and the rest of the world—remains open to serious doubt.

Cross-fertilization with Arabs led numerous young Malay men to travel to the Middle East to study Islamic asceticism, which they brought back home and relayed to an impressionable audience.

A no-visa welcome mat laid out for Arabs made Malaysia a safehouse for Saudi terrorists like Khalid al-Mihdhar and Nawaf al-Hazmi, two of the 9/11 Pentagon bombers. Four al-Qaeda adherents chosen to carry out an abortive plot to hijack a plane and crash it into the US Bank Tower in Los Angeles in 2002 were Malaysians.

While Mahathir's race- and religion-based policies stirred controversy, they helped meek Malays achieve a level of self-confidence and prosperity that they had never imagined. In a single generation, Malays whose parents scratched out a bare-bones existence raising cassava and living in thatched attap huts owned concrete bungalows. They rode motor scooters and drove Protons, built by a national car company that Mahathir muscled into existence. Government-mandated low-interest loans, favorable to Malays, made it all possible.

So, while Malaysia's economic skyline continues to soar, its Muslim street is moving in a different direction. During my years there, Malays commonly identified themselves foremost as Malays. Today, they're more likely to describe themselves as Muslims first, alongside Saudis, Palestinians, Iraqis, Iranians, and others in the greater *umma*, the Islamic world.

Back then, it was unusual for Malay women to cover their hair or to wear anything more modest than the traditional *sarong kabaya*, a hip-hugging, ankle-length skirt, and snug blouse. Typical for men were lightweight trousers and loose batik shirt, a cool, relaxed style reminiscent of the Hawaiian aloha look. Today, Middle Eastern dress, popularized by Arab travelers who visit for business and pleasure, is unremarkable for both sexes. More than 80 percent of Malay women wear a closely wrapped headscarf. The black, shroud-like niqab is commonplace. Female genital mutilation has gained in popularity. According to one study, 93 percent of Malay girls and women undergo ritual genital mutilation.

In our day, the aristocratic Tun Razak danced foxtrots and rhumbas at parties with other men's wives, Carol included. And his wife danced with other women's husbands. I was one of them. No one gave it a thought. None of it would be acceptable today. I once related this to Razak's son, Abdul, when he, too, was prime minister, expecting him to be amused. A black cloud crossed his face, and he abruptly changed the topic.

Islamic religious police now pounce on Muslim men caught drinking in public and women in revealing outfits. Non-Malays remain unmolested. The news media seldom discuss sensitive racial or religious issues. Attendance at mosques is up sharply, as are Arabic-language classes, puritanical interpretations of public behavior, and the intervention of Sharia law into civil affairs.

With all these and more heavy-handed restrictions locked in place, serious racial violence has not returned to Malaysia since 1969. But, as was so horrifically demonstrated that landmark year, not all human emotions can be restrained by government diktat for all time. Those bottling up their emotions today very well may run amok tomorrow.

## Chapter Seven

# My Favorite Dictator

With Malaysia quieting down, I began hearing noise coming from the south. Not the gunshots that had ricocheted through the streets of KL, but jackhammers and piledrivers. Singapore was rising. As I turned my attention there, I would learn the strengths and weaknesses inherent in a dictatorship, even a scrupulous and munificent one.

In the early 1960s, Singaporeans half-joked that the loudest sounds heard on their sleepy little island were the click of chopsticks and the clack of mah-jongg tiles. One man, though, seemed never to sleep. Yet he dreamed. Then he made his dreams come true. Lee Kuan Yew was indisputably the sire of Singapore. Given the scale of the place—one thirtieth the size of little Israel, to which he frequently compared it—Singapore is, quite literally, The House that Lee Built.

He drove himself mercilessly to succeed, for the benefit of his seemingly hapless island, and for his own insatiable ego. Once he battled his way into the prime minister's office, he devoted the rest of his life to molding Singapore in his own image. For more than three decades, Lee single-handedly established and enforced almost every aspect of life for the island's six million obedient citizens, from reproduction to chewing gum.

Like dictators everywhere, he was a bully—brutal, ambitious, malicious, ruthless, willful, unforgiving, and arrogant. Unlike other dictators, he was puritanically incorruptible. And he was brilliant. The extreme contradictions between heavy-handedness and beneficence made him unendingly fascinating to me. I frequently asked to interview him when I was in town. He seldom refused.

The goal Lee set for himself seemed impossible: to build a modern city-state on a dot of land at the tip of peninsular Malaya's exclamation point. In the eighteenth century, this barely-there speck was a pestilential, malarial swamp. It was controlled, to an extent, by a minor Malay sultan who, for a price, offered it as a haven to pirates pillaging the South China Sea.

The one advantage the island had going for it was its superb natural harbor on the strategic Strait of Malacca. The imperial British, desperate to control the waterway, cut a deal with the sultan and made Singapore a vital outpost of the empire. They lined the coast with heavy artillery and, under the misguided belief that this made them safe from a potential attack, developed the anchorage into a thriving entrepôt. Today, the straits of Malacca and Hormuz, which link the Persian Gulf with the Gulf of Oman and the Arabian Sea, are the world's two most vital oil arteries and choke points.

On February 8, 1942, Japan staged a shocking surprise attack from its own newly captured stronghold on the Malay peninsula. The Japanese, vastly outnumbered but far shrewder than the British command, overran Singapore in a single week. The stunning defeat resulted in the surrender of eighty thousand troops, the greatest British military humiliation in history.

After occupying Singapore and Malaya for three years, a then-ruined Japan handed them back to Britain at the end of World War II. Britain unified Malaya with its two colonies on Borneo, Sarawak, and Sabah. The Malayan Union was created in 1946. Singapore, which the British retitled a Crown Colony, similar to Hong Kong, was left out. The Union quickly splintered and was replaced by the Federation of Malaya, to which Britain granted independence in 1957. Finally, in 1963, the Federation bonded with Singapore and renamed itself Malaysia; the "si" inserted into Malaya in recognition.

Another crisis erupted almost immediately. The inclusion of Singapore, with its ethnic Chinese majority, meant that the Malays of the newly unified nation would be a minority, second-class in their own homeland. The Malays rebelled and for two months the worst and most prolonged race riots in Singapore's history racked the island. Dozens were killed and hundreds critically injured.

The violence encapsulated the mind of the young Lee Kuan Yew in a dark nightmare from which he never fully emerged. With his island pincered between overwhelmingly larger Malay-Muslim Malaysia and Indonesia and with its own 15 percent Malay population discontent, he lived in constant fear of a recurrence.

Adding to Lee's psychological predisposition, he and Prime Minister Tunku Abdul Rahman—as opposite as two politicians could possibly be— were incapable of overcoming their intense distaste for each other.

"Mr. Lee Kuan Yew is too clever by half," the Tunku sneered in intellectually outgunned frustration. One year after unification, the Tunku forced Singapore out of Malaysia.

The expulsion was Lee's first, and by far worst, political failure. It drove him into deep depression from which he doubted he would ever escape. But he did, with renewed vigor that never again flagged. By the time I made my first reporting trip to Singapore, in 1967, he had begun to reimagine the island, to transform it into a shining prototype for the developing world.

In a taxi from Changi Airport to the center of town, I asked the chatty, gray-haired Chinese driver why the road was lined for miles with plywood sheets, painted sky-blue, entirely blocking the view.

"We're expecting a royal visitor," he replied with a chuckle, "and Mr. Lee Kuan Yew is embarrassed by what she would see."

What this visitor, Queen Elizabeth's cousin, Her Royal Highness Princess Alexandra, would have seen behind the blue wall were stretches of weedy flatland and jungle dotted with derelict tin-roofed shacks and kampongs, or villages, of decaying shophouses and attap palm huts, in which 90 percent of the population lived.

Just a decade later, had the princess returned, she would have been stunned, as I was each time I came back. A new Singapore had emerged, a futuristic metropolis of state-of-the-art architecture soaring into the cloudless sky. Blocks of tidy, utilitarian apartment buildings now housed 80 percent of Singapore's citizens in government-subsidized flats. Fully 90 percent of them owned their homes.

From Changi, annually rated the world's finest airport, the princess's limousine would have rolled along silken, multilane boulevards lined with multihued gardens of bougainvillea, frangipani, and swaying palms. She would be startled to find that the cramped island she recalled from her first visit had expanded into the sea by a quarter of its landmass, with over fifty square miles of dredged sand, imported from Indonesia, added to its natural boundaries.

She'd be amazed to find Singaporeans traveling belowground on a subway system that left, and to this day still leaves, those of London, Paris, and New York in the dust. Rail cars hum on rubber wheels, arriving and departing on the minute, doors whooshing open precisely at the same spot on the platform. Station walls are hung with posters challenging passengers with math and science brainteasers.

While they rest assured that their trains run on time, Singaporeans also are pointedly aware of a raft of government rules controlling nearly every aspect of their lives. One of the more disgusting sights and sounds of earlier Singapore life is no longer seen or heard. "Hawking," a public-health travesty whereby Chinese noisily clear their lungs and expectorate the disgusting result in public, is now a crime, subject to a $750 fine. In addition to spitting being outlawed, public toilets must be flushed after each use; smoking, gum chewing, and littering are not permitted; homosexual acts are illegal, as is pornography. Some laws infringe on the absurd: urinating in public elevators is against the law and naked residents in their own homes must not be visible to neighbors.

Punishments range from significant fines ($150 for an unflushed toilet) to two years in jail (gay sex). Anyone bold enough to spray graffiti on public property may expect to be beaten with a bamboo cane. I made sure to have my hair cut before leaving KL for Singapore because "hippy"—i.e., over-the-collar—hairstyles for men were forbidden and I could have been turned away at the airport. (Lee lifted this ban in the 1990s.) On one trip, Carol halted in her tracks, fearful of jaywalking with a group of American friends who were visiting for the first time, knowing they could be fined $38 each.

Lee imposed these and numerous other sanctions as he polished his once-slovenly little nation into a glittering ornament and a finely tuned engine of finance and industry. He succeeded beyond anyone's wildest expectations, possibly even his own. Singapore today boasts the world's freest economy, making it a prime target for the world's wealthiest nations and private investors.

I was excited and a little nervous about my initial interview with Lee. Colleagues had warned me that he was a tough customer, did not suffer fools, and would seek out my weaknesses and pounce on gaps in my knowledge.

In reading up on his background, I learned he had attended the London School of Economics and graduated with distinction from Cambridge University. He was married to a brilliant Singaporean who also graduated from Cambridge, with honors even higher than his. The couple had a daughter and two sons and lived in a substantial but unpretentious century-old house in the leafy Oxley Road neighborhood.

Lee's parents, like he and his wife, were devoted Anglophiles who spoke English as their first language. His paternal grandfather named him Harry, hoping it would help the boy insinuate himself among the island's ruling class. Harry Lee was the quintessence of what British imperialists mockingly called a WOG, a Westernized Oriental Gentlemen. On entering politics, though, Lee turned from aping the Brits to his ethnic roots. He studied Mandarin with a tutor in order to better communicate with Chinese voters. Similarly, during World War II, although he despised the Japanese, he learned their language and used it to get a job with the occupation's propaganda arm.

After forming the People's Action Party and campaigning for parliament on a platform to end colonial rule, Lee let it be known that his given first name, which appeared on his birth certificate, was no longer to be used in public. Friends and family, though, continued to call him Harry.

By the time I met him, he had established a well-deserved reputation as a hard-nosed politician. Many Singaporeans used far more pejorative terms, but only in whispers. The term nearly all agreed on, whether willingly or reluctantly, was "incorruptible." In 1961, a CIA agent offered Lee a $3.3 million bribe (that would be $25 million in 2020), to keep quiet about an unsuccessful agency operation in Singapore. Lee refused and forced the CIA to confess publicly that it had attempted and failed to buy him off.

He built a government and a civil service based on the ancient Mandarin system of meritocracy. Because of his constant fear of racial unrest, he championed multiracialism in government, public housing, and education. He made English the common language in an effort to integrate the multilingual, multiracial, multiethnic society and to facilitate trade with the West. But, to preserve ethnic identity, he also required schools to teach students their ancestral languages.

He had his shortcomings, and they were legion. Critics at home and abroad never lacked for issues on which to fault him. He curtailed civil liberties through strict limits on public protests and harsh media controls. He dabbled in eugenics, convinced that purposefully breeding highly educated men and women would create superior Singaporeans, and spoke openly about it in starkly debasing terms:

"Not that all the children of gardeners or laborers are duds. Occasionally, two grey horses produce a white horse, but very few. If you have two white horses, the chances are you breed white horses. It's seldom spoken publicly because those who are not white horses say, 'You're degrading me.' but it's a fact of life. You get a good mare; you don't want a dud stallion to breed with your good mare. You get a poor foal."

While shunning any hint of political correctness in dealing with others, he was exquisitely sensitive to criticism of himself. He had offensive articles in foreign publications smeared with black ink, blocked their circulation, and sued them. He jailed political foes for years without substantiated evidence or trials. He argued that tough discipline was essential for political stability and economic progress. "Anybody who decides to take me on needs to put on knuckledusters," Lee threatened. "If you think you can hurt me more than I can hurt you, try."

When I interviewed Lee that first time, the Vietnam War was peaking and he was preparing for his first official visit to Washington, to meet with President Johnson. His office in the British-built Supreme Court building, a replica of London's Old Bailey, was huge but sparsely furnished. I found him seated behind a desk at the far wall. He did not rise to greet me. Nor did he smile.

"Sit there," he commanded, sweeping the back of his hand toward a worn, leather club chair so distant from him that I was forced to raise my voice and strain to hear him. He knew exactly how to intimidate a young reporter.

He was wearing the white trousers and open-collared, short-sleeve, white shirt that constituted his party's uniform. He also wore a beige golf jacket. Although he was a lifelong Singaporean, he couldn't tolerate the humid heat.

He insisted on air-conditioning everywhere he went, thermostat set precisely at 22°C, 71.6°F.

I would interview Lee a half dozen times before he died, in 2015, at the age of ninety-one. But the impressions he left on me that first time stuck. He didn't like foreign correspondents and made no effort to pretend otherwise. He was, in a word, tough. He looked it, too: face, large and pockmarked; receding black pompadour accentuating a broad, soaring forehead; unblinking dark eyes with hooded lids above and puffy bags beneath. A British official once referred to him as looking like "a bit of a thug," and it was rumored that, as he studied his image in the bathroom mirror one morning, Lee reluctantly concurred.

Lee had taken Singapore into the Non-Aligned Movement, calculating that a foreign-policy position somewhere between the Cold-Warring USA and USSR would most benefit his fledgling government. Like leaders of other Non-Aligned nations, principally India and Indonesia, he frequently criticized the Johnson administration, winning favor among his new teammates.

But he tended to hold his tongue on America's war in Vietnam. He loathed communism and believed firmly in the Domino Theory, fearing that if the United States was defeated or withdrew from Indochina, the rest of Southeast Asia—Singapore included—would turn red.

By delicately balancing criticism of America with accommodation, Lee gained immense economic and strategic dividends for Singapore. Fifteen percent of its income derived from US military procurement for the war in Vietnam. Lockheed set up shop on the island to repair and maintain aircraft crucial to the US war machine. American private investment rose by $100 million a year. Lee, the pragmatist's pragmatist, played his cards brilliantly.

In response to my opening question, on whether he believed that LBJ should continue bombing North Vietnam, a policy then fiercely criticized by many Americans, he finessed, saying, "If Americans think that halting the bombing would lead directly to peace talks with the North Vietnamese, they are sadly mistaken. And if President Johnson thinks that this would happen in time to have a positive influence on his reelection, he, too, is wrong. North Vietnam has no reason to rush to the conference table. . . . You could halt it or continue it without much influence on the future of the war or of peace negotiations."

Curious to know how he, with his liberal, Western education, rationalized governing as an authoritarian, I asked whether he foresaw an end to his harsh rule. This time his answer was extensive but blunt. "You Americans believe that we should follow your liberal democratic standards. I have no doubt that you mean well. But you are wrong. Your standards do not apply here. We must abide by Asian values. Call it filial piety or father knows best. In a society that is 80 percent Chinese, one must lay down the law. There is no other way to govern a Chinese society."

More than three decades of iron-fisted rule proved he meant it. American-style democracy, according to Lee, had no place in his country or anywhere else in the developing world. Checks and balances interfered with governing under circumstances "where executive action must be swift to forestall disorder."

"Western newsmen often accuse me of interfering in the private lives of our citizens," he said. "Yes, I do. Without that, we wouldn't be here today. We would not be making the economic progress we are making. It is true that if I had not played my cards correctly and had not laid down the law on some very personal matters, we would be finished. So, yes, I have told people, especially the educated class, to have more children, to stop spitting and smoking, to learn English, to keep the noise down, to respect your neighbors, whoever they are. Never mind what people think. It is my responsibility to decide what is right."

I had interviewed barely a handful of national leaders at that stage in my career, but I knew that very few would be as candid as Lee. His rationale for "Asian values" led me to reconsider my youthful conviction that Western democracy was what all people wanted and that it was workable in all societies. Neither is so.

Ironically, Lee's methods in one of the world's smallest countries have worked well in the largest. Decades ago, China's communist leaders began dispatching technocrats from Beijing to Singapore. They sat at Lee's feet, like eager acolytes before the Buddha, soaking up his wisdom. The disciples carried proof back to Beijing that a tough government could buy the loyalty of a rational Chinese population by delivering a living wage, sufficient food, and abundant consumer goods. Deng Xiaoping awoke to this wisdom in the aftermath of the 1989 Tiananmen Square Massacre. Today's China is in many ways a massive replica of tiny Singapore. Lee, in turn, based on what he learned from his visitors, became the first national leader to forecast China's stunning emergence. He delivered the message, with limited success, to Johnson and future US presidents. Henry Kissinger became a Lee Kuan Yew devotee.

Lee remained in office for thirty-one years, until 1990, when he stepped aside. But not down. This was a unique case of a strongman confounding the Chinese proverb that "he who rides a tiger is afraid to dismount." In 2004 his elder son, Lee Hsien Loong, took charge and relaxed a few of his father's more stringent rulings. But Singapore continues to march rigidly along, its people by and large, though not universally, content with abundance in lieu of liberty.

Lee Kuan Yew was a rare specimen of that rarest breed, the benevolent dictator. His compulsion to improve the lives of Singaporeans abetted by his unquestioned incorruptibility distinguished him from the worldwide rogues' gallery of strongmen. Such unique qualities convinced Singaporeans to forgo freedom of speech and of the press, and other democratic ideals for the more tangible benefits he delivered.

American visitors, impressed by the orderliness and prosperity, commonly question why their government can't replicate what Lee did. The essential reason, as we learned during the COVID-19 crisis, is that no matter how obvious the benefits, Americans don't like being told what to do. And yet, when a president whose authenticated lies are legion told them that the news reported by their free press—a press Singaporeans long for in frustrated silence—was "fake," they rolled over like obedient puppies.

With a year remaining of my assignment in KL, I began weighing potential options for the future.

As an AP correspondent, I had grown and learned a great deal: how to report from the field and dictate an accurate, coherent story with little more than a glance at my notebook; to compete with other wire service correspondents on critical minute-by-minute deadlines; to tell a complex story in the fewest possible words; to recruit reliable stringers in outlying towns and massage their material into usable copy.

I had also learned that an AP bureau chief was responsible not only for covering the news but also for selling wire-service products to clients. I spent hours in the cluttered offices of editors of English, Malay, Chinese, and Tamil dailies, drinking countless cups of tea while touting AP Radio Photos and ancillary feature services. And reminding them that, by the way, their bills were overdue.

I had not signed up to be a salesman or a bill collector.

Back in the spring of 1964, as I was walking out the door at Columbia to begin work the next day with AP, Dean Richard Baker had offered me a bit of career advice. "Don't stay too long or you'll be labeled a wire-service reporter and you'll find it hard to move into newspapers or magazines."

It was now seven years. Long enough.

## Chapter Eight

# The Council, the Papers, and the *Post*

I could be doggedly persistent when I decided circumstances warranted. But patient? That was another matter. Persistence meant doing something to make something else happen. Patience required not doing something. It meant waiting. I was not good at it.

Stan Swinton, my AP boss, seldom kept me waiting. If I sent him a telex overnight, I knew an answer would be on its way minutes after he arrived at his office in Rockefeller Center at 7:00 a.m.. No patience needed.

Stan was an AP lifer. For half of his forty-two years with the news agency, he ran AP World Services, which meant he was in charge of all foreign bureaus and foreign correspondents. He'd been a frontline reporter during World War II and afterward was based in Rome. So he knew what it was like for a correspondent far from home to be hung out to dry while an editor was enjoying cocktails on the other side of the world.

As my KL assignment wound down, Stan invited me to a meeting in Bangkok of Asia-based correspondents. One sultry evening, as we were chatting on the deck of the riverfront Oriental Hotel, he passed along a well-worn bit of philosophy he'd first heard from Ambassador Clare Boothe Luce, the famous author as well as the wife of Time Inc. founder Henry Luce. "It's not what you know; it's who you know."

Stan had built his career on hard work. But friends in high places helped him advance. When I told him I meticulously separated friendships from my reporting, he suggested a work-around. "The Council on Foreign Relations has an excellent program for mid-career correspondents. If you got it, you'd get to know just the kind of people I'm talking about. And you could still stay within your boundaries."

Acting on his advice, I applied for the Edward R. Murrow Fellowship and got it. That year, 1969–1970, turned out to be one of the most valuable of my life. I met people I wouldn't have otherwise and gained invaluable insights

The *Pentagon Papers* blew the sham wide open. Among its revelations was that, as far back as 1965, Undersecretary of State George Ball had presented the following grim assessment, replete with racist innuendo, to President Johnson: "No one can assure that we can beat the Viet Cong or even force them to the conference table on our terms, no matter how many hundred thousand white, foreign (US) troops we deploy."

The next year, McNamara produced his own evaluation, which demonstrated that the communist side was prepared to outlast Americans' willingness to remain on the ground in Vietnam: "Enemy morale has not broken—he apparently has adjusted to our stopping his drive for military victory and has adopted a strategy of keeping us busy and waiting us out (a strategy of attriting our national will)."

Having put his job and reputation on the line by stealing the papers, Ellsberg understood he had reached the in-for-a-dime, in-for-a-dollar point. He decided to go public. He offered the papers to Democratic Senator J. William Fulbright of Arkansas and several other anti-war legislators. None was willing to hold hearings.

Frustrated, Ellsberg determined he had no choice but to pass the hot potato to a journalist. He leaked the tome to *New York Times* reporter Neil Sheehan, who had distinguished himself as a correspondent in Vietnam. The *Times* began publishing on June 13, 1971. The *Washington Post* quickly caught up.

The Nixon administration was livid beyond fury. It charged Ellsberg with espionage. He faced up to 115 years in prison, but, once federal investigators learned that Nixon's infamous "plumbers" had broken into the office of Ellsberg's psychiatrist and stolen his medical records—stealing records about a man who had stolen records—the judge had no choice but to dismiss the case.

Along with the *Post*'s exposé of the Watergate scandal a year later, the publication of the *Pentagon Papers* sowed deeper doubt and distrust of the government among more everyday Americans than any event in prior history. At the same time, the revelations by Sheehan and the *Post*'s Carl Bernstein and Bob Woodward elevated investigative journalism to a higher level of respect than ever before. Enrollment in journalism schools shot up and applications for journalism jobs increased.

Vietnam hawks and Nixonians reacted by attacking journalists as unpatriotic. Liberal doves praised them as heroes of democracy. The fact remains that without the *Times* and the *Post*, neither hawks nor doves would have learned that the people we elected to office in full expectation that they would look out for our best interests were, in fact, unconscionably sacrificing our sons and brothers, husbands and fathers. They lied to us every day for fourteen years.

Whether or not one believes that journalists live up to their responsibility to readers and viewers, there is no denying that the *Pentagon Papers* comprise confessions of lies by those who told them. By publishing, journalists revealed the truth behind the lies. If Americans don't consider that a service, they are mistaken. They are deliberately hiding from the facts.

My own view as a practitioner for over fifty years is that it is our duty to shine a high beam into government's darkest corners and expose whatever is hidden there. The free press is the single most powerful instrument the framers handed directly to citizens as defense against government deceit. Citizens who accept politicians' lies that all journalists lie are swallowing whole the lies of professional liars:

No, we are not perfect. Yes, we do stumble, sometimes fall, and occasionally drop the ball altogether. But, attempting to undermine the credibility of the press as a body and to smear all journalists—except for those who actively support the politician in question—ranks first on any authoritarian's to-do list. By conditioning the public's mind to reject criticism of him or her, the strongman sets the stage for further control.

The question of what I was going to do next nagged at me during the fellowship year. By the time it drew to a close, I felt prepared for a step up. Phil Foisie, who oversaw foreign coverage at the *Washington Post*, offered me a job on his growing staff.

Phil was the younger brother of Jack Foisie, the *LA Times* correspondent with whom I'd walked into Hue during the Tet Offensive. Unlike the puckish Jack, Phil was withdrawn, gloomy, a chain-smoking, gin-drinking, pill-popper. He habitually paced the newsroom with a mask of discomfiture on his large, round face, wire-rim glasses pasted to his high forehead, cigarette pinched between extended fingers, lost in ceaseless, burdensome worry.

Phil was remarkably accomplished. He had been a championship tennis player in his youth and was a graduate of Harvard and a fluent Japanese speaker. He served as a military intelligence officer on the China-Burma frontier during World War II. The experience left him with a soft spot for Asia. We shared that, though not much else.

When Phil joined the *Post* in 1955, it fielded no foreign correspondents and most of the international news it published came from AP and other wire services. If the *Post* was to compete with the *Times* and a handful of other serious newspapers, Phil knew, it must have its own foreign staff. Not that readers particularly cared; surveys revealed that interest in foreign news ranked below the funny pages. It was a matter of prestige, like owning a Rolex when a Timex tells the time just as well.

In 1957, Phil opened the *Post*'s first bureau, in London, on a shoestring. A decade later, he'd grown the staff to twenty-three correspondents in fourteen countries. He hired me with the understanding that I would be posted to Asia. When and where to be determined.

The step from AP to the *Post* was a big one for me. Wire service reporters, despite being some of the best in the business, generally function in near anonymity. Their bylines, if and when they appear on the wire, are often removed by newspaper editors. Some editors feel free to blend the copy of various services. A newspaper's own correspondents' bylines normally are printed, in boldface, above the dateline and become known to readers. Since presidents, cabinet secretaries, members of Congress and their influential staffers read the *Post*, these reporters may contribute to shaping the country's policies. Heady stuff for a kid from Paterson.

I was energized as we drove down Interstate 95, from Manhattan to Washington, in May 1971. In my excitement, during a pit stop I left my briefcase containing every piece of paper that affirmed our existence on the planet—passports, medical and insurance records, checkbook—on the roof of our car. It flew off somewhere on the Beltway. By the time we arrived at the *Post*, a kindly truck driver, having found my letter of welcome from Foisie inside, had delivered the battered case to the newsroom. I took it as a sign of good fortune to come.

We sublet a house for the summer and then bought a place of our own in suburban Bethesda. For the next nine months, I edited copy on the foreign desk, much as I had at AP prior to going to Vietnam. It wasn't long before stories from South Asia piqued my interest. I began noticing wire reports about increasing unrest on the Indian subcontinent. A story with major international ramifications was building in East Pakistan and the *Post* had no correspondent there. So, I took it on myself to contact specialists at State and Defense, universities and various foreign embassies around town. I tapped into their expertise, using it to write analyses that added depth and context to the straightforward wire reports.

This was the picture: Ethnic violence, fueled by political dissent, was breaking out in the poverty-stricken, eastern wing of Pakistan. Britain had created the oddly bifurcated nation in the summer of 1947, when it granted independence to Hindu-majority India and carved out a new homeland for the subcontinent's ninety-five million Muslims. A 1,200-mile swath of India separated East and West Pakistan. It was as though New York and California were one country and everything in between was another.

"Partition," as the crude geopolitical surgery was called, overnight uprooted fourteen million panicked Hindus and Muslims. As many as two million were slaughtered by zealots of the other faith as they attacked villages and raided overloaded refugee trains. The cataclysm pitched the subcontinent into recurring spasms of tension and violence that continue to this day. The Indo-Pak relationship remains one of the most antagonistic in the world.

In addition to hostility between Hindus and Muslims, within the newly created Muslim nation, West Pakistanis—principally "wheatish" or fair-complexioned, ethnic Punjabis—imposed political, economic, and military control on the darker-skinned Bengalis of the East. West Pakistan's sixty million people looked down on their sixty-eight million compatriots as racially inferior and their Islamic practice as adulterated.

The conflict now building steam was inevitable. It was triggered by a charismatic Bengali politician by the name of Sheikh Mujibur Rahman. He and his Awami League party had won Pakistan's first nationwide elections in a landslide in December 1970. The military dictatorship in West Pakistan refused to allow them to take office.

West Pakistan was poor, but East Pakistan was dirt poor. Subject to the whims of nature and politics, it was the epicenter of what foreign correspondents referred to as South Asia's "disaster belt." A monster cyclone had devastated much of low-lying East Pakistan a month prior to the polls. The storm claimed as many as half a million lives, ranking it among the world's worst-ever natural disasters. The central government ignored the plight of over half its population and delayed assistance until international pressure shamed it into acting. Bengalis were enraged.

A no-less-provocative issue was West Pakistanis' insistence that their primary dialect, Urdu, be made the official tongue of all Pakistan. Bengalis had their own language. Being forced to speak Urdu would have added an unbearable burden to the disadvantages they already suffered as second-class citizens of a country in which they were the numerical majority. When the elections came, they voted against Urdu and for Sheikh Mujib, as he was known, handing him a better than two-to-one victory. But the military-backed power elite stood firmly against permitting a Bengali to rule.

On March 7, 1971, at the Ramna Race Course in central Dacca, Mujib delivered what would be the most consequential speech of his life. Speaking before a huge crowd of agitated Bengalis, he declared that he would lead a fight for freedom, not from Britain, not from India, but from West Pakistan. "The struggle this time is the struggle for our emancipation!" he said. "The struggle this time is the struggle for our independence!"

Awed Bengalis were already referring to Mujib as Bangabandhu—Friend of Bengal, or Father of the Country—and his words carried far greater weight than those of a conventional politician. His speech touched all the hot buttons and electrified Bengalis. It set in motion a series of actions and reactions that would result first in a tragedy of historic proportions and eventually in a stunning, though tenuous, victory.

As soon as Mujib finished speaking, workers and students spilled from the racetrack into the streets of Dacca, protesting loudly but peacefully. Troops

the message. It remains to this day the strongest official statement of internal, diplomatic protest in the history of the State Department: "Our government has failed to denounce the suppression of democracy. Our government has failed to denounce atrocities. Our government has failed to take forceful measures. . . . Our government has evidenced what many will consider moral bankruptcy. . . . Private Americans have expressed disgust. We, as professional civil servants, express our dissent . . . And fervently hope that [the government will] salvage our nation's position as a moral leader of the free world."

The administration's self-muzzling drew condemnation up and down the halls of the State Department, in Congress and from the press. Kissinger's reaction to the cable, Blood later said, was "deafening silence." In fact, though, he and Nixon were purple with rage. The Blood Telegram threatened to upset their painstaking China plan. As payback for Blood's candor, Kissinger recalled him from Dacca and hid him away at an obscure desk in the department's personnel office. His career was ruined.

The slaughter would end nine months later. At least two hundred thousand and possibly as many as three million Bengalis would be dead. Nixon and Kissinger earned their survivors' eternal hatred.

Before that happened, with trans-Pakistan hostilities intensifying, alarm deepened in India over the security of its borders with the two wings of the Muslim homeland. Ten million terrified refugees poured from East Pakistan into Calcutta. The teeming, destitute city staggered under the strain. The government erected a vast tent encampment on Salt Lake, a sunbaked, dry lakebed on the outskirts of the city. Overcrowding, lack of sanitation, insufficient water and food were intolerable. Refugees became sick and died.

The East Pakistan story seized the public's consciousness in the United States. Americans were incensed by press reports, like those in the *Post*, about the refugees' conditions and Nixon's refusal to help. Former Beatle George Harrison and Indian superstar sitarist Ravi Shankar organized "The Concert for Bangladesh" on August 1, 1971, at New York's Madison Square Garden, to raise funds for relief. Forty thousand people turned out, eventually contributing $12 million. Exulted Shankar, "in one day, the whole world knew the name of Bangladesh. It was a fantastic occasion."

As India prepared to go to war, it hastily formed and armed a Bengali paramilitary force, the Mukti Bahini or Freedom Fighters. These poorly prepared guerrillas battled the Pakistani army. All that distinguished the carnage from the Holocaust was that it was carried out not by Germans on Jews but by Sunni Muslims on Sunni Muslims.

The second boot dropped with a sudden crash on the evening of December 3, 1971. Pakistani planes attacked eleven air force bases in northern India and the disputed state of Kashmir. Mrs. Gandhi immediately declared war. India's

Soviet-built MIG-21s launched in minutes, followed by full-scale air, land, and sea invasions of both of Pakistan's wings.

Foisie dispatched Lee Lescaze, the *Post*'s Hong Kong–based correspondent, to Dacca. He provided superb coverage of some of the war's most horrendous incidents. Lescaze later became the paper's foreign editor and my immediate supervisor.

With a crushing Pakistani defeat at the hands of India's far more powerful armed forces looming, Yahya demanded the United States provide more meaningful help. Although Kissinger now enjoyed his own, direct communication with China and no longer needed the beleaguered Pakistani's help, he persuaded Nixon to rattle a saber or two, if only for show.

The president ordered ships of the US Seventh Fleet to sail from Vietnam's Gulf of Tonkin to the Bay of Bengal. The battle group centered on the nuclear-powered aircraft carrier USS *Enterprise*, which was accompanied by nine other vessels, including a nuclear attack submarine. The flotilla arrived off the coast of Bangladesh on December 15, too late to matter. The effort served only to further antagonize Indians and Bengalis. Pakistan, outmanned, outgunned, and out-strategized, surrendered the next day.

The Indo-Pak war had lasted just thirteen days. Pakistan suffered grievous military losses—eight thousand troops killed, twenty-five thousand wounded, and ninety-three thousand taken prisoner. India's casualties were less than half that. Shorn of its eastern wing, Pakistan emerged a crippled bird that wouldn't fly right again.

## Chapter Nine

# Molested at Birth

It was time for Lescaze to leave Bangladesh and Foisie plucked me off the desk to replace him. I had never set foot in India or Pakistan and going solo on short notice without knowing a soul at the destination was at once daunting and exhilarating. It was a chance to prove myself. Or fail.

Testing moments like this become routine in a foreign correspondent's life. But, in my experience, they never become easy. Something happens somewhere and someone needs to be there to cover it. Whether you know the place well or are a complete stranger, whether a colleague is waiting to help or you're on your own, whether people are killing each other in the streets or casting ballots at the polls, like a firefighter, police officer, or soldier, you go.

With one foot out the door of our house and a taxi driver impatiently honking his horn, I remembered to call our friend Nancy Pelletreau at the State Department. She'd previously been based in Bombay and New Delhi and had close Indian friends.

"Take down this number," Nancy said. "Call when you get to Delhi. Bim will take care of you."

My flight landed in the dead of night. Even though the war was over, strict blackout rules were still in effect and the low-slung capital city was obscured in darkness. In the mobbed terminal, I caught a cloying whiff of sandalwood incense. Instantly, it became my forever-scent of India. Immigration and customs formalities were chaotic and dragged on for hours. By the time I got into a boneshaker Ambassador taxi that looked like it had begun its long life in service to the Raj, a brassy sliver of morning sun was glimmering through the murky air, casting faint light on a ghostly montage.

Hundreds, maybe thousands, shrouded in white homespun rose like zombies from woven-rope charpoys scattered along the road. I'd never seen anything so otherworldly. Clutching small brass jugs of water, some straggled into weedy fields to squat. Others hunkered at ramshackle stalls, slurping steaming glasses of sweet, milky chai, cooked on cow-dung fires.

Minutes later, my taxi delivered me to the palatial, red-sandstone Ashoka Hotel. From the squalor of the millions to the luxury of the few. The brief journey summed up for me the terrible contradictions of India.

I was drained by the twenty-hour flight, but my brain was wired, and sleep proved impossible. I paced the Ashoka's soaring lobby, under the baleful stare of a lone overnight watchman. At a decent hour, I called the number Nancy had given me and introduced myself to Bimla Bissell. She had been a highly effective social secretary to several US ambassadors and was now working at the World Bank's Delhi branch. On the side, she ran Playhouse School, her nursery that catered to local and expatriate children. Bim's husband, a Connecticut Yankee named John Bissell, had founded Fabindia, a small, socially conscious company that promoted and sold handcrafted textiles and clothing.

"Come to dinner tonight," she said without missing a beat.

Bim knew everyone. She had assembled a dozen luminaries around the dinner table: foreign and defense ministry officials, newspaper editors, diplomats, and academics. They provided me with a multifaceted seminar on Bangladesh, the war, and its politics, more detailed than I could fully absorb. As I scribbled furiously, they contributed a Who's Who of contacts in Calcutta and Dacca. I also received this vital tip from one guest, "Straightaway, when you reach Calcutta, be sure to see Mr. Chatterjee at Writers' Building. He's the key."

I spent the next two days prowling Delhi's government offices, acquiring the complex paperwork and passport stamps essential to function as a journalist in India and to continue to Calcutta, where I would apply for yet more documentation and a permit to cross into Bangladesh.

I transited the broad shoulders of India to Dum Dum Airport, on the edge of Calcutta. It was at Dum Dum, around 1896, that the British army invented the eponymous hollow-tip bullet it used as a manstopper against rebellious Indians.

The taxi ride into the city assaulted my every sense. Traffic was crazed. A mad merry-go-round of humanity—on foot, bicycles, and motor scooters, packed into and atop buses, trains, ancient automobiles, trucks garishly painted with Hindu deities, sputtering tuk-tuks, two-wheeled rickshas hauled by bare-footed runners—clashed with picket-ribbed holy cows, mange-infested dogs, goats, pigs, camels, and the occasional elephant, all struggling to maneuver in the gridlocked streets.

Earsplitting horns blared incessantly, competing with a cacophony of moos, barks, squeals, oinks, growls, bleats, bellows, roars, and trumpeting of the menagerie.

Mothers crouching at curbside drew the ends of their saris across their faces as curtains of privacy while they suckled infants. Little girls carried naked siblings astride their hips. Other children, noses oozing, eyes crawling with flies, squatted in gutters, defecating. The stink of human and animal waste mingled with engine discharge was nauseating.

Beggars, some of whose parents had horrifically deformed them at birth in order to raise their pity quotient, pleaded for a few paise. I had to choose between the smells, noise, and cripples thrusting their maimed limbs at my face and cranking up the window and suffocating. I alternated. If Hell were located in India, I decided, it would be in Calcutta.

As at the Ashoka in Delhi, I left Hell behind on the street when I checked into the Grand Hotel, a once-elegant hostelry on once-elegant Chowringhee Road. Though decayed, the Grand retained a few touches of its former grandeur. Its sooty facade stretched along most of an entire block. A concrete canopy propped on mock Ionic columns sheltered passersby from broiling sun and pouring rain.

In every city where foreign correspondents flock to cover a major story, one hotel becomes their preferred base. In Saigon, it was the Continental. In Phnom Penh, Le Royal. In Rangoon, the Strand. In Calcutta, it was the Grand. I jostled my way through the narrow lobby, clogged with television crews and their bulky equipment. Producers were dishing out wads of rupees to telex operators and taxi drivers, buying access and to block the competition.

My first task was to gain permission to cross the border and carry on to Dacca. Following the tip I'd picked up at Bim's dinner, I headed to the Writers' Building and the indispensable Mr. Chatterjee. Before me sprawled a splendid pile of vermilion edifices in more or less Greco-Roman style, lumped together over the centuries since 1775. Calcutta then was the capital of British India, and Writers' was where the Raj trained its Oriental-languages experts. With independence, it became home to India's West Bengal state administration.

As I stepped down from a ricksha and handed the puller a few sweat-dampened rupees, I noticed scores of scriveners hunkered on the sidewalk ringing Writers', pecking away at ancient typewriters, *writing* official documents for illiterate applicants seeking permits and licenses or filing complaints.

Once inside, I was lost in a musty, dim maze of rough-fibered jute-carpeted hallways lined with seemingly uncountable offices. Some were tiny, some larger, but all were packed from wall to wall and floor to ceiling with papers—papers held together with straight pins, the stapler apparently still undiscovered in India; papers piled to the point of toppling over onto floors, tables, desks, and chairs; papers shoved into brown file-folders bound with red cotton ribbon, the original "red tape," that British government servants began using in the seventeenth century.

This was my introduction to bureaucracy Indian style. In addition to the railroad, the bureaucracy was Britain's great parting gift to the colony that for three hundred years had been the most brilliant jewel in its imperial crown. By training Indians to do most of the government's day-to-day work, the Brits were able to run the vast subcontinent with a relative handful of expat civil and military officers. The system ballooned over the centuries to the point where it now comprises some twenty million workers at the federal level alone. (The US government employs a paltry two million.) Platoons of officers direct regiments of clerks known as "babus," who command corps of menial workers called "peons" (pronounced "pyoons"). The result looks and sounds clumsy and tumultuous and frequently is. Somehow, though, it works.

Sort of.

In one of the dim hallways, I approached a man in a peon's high-necked dark-blue uniform smoking a pungent *bidi* and asked if he would please direct me to the office of Mr. Chatterjee. He was flustered and stared blankly at me. *Language problem*, I surmised. Summoning my full command of India's twenty-two officially recognized dialects, I tried again: "Chatterjee *sahib*?" Nothing.

At that moment, a gray-haired gentleman with a neatly trimmed mustache and wearing an immaculately pressed, long-sleeved cream shirt, dark slacks, and sockless leather sandals, *chappals*, appeared out of the gloom.

"May I help?" he asked.

"Thank you," I replied. "I'm looking for Mr. Chatterjee."

He burst into laughter. After regaining his composure, he explained. "You asking for Mr. Chatterjee in Calcutta would be like me standing in the middle of Times Square on New Year's Eve and shouting for Mr. Smith. Their numbers are boundless."

Once I outlined my border-crossing mission, though, he was actually able to direct me to *the* Mr. Chatterjee. I found this worthy person seated at a paper-strewn desk in front of a tall window, dust motes dancing on sun beams backlighting him in a golden haze. The light blurred his features, but I made out straight, silvery hair neatly trimmed and parted.

"Your good name, please?" he asked wearily, pushing his glasses up from the tip of his nose and raising his eyes in my direction.

*My*, I thought, *how nice. How respectful.* I later learned that this inquiry was something other than a courtesy. It was literal. In Bengal, one's "good name" is one's official given name as it appears on one's birth certificate and other legal documents.

"Lewis Simons," I answered.

"You are from?" he asked.

"The *Washington Post*," I replied.

Not everyone was so fortunate. A correspondent from *US News & World Report* had been in to see this same Mr. Chatterjee some days earlier. He was Joe Fromm, a highly regarded journalist, and he was accompanied by a colleague whose name I've forgotten. Let's call him Brown. The conversation went something like this:

Chatterjee to Brown: "You are from?"

Brown: "No, I am Brown. He is Fromm."

Chatterjee to Fromm: "You are from?"

Fromm: "Yes, I am Fromm."

Chatterjee: "No, you are from?"

Fromm: "Yes, I am Fromm and he is Brown."

On and on it spun, a Bengali take on Abbott and Costello's classic "Who's on First" shtick.

I told Chatterjee I needed a permit to cross the frontier. "Certainly," he said. But first I would have to see Mr. Bannerjee. He gave me directions and I set off. I got lost again but eventually located the correct Bannerjee—an appellation no less ubiquitous than Chatterjee—and we went through the same "good name" and "from" routines. Unfortunately, Bannerjee said I needed to see Mr. Mukherjee.

Directions. Search. Get lost. Find the correct Mukherjee. Repeat routine:

"Sorry, see Bannerjee."

"Just did."

"No, no, not *that* Bannerjee."

Plunge back into the halls that lead nowhere. Find the right Bannerjee. Repeat routine, stupefied:

"Ah, you must see Mr. Chatterjee."

"I did! About four hours ago!"

"Well, he's the only one who can help you."

Maddened, I stormed back into Chatterjee's office, planted my feet in front of his desk, and blew my stack. His face turned chalky and his jaw sagged. He maintained silence until my steam dissipated. Then he fixed me with eyes gone cold and, in a stern but measured voice, taught me a lesson that would guide me through Asia for the next forty-five years.

"You are a young man, Mr. Simons," he said, "just starting out in your career. I am much older than you. In Asia, we respect age. And we practice patience and good manners. You have been very rude to me, and you have been impatient. You know nothing about me, but I am in a position to end your career here and now. It would mean nothing to me to deny you permission to travel. You would be unable to get to Dacca and carry out your assignment. Now, I suggest that you sit down, take a few deep breaths, and consider your situation."

My knees turned to jelly. My stomach churned. Mortified, I sank into a sagging cane chair and, panicky, breathed. My first thought was that having flown halfway around the world, I had screwed up. Royally. I could be finished before I got started. What would Foisie say? My second thought was that I had indeed been disrespectful. Here I was, a smart-ass kid from Nowheresville, New Jersey, in a country with a cultural history of ten thousand years, about which I knew nothing, insulting a person who held my future in the palm of his hand. What I had done was not just inexcusable. It was stupid.

I bared my soul to Chatterjee, all but kowtowing on his dusty floor, offering him the sincere apology he deserved. "I'm grateful for your setting me on the right path," I told him, with all the sincerity I could collect. "I won't forget what you said. I am sorry and I beg your understanding and your pardon."

With admirable grace, he forgave me. Minutes later, I backed out of his office clutching all permits, duly signed, stamped, and pinned.

I celebrated my narrow escape from ignominy that evening with an extravagant meal in the gloomy dining room of the Grand. Not knowing *palak paneer* from *aloo gobi*, I asked the tuxedo-clad waiter for his recommendations.

"Sahib, you are having son?" he inquired solicitously, head bobbling. "No," said I, wondering where this was going, "Two daughters."

"Ah," he responded, as though surmising as much. "Then you must be eating mutton-brain *masala*. It is being made with pure gold. It will be making you very strong. Son is guaranteed."

My selection was obvious. Glistening gray matter topped with gold leaf as filmy as a summer breeze, it was spicy and delicious, though my inexpert taste buds failed to detect a precious-metal flavor.

Our son was born seven years later. Still . . .

Dacca's rundown airport was bedlam when my one-hour border hop landed at midday on December 18, the day after Pakistan's commander formally surrendered to his Indian counterpart at a ceremony at the Ramna Race Course, where it all had begun. Word had reached the city that Pakistan's new president, Zulfikar Ali Bhutto, had released Sheikh Mujib from prison and that he would soon return to Dacca.

Joyous anticipation saturated the steamy air. Jubilant citizens of the newborn nation were flying in from around the world, as were journalists. Pedicab drivers were enjoying outrageous fees—$5 or $6—for the short ride into town. I grabbed one. The driver, a scrawny man with ropy calves and a graying, Lincolnesque beard, was bubbling over with anticipation about the imminent arrival of his hero. "He is coming home, Sahib! He is coming!"

As I registered at the Intercontinental Hotel, a correspondent I recognized was heading for the door and told me that a victory rally was underway at the ubiquitous racecourse. I dropped my bags at the front desk and ran the few blocks. What I found instead of a celebration was a horror show.

A dozen frenzied Mukti Bahini, armed with dated Enfield rifles and fixed bayonets, were torturing four terrified victims, cheered on by a mob of hysterical men. The freedom fighters had been lauded at home and inspired admiration abroad for their courage during the nine-month independence struggle. Now they were taking barbaric revenge on the four, members of a non-Bengali Muslim minority known as Biharis. The Biharis were hardly innocents. Thousands had collaborated with Pakistani troops, committing murder, rape, and looting.

Helpless and nauseated, I stood on the grassy maidan in the center of the racetrack, as the Mukti Bahini dragged out the horrifying retribution for hours, poking and prodding with their bayonets, knives, and lit cigarettes. The sickening nadir was reached when adored Mukti Bahini hero Kadir "Tiger" Siddiqui bayoneted a petrified captive through the gut. The crowd roared its approval. Then, in an eruption of crazed brutality, the guerrillas seized an adolescent boy, supposedly a cousin of one of the four Bihari men, slammed him faceup, gaping, to the ground and stomped him to death.

Have you ever seen a human stomp another? *Stomp*? Smash the heel of his boot into noses and eye sockets, over and over, until the fragile bone crunch and shatter? Have you ever watched deep-red blood and pink intestine spill from a bayonet slash to the stomach? Have you heard the unholy screaming? Have you looked into the maddened, sweating face of a grey-bearded man as he slams the butt of his rifle into the throat of a teenaged boy splayed on the ground? Over and over again? Have you stood there, close enough to touch either of them, said nothing, while writing in a notebook?

I have.

Much of the world had been sympathetic toward Bangladesh throughout the war and stood by it in victory. But the racetrack nightmare signaled a worrisome beginning for the new nation.

Though I did my best to keep my own reactions out of my copy, the story I filed that evening couldn't be read as anything other than negative. It ran on the *Post*'s front page alongside Horst Faas's and Michael Laurent's shocking AP photographs. The coverage alarmed Prime Minister Gandhi. With Indian forces still in charge of Bangladesh's security, she ordered her commanders immediately to have all killing of collaborators halted.

It continued.

Over the next three weeks, while awaiting Mujib's return, I wandered the streets, alleys, and warrens of Dacca. I drove past primitive, smoke-spewing brick kilns to outlying villages, speaking with peasant farmers, laborers, fishermen and, that favored source of foreign correspondents everywhere, taxi

Calcutta, established a Dacca shelter for pregnant raped women and sent their babies to adoptive parents around the world. Carol delivered donated cans of powdered formula from Delhi to the shelter.

Rumors circulated that the Pakistani soldiers raped men, too. For humiliation. But the Pakistanis were not alone in brutality. India's Hindu troops raped Muslim women. Bengalis raped Biharis, and Biharis raped Bengalis. In turning their backs, Richard Nixon and Henry Kissinger were complicit in one of the great abominations of the twentieth century.

On Monday afternoon, January 10, 1972, Sheikh Mujib returned in triumph to the nation he had created, a nation born in ruins. Ecstatic Bangladeshis swarmed from the center of Dacca to the airport, and I allowed myself to be carried along like a cork bobbing on a tidal wave. They were beside themselves with glee, chanting what only weeks before had been a battle cry and now was a cheer of exultation:

*Jai Bangla!* Victory to Bengal!

We were so tightly packed together that arms and legs twined. Laughing and shouting, we tripped and tumbled, stepping on each other's feet. Hundreds of broken flip-flops and sandals littered the mile-and-a-half route.

From where I was pinioned in the midst of this exultant throng, just inside the airport grounds, it was impossible to hear what, if anything, Mujib may have said to those who embraced him as he stepped onto the gangway from a British Royal Air Force jet. Bhutto had released him two days earlier. He'd flown first to London, where Prime Minister Ted Heath received him, then to New Delhi, where he met Mrs. Gandhi for the first time. Bhutto had arranged the indirect route as a face-saving means of avoiding humiliating interaction with his archfoe, the victorious Indira Gandhi.

I watched thousands hurl garlands of orange and yellow marigolds in Mujib's direction. Untold numbers, it could have been millions, lined the road, shouting themselves hoarse as he waved from the back of an open trailer-truck draped in blue and red bunting, inching into the city.

Later in the day, Mujib completed a historic circuit, appearing at the Ramna track, where he had declared independence ten months earlier and where I had watched his supporters weeks ago murder their enemies. Standing on a towering, wooden platform, he gazed out over a jubilant multitude, packed shoulder-to-shoulder and face-to-back. An ocean of black-haired heads, rolling beyond the horizon, glistened in the brilliant sun.

I asked a khaki-uniformed senior police officer alongside me on the platform to estimate the crowd.

"At least one million," he said confidently.

I had no sense of what a million people looked like, or half a million for that matter. I did know that this was by far the most people I had ever seen in one place.

It also was the first time I saw Mujib. I jotted in my notebook, "Unusually tall (6 ft?) & heavy for Bengali, gray hair slicked back, dense moustache, large, trendy black-rim glasses."

He was dressed in a traditional black vest over a long, white cotton shirt called a "panjabi," and a matching, elaborately tied sarong, a "dhoti." His voice cracked several times, and he removed his glasses to wipe tears away. He shouted in Bengali into a mass of microphones, "My life's goal has been fulfilled! My Bengal is independent!"

Apparently having been told of the atrocities recently committed where he now stood triumphant, Mujib appealed to his people to resist their overwhelming desire to retaliate against those who'd massacred friends and relatives, "Forgive them," he said. "Today I do not want revenge from anybody. There should not be any more killing. . . . The Bengal that will eat, smile, sing, and be happy is my Bengal. Everyone in Bengal is now a Bengali, and we must live together."

Though many anticipated it, few but the most cynical would have admitted on that glorious day that Mujib's promise of a *shonar Bangla*—the "golden Bengal" of Rabindranath Tagore's Nobel Prize–winning poetry—no matter how well-intended, would prove hollow.

The next morning, Mujib initiated what would become a custom of holding court in his bedroom. Historically, rulers and other revered figures throughout South Asia received supplicants seeking favors and influence in a tradition known as "darshan," and it carried over to contemporary government officials. Mujib's twist on the ancient theme was to greet the petitioners while propped in bed, not seated on silk cushions or a gilded throne.

I elbowed my way into a swarm of well-wishers cramming the small room. Mujib was jovial, laughing, shaking hands. He attempted to eat the two soft-boiled eggs, toast, and tea his wife brought in, but to no avail as we pressed around him.

Looking at the Western newsmen, he thanked "my foreign correspondents" for the supportive coverage he'd received. I noted that in less than twenty-four hours, Mujib had made reference to *my* Bengal and *my* journalists. *Were these spontaneous expressions of paternal warmth or ill-considered hubris*, I wondered.

Mujib had grown accustomed to media adulation while imprisoned and was elated by the monumental welcome. He wasn't prepared for his world to come crashing down. He failed to anticipate that long-suffering Bengalis expected him to deliver results quickly and that journalists tend to back the underdog. Once a new leader acquires power, once the underdog becomes top dog, the rules of the game change.

Americans who disparage the press for criticizing their favored leader would do well to learn that game. Like most Americans, journalists admire those with the strength to survive hardship and overcome adversity. But many of us also are soft touches who sympathize with those who lack that fortitude.

Our form of democracy anticipates that government will lend a hand to the weakest among us. So, it's natural that the press reports when such help is given and when it's withheld. But, if journalists don't want to squander our legitimacy, we can—we must—avoid taking sides in print and limit our reporting to the facts. Doing otherwise, whether with delicacy or by swinging a hammer, is offensive to readers, making them feel manipulated.

Let the reader judge.

Opinionated journalism peaked in the United States during the Trump administration. I understand why. But it cost us countless readers and viewers. By following the facts and reporting them, we may be able to recoup some. The press, the public, the nation, all will benefit.

*Chapter Ten*

# Delhi Wallah

By late January 1972, when I returned to the newsroom from Bangladesh, Foisie had convinced Executive Editor Ben Bradlee to reopen the *Post*'s New Delhi bureau, which he'd shut five years earlier. Readers' interest in the Indo-Pak war and the prospect of Gandhi and Bhutto continuing to be at each other's throats indicated that the subcontinent could compete for page one.

Foisie offered me the job. I was ecstatic. Not that Washington-obsessed *Post* staffers were lining up for dibs on moving to Delhi. When I told colleagues I would be going to India, one national reporter responded nonchalantly, "Why?"

Her indifference was symptomatic of attitudes about India among many Americans, who perceived the country only in terms of its dehumanizing poverty. The suffering was an inescapable reality, especially for the short-term visitor. But for those who have the privilege of living there longer, the dreadful state of most Indians' lives is moderated by generosity and welcoming at every social level and by people's openness and willingness to engage.

Our first friends, the Bissells, were—still are—extraordinary people, but they weren't alone in opening themselves and their home to us. Indians we befriended during our three-year stay remain friends today, as do their children with ours. For that reason, when people ask which, of all the countries we've lived in, is our "favorite," (we enjoyed them all), Carol and I invariably answer India.

Since I would be setting up a news bureau and household from scratch, I went looking for advice from people who had worked and lived in Delhi— diplomats at the Indian embassy and the State Department, businesspeople, and fellow journalists. Syd Schanberg of the *Times* currently was based there and was reassuring.

"Don't worry," he wrote me, "the Indians discovered fire and the wheel centuries ago."

Still, I knew we faced upheaval and trial. We had barely settled into our house in Bethesda and suddenly we were dropping everything and starting

punitive tax, everything would be settled to everyone's satisfaction. He would leave us in peace, and we could go about settling into our lovely home.

Temptation flickered, then sputtered out. I could hear the gossip: "The new *Washington Post* correspondent bribed an official of the government of India. Simons paid baksheesh to avoid paying taxes, desperately needed by the poverty-stricken country, on a bullock cart's worth of imported luxury goods."

"Sorry," I said. "I cannot do that. I will pay the duty."

Bewildered and bitterly disappointed, he stormed out of the brimming bedroom, slammed the door, and sealed it shut with a blob of heated red wax.

"You must not be breaking seal until duty is paid in full!" he ordered curtly, then departed.

The *Post* transferred the money, and I went to the bank to collect the immense heap of rupees. As I approached the rear of a long queue, clutching an empty suitcase, a middle-aged man in white, cotton, homespun garments took my elbow and offered a gracious welcome I would hear often during my years in India, "Sahib, you are our honored guest."

He led me directly to the cashier. Heads up and down the queue bobbled in mute approval.

The teller blanched when I handed him the money order. He retreated to a back room, then emerged with stacked bricks of tattered rupee notes, many of them worm-holed and bound with grimy string. Shuffling and counting took him and a colleague so long that the growing line of customers behind me had to be shifted to another window.

I lugged the suitcase, now packed with a maharajah's ransom of cash, to the customs office and presented it, with all the poise I could summon, to Customs Man himself. Every rupee, of course, had to be counted again. Then recounted. Staff members were astounded: So much duty actually being paid! Normally timorous peons slipped from the shadows and gawked, as did supercilious office wallahs, pretending to stamp and sign official documents that they pretended to be reading. There would be much chin-wagging when they reached home that evening.

A chai wallah was summoned and poured me cup after cup of his sweet, milky brew. Also, sweet Parle-Gluco biscuits. At long last, a round of head bobbles and grudging *tikke*s (okays) confirmed visually and verbally that the final rupee count passed muster. I was given a handwritten receipt and set free. Customs Man, crotchety and making it clear with blazing eyes that I was a chump for not cutting him in, accompanied me to our house and cracked the seal on the door. Our stuff was officially ours. We were home.

We were ready to become Delhi wallahs.

Ensconced by the front windows of my office, I set about cranking out India 101 stories, "snake charmers," I called them. Every new foreign correspondent everywhere feels obliged to reinvent the wheel. It works out because for every new writer there's a new generation of readers ready to cluck over something amazing. India is a treasure trove of such stories.

With these basics out of the way, several months later, I drove to Dharamsala, a small town in India's cedar-forested Himalayan foothills, to interview the Dalai Lama. I had read the dramatic story of his flight from Tibet in *Life* magazine in 1959. With the help of the CIA, the then-twenty-two-year-old Buddhist god-king had escaped his isolated homeland on horseback in the midst of a violent uprising against Communist China. Some eighty-seven thousand Tibetans and two thousand Chinese soldiers were killed. The Dalai Lama and a hundred thousand of his most reverent followers were granted asylum by India and have remained there since. For me, interviewing him would be a dream realized.

He now lived in a stucco cottage, a far cry from the hulking thousand-room, Potala Palace he and his predecessors had occupied since the mid-seventeenth century in the Tibetan mountain city of Lhasa. He appeared as down-to-earth as his surroundings. His head was freshly shaved and he was wrapped in a monk's carmine wool robe. He wiggled off his sandals and, sitting cross-legged on an upholstered chair, fiddled with his bare toes. His alert eyes twinkled mischievously behind gold-rimmed glasses. He giggled often and spoke English haltingly. A bilingual young monk stepped in repeatedly to interpret.

Unaffected though he seemed, I felt something mystical surrounding the Dalai Lama, as though his smooth face was ringed in an aura, as in paintings of early Christian saints. I would interview him three more times and, each time, I felt the same transcendent force, a force beyond my ability to fathom. By our final meeting, many years later, after he had stepped down as leader of the Tibetan government in exile and I had moved to magazine journalism, I realized that while he was human, and flawed, he was as selfless a person as I knew.

In this first interview, I limited my questions to political matters. We discussed his hope, still alive then, of one day returning to Tibet. He surprised me by admitting readily that, under his rule, Tibetans had suffered economic privations through the avarice of the Buddhist priesthood. He also acknowledged that the Chinese Communists had done much more to improve Tibetans' living standards and the country's infrastructure than he had.

After the interview the Dalai Lama invited me out to the garden, where we mingled with a handful of young European backpackers, gathered for his weekly darshan. They bowed before him and pressed their palms together as they stood in the shade of tall, purple rhododendrons. A Scandinavian girl with stringy, blonde hair approached hesitantly and told him she was terrified of dying. He responded in a near-whisper, "No, no. There is nothing to fear about death. It comes to us all because it is a normal part of life. Do not fear death. Welcome it."

I drove back to Delhi the next morning and stopped at the Reuters office to pick up my messages. One, forwarded by the foreign desk, was from my mother. My father, who had been seriously ill for a year, had died. He was seventy-six. Still under the spell of the Dalai Lama, I was shaken yet accepting.

Today, having surpassed my father's age, when the subject of death comes up, as it does more frequently than it did back then, I recall those words and feel reassured. "It comes to us all because it is a normal part of life."

India was planning a grand celebration to mark its twenty-fifth year of independence from Britain. The occasion would provide me with the perfect peg for an overarching story I'd been wanting to do. I phoned S. K. Singh, the external affairs ministry official who dealt with foreign correspondents, to request several interviews.

"As a newcomer," I began, "I'm embarrassed to suggest that I'm sufficiently well-versed to take on the story of what India has achieved—and failed to achieve—in the past quarter-century."

"Nonsense," S. K. interrupted in his peculiar, high-pitched voice. "No one else would even try."

The *Post* ran the piece on August 16, 1972, under the headline, "India, Free 25 Years, Enjoys Stability Amid Poverty."

It told how, following the earthshaking civil disobedience campaign against the British led by Mahatma Gandhi, Prime Minister Jawaharlal Nehru had built respect on the world stage for an independent India; how Nehru's daughter, Indira Gandhi, elevated that status through her blitzkrieg victory over Pakistan, just eight months before the independence commemoration; how vibrant democracy, an extremely rare genre in the Third World, was on display in full-throated parliamentary debate; how the press was free and dependably critical.

It also explained that the accomplishments of Nehru and Gandhi and their Congress Party, the only faction to rule since independence, fell far short of raising the masses from millennia-long destitution and that the economy was mired in the doldrums of Nehru's Fabian Socialist philosophy that government must occupy the "commanding heights" of industry.

"As a government," I wrote. "India has advanced far toward the recognition its leaders dearly crave from the world beyond the subcontinent. Political stability is so much a fact of life that opposition is almost nonexistent. . . .

"As a people, the great Indian masses are as impoverished today as they were on this day in 1947, the day Britain set them free. To the outsider, witnessing this phenomenon of advancing government and lagging populace can be like watching a lumbering bullock cart. But on this cart, sometimes one wheel rolls forward and one stands still, and the cart turns in a circle."

At midnight on August 15th, cannon thundered and bugles blared from atop the red, sandstone walls of parliament. Addressing dignitaries within the imposing structure that the raj had erected to its own eternal glory, Indira Gandhi spoke. "The struggle for freedom began when the first man was enslaved," she said, "and it will continue until the last man is freed, not merely of visible bondage but of the concepts of inferiority due to race, color, caste, or sex."

The audience responded with rousing cries of *Jai Hind!* Victory to India!

Outside the halls of power, though, half a billion Indians felt anything but victorious. Their India would be wholly recognizable by their ancestors in centuries past:

Millions of low-caste Hindus—Untouchables—suffered humiliation and deprivation.

Millions more were captive in an ancient system of bonded labor.

When their husbands died, widows committed "sati," throwing themselves onto the funeral pyres.

Peasant families lived in huts made of mud, straw, and cow dung, the same dung the women formed into fuel patties for cooking.

Tens of thousands of children died each year of inadequate nourishment.

As the power elite in Delhi celebrated that stifling August night, the curse of drought lay once again upon the land. Famine and starvation trailed close behind.

The food crisis shocked the nation. After several seasons of benevolent monsoons and a bumper crop in the early 1970s, India had been declared self-sufficient by the government and was even considering exporting food. North Vietnam was negotiating a large rice purchase. Bursting with pride, the government of Maharashtra State banned the use of the word "famine." Nothing terrified Indians more than that word, with good reason:

Between the eighteenth and twentieth centuries, more than sixty million people had starved to death.

Suddenly, the lie was stripped bare. Instead of nearly ten million tons of surplus grain in government storage, as claimed, there was less than four million. Rats had gorged on much of it; much more never existed outside the imaginations of self-aggrandizing government ministers.

There would be no exports. Instead, India would have to *import* more than two million tons. The only source of that much grain was the United States. And, as the Bangladesh war had made clear, no love was lost between Mrs. Gandhi and Mr. Nixon. In addition, the Soviet Union, India's great ally, had

was telling it like it was. Gandhi bought American wheat; famine was averted and lives were saved. The grateful public dismissed her embarrassment and praised her for taking effective action.

For this, and for decisively winning the war, she acquired a host of adoring nicknames at home and abroad. Admirers called her "the only man in the cabinet." Even the antagonistic Kissinger once admitted, grudgingly, "I wish we had a man as strong as she in our cabinet."

But there was actually nothing macho about Gandhi. Petite, soft-spoken, draped demurely in homespun saris, she projected strength by sheer force of will. As her hair color faded, she had it dyed black, except for a steely streak running along one side.

The affectation led to another flattering title, "The Iron Lady of India."

The president of her Congress Party, D. K. Barooah, laid the ultimate, fawning declaration of power at her feet.

"Indira is India," he proclaimed, "and India is Indira."

This was a far cry from her early days as prime minister, beginning in 1966, when a skeptical press mocked her as a *goongi goodiya*, a dumb doll.

Political enemies confessed amazement at the transformation. One hailed her as a reincarnation of one of polytheistic Hinduism's most venerated deities, the goddess Durga. The multiarmed protector of all that is good and harmonious in the world, Durga often is portrayed astride a lion or tiger, battling the forces of evil.

Gandhi herself was riding what the Indian press called the "Indira Wave." This was her moment. Indians I knew, even those who weren't fans, conceded that the country was hers to do with as she wished.

She could have devoted serious yet humane attention to reining in runaway population growth, then at an unsustainable 2.3 percent; tackled the crippling problem of illiteracy, which disadvantaged a staggering 65 percent of Indians; put teeth in the widely ignored *Dalit* laws to diminish the stigma of untouchability; or tightened screws on the country's notorious tax evaders, who paid bribes, like that Customs Man had tried to weasel from me, hoarded gold and silver, or ignored income taxes completely, cheating the government of billions.

She could have done all this and more. Instead, like Imelda Marcos and her "City of Man" catchphrase for Manila, she created a beguiling, but ultimately meaningless, political slogan: *Garibi hatao.* Meaning "eradicate poverty," it was designed to nail down an insurmountable voting majority among the poorest of the poor, giving them a voice they never had. It could have produced a win-win result: The masses would be lifted, if only a little, and they would vote for Gandhi.

But she dropped the ball. Instead of monitoring the program, she passed responsibility to senior members of her party. To no one's surprise, they siphoned off much of the anti-poverty money and spread it among themselves and a network of cronies. The rich grew richer, the poor remained miserable.

In fairness, resolving many of India's gravest problems lay beyond anyone's ability. The economy staggered under crushing inflation, increased by Bangladesh war-related expenses. Despite successful anti-famine measures, drought still plagued much of the country. The 1973 Arab oil embargo sent fuel prices skyrocketing worldwide. Gandhi had no control over these catastrophes.

In the end, she learned the same harsh lesson that sooner or later befalls leaders everywhere: You get credit for the good times and blame for the bad.

Life for our family was a wobbly teeter-totter of luxuries and hardships. We were afloat in servants. In addition to Catherine, who had traveled with us from Washington and looked after the children and cooked, we had a *sweeper*, who did the heavy household work; a *syce*, who drove the office Mercedes; a *mali*, who tended the garden; and a *chowkidar*, who supposedly provided security at night by banging a stick on our fence, alerting would-be miscreants that he was awake. Our wringer-washer spared us the laundry services of a *dhobi*. But a *durzi* visited from time to time, sitting cross-legged on the floor, stitching dresses for Carol and the girls and bush shirts for me.

In the States, only Vanderbilts and Rockefellers might employ household staffs of this magnitude. In India, it was standard operating procedure for middle-class-and-up locals and expats. And, like the pampered everywhere, we soon complained that finding good help was difficult. Ours came with seemingly limitless extended families, members of which allegedly and repeatedly fell down wells or lay feverish at death's door, requiring time off and travel money. When, as gullible newcomers, we succumbed to this bamboozling, Indian friends warned that we were "spoiling the servants."

Carol never became comfortable managing the staff and often said she'd prefer a good vacuum cleaner to the sweeper and a power mower to the mali. But that's not the way things were done in India. People who could afford to were expected to hire workers, allegedly their contribution to the economy.

Someone in our family was almost always sick. Becca, who was two when we arrived, suffered from parasites that took up permanent residence in her tummy and remained there until we left India. Stool tests and antibiotics became routine.

As young as they were at the time, our daughters still recall scenes of shocking poverty. For a number of weeks, a gang of laborers excavated a trench in the street outside our house in preparation for installing a huge concrete storm drain. While the men dug, their wives set up housekeeping inside the pipes, which provided a rare solid roof over their heads. Justine still recalls the scene as one her most lasting impressions of what abject poverty looks like.

Food preparation was an unending time-suck. Smelly tap water had to be boiled. Fruits and vegetables, fertilized with human waste, required soaking in a reddish concoction of boiled water and bleach. We named the two types of water, "stinky" and "pinky." The outdoor meat market was a sight to put off even the most voracious carnivore: bloody hunks of mutton and water buffalo, swarming with flies, hung from hooks in the suffocating heat. The butcher sat on the ground, a large knife clenched vertically between his bare toes, running slabs of raw flesh up and down against the blade with both (unwashed, I'm sure) hands. Fish, shipped from Bombay, was risky. Except for the occasional chicken biryani, we became vegetarians, everything meticulously soaked in pinky.

A British woman who'd recently married a mid-level Indian civil servant invited Carol to their government-subsidized apartment one afternoon. She served iced lemonade. Soon afterward, Carol—in the early weeks of pregnancy—felt sick, nauseous, and unsteady on her feet. She presumed it was morning sickness. It was hepatitis. Our doctor, a genial Sikh named N. P. S. Chawla and known as "Duke," warned us that maintaining the pregnancy could be risky. We agreed and scheduled an appointment for the next day. Moments after the procedure began, the lights blinked off in the small surgery at the rear of Duke's home. Brownouts, lasting hours or days, were a regular feature of Delhi life, particularly during summer's brutal heat. Duke called me to the dark operating room. My job was to hold a flashlight.

Within days, I, too, came down with hepatitis. Our faces and eyes turned yellow with jaundice, we were severely nauseated, incapable of eating, too weak to get out of bed. Duke recommended tinned pineapple juice. Unable to keep down the only version available on the local market, we phoned Liz Moynihan, the wife of US Ambassador Pat Moynihan. Liz appeared with a case of Dole from the embassy commissary, a kindness we never forgot. Gradually, we both recovered.

Months later, we ran into the Lemonade Lady. It turned out that she, too, had been sick. Only then did she confess that she'd made the drink and the ice with untreated tap water. She was trying to develop antibodies she believed Indians possessed. That was a miscalculation. Millions of Indians spend their lives afflicted with the same "Delhi Belly" that foreign tourists and visitors commonly suffer.

Staying healthy while not insulting our Indian hosts was a delicate business. During an interview I had with an Untouchable family in Punjab, while seated on the hardened-dung floor of their mud hut, the lady of the house offered me a glass of water. The temperature was well over 100°F and I was dehydrated, light-headed. Peering into the glass, I saw that its bottom was coated with a gray-green substance of indeterminate origin. What to do? I couldn't dump it surreptitiously into a potted plant because there was none. Besides, I was cotton-mouth thirsty. So, I thanked my hostess, *shukria*, smiled, and bottoms-up. And lived to tell the tale.

On the morning of May 18, 1974, a Saturday, I was in my office, drinking coffee and listening to government-run All-India Radio when the newscaster interrupted the regular program. In the plummiest BBC-style English, he intoned that India had just conducted "a peaceful nuclear explosion experiment" beneath the Rajasthan Desert, near the border with Pakistan. This was, literally, earth-shattering news. In that instant, India joined the world's mightiest powers—the United States, the Soviet Union, China, Britain, and France—as the sixth member of the nuclear weapons club.

Considering its pervasive and long-standing poverty, India had seemed an unlikely competitor in the worldwide nuclear weapons sweepstakes. But its leaders, worried that Pakistan would reach the goal first, putting India at an impossible disadvantage, began secret experiments. In fact, India had signaled its intentions years earlier. Way back in 1946, Indira Gandhi's father, Jawaharlal Nehru, had declared, "As long as the world is constituted as it is, every country will have to devise and use the latest devices for its protection. I have no doubt India will develop her scientific researches, and I hope Indian scientists will use the atomic force for constructive purposes. But if India is threatened, she will inevitably try to defend herself by all means at her disposal."

India's defeat by China in a brief Himalayan border war in 1962 added to the impetus. Indian scientists, many of them trained abroad, never were in short supply. Ten years after Nehru spoke, some of those scientists built the country's first nuclear research reactor, using plutonium produced in a Canadian-supplied reactor that Indian scientists secretly diverted from its intended peaceful purposes.

With a few hours to go before the *Post*'s deadline, I telephoned Indian and foreign experts, asking for their reactions. Many had not heard the broadcast and were shocked. Some insisted I must have misunderstood. None accepted the official claim that the explosion was for peaceful purposes. One mocked the operation's duplicitous name, "Smiling Buddha." All foresaw that India's closest neighbors, Pakistan and China, would consider the development hostile. How they would respond, beyond pro-forma condemnation, was less predictable.

Most analysts failed to anticipate just how far beyond South Asia Smiling Buddha's impact would be felt and what the long-term, worldwide implications would be. In fact, India's explosion, of about the same magnitude as the "Little Boy" bomb that the United States dropped on Hiroshima in 1945, generated reactions still being felt today.

The effect resembled the rings that ripple across a pond when a child tosses a stone. The bigger the stone, the higher the ripples and the farther they travel. This was a rock.

Within the first innermost circle was New Delhi and, specifically, Prime Minister Gandhi. Front pages bannered the nuclear test story and hailed her for elevating India's status to that of the great powers. The teenager who delivered newspapers to my office on his bicycle that afternoon was beside himself, shouting to me as he tossed the bundle to my door. "Now we're the same as America and Russia and China! We have the atomic bomb!"

The second circle rippled across the border into Pakistan, where Prime Minister Bhutto reacted furiously: "Pakistan will fight, fight for a thousand years. If India builds the bomb, we will eat grass or leaves, even go hungry, but we will get one of our own. We have no alternative."

He meant it. A year after the Rajasthan test, Bhutto recruited Abdul Qadeer Khan, a brilliant young Pakistani metallurgist who was working in the Netherlands. Bhutto brought him home, with instructions to establish the nation's nuclear bomb program and funded him to his heart's content.

A. Q. Khan brought with him state-of-the-art plans and materials he had stolen in Europe. Developing the Islamic Bomb in strict secrecy took Khan twenty-four years. On May 28, 1998, he supervised five simultaneous underground nuclear explosions. The great equalizer, for which Pakistanis had sacrificed, if not quite eaten grass, became a reality.

The third circle lapped across Afghanistan and trickled into Iran, neither of which was planning its own nuclear weapons. Iran then was under the iron rule of Shah Reza Pahlavi, a coddled pet of the United States. I visited Tehran shortly after the Indian test and, after interviewing Prime Minister Amir-Abbas Hoveyda, reported that the shah was spending lavishly to build his Shiite kingdom into a regional power. He was buying billions' worth of weapons in the United States, Britain, and Western Europe. But they all were conventional. Three decades passed before Iran, by then a rigid theocracy, began developing its own nuclear arms. The critical link was none other than A. Q. Khan. He sold his secrets, at immense personal profit, to Ayatollah Khomeini, as well as to Libyan dictator Muammar Gaddafi. Neither country, however, has yet achieved its goal.

The fourth circle splashed ashore in North Korea, another Khan client. The Kim family–run Communist state succeeded in developing a still-growing nuclear arsenal, with missile delivery systems now able to reach parts of the United States.

And so it was that India, the wellspring of Gandhian nonviolence, peaceful protest, and civil disobedience, escalated the deadliest form of warfare known to humanity. Prime Minister Gandhi's action made clear that her only link to the Mahatma, the "Great Soul," who had proclaimed that, "nothing enduring can be built on violence," was a name she had acquired through a short-lived marriage.

Saved by the bomb, Indira again rocketed back up India's political roller-coaster. But the carnival ride was a rickety contraption balanced on shifting sand. In a news analysis the day after the Rajasthan test, I wrote, "Gandhi's glory is likely to be short-lived. As the brutally hot summer wears on and food prices climb, the man in the street and the village lane will cease to find comfort in his country's nuclear capability."

Sometimes you call 'em right. One year after the Indian test bent the shape of international military power, Indira Gandhi would fall from grace. To save herself, she would lock her country behind the bars of martial law. My own troubles with my favorite foreign country soon would follow.

The conceit that one reporter can cover a country as vast and bewildering as India and make it comprehensible to nonchalant readers halfway around the globe touches the far end of hubris. Yet my area of responsibility also included all the real estate and people from Burma to Iran and from Afghanistan to the teardrop island of Ceylon, which recently had changed its name to Sri Lanka.

So, I was in the air and on the road much of the time. My most frequent destinations outside India were Bangladesh and Pakistan. Only a handful of Western news organizations maintained foreign correspondents in either country, most relying on Delhi-based staffers like me to provide periodic reporting. I thought of these visits in terms of a country doctor's house calls—temperature, blood pressure, take two aspirin twice daily, and call if the pain persists.

In Dacca, the prognosis was poor. Sheikh Mujib had succumbed to the temptations faced by populists everywhere—authoritarianism, corruption, cronyism, and susceptibility to the flattery and entreaties of courtiers. He was proving himself wholly inept at managing Bangladesh's death-dealing economic and societal crises. Postwar euphoria had faded.

The outlook in Islamabad was somewhat more promising. As his country struggled to recover from the loss of its eastern wing, Prime Minister Zulfikar Ali Bhutto showed himself to be a shrewd operator. He recognized that Pakistanis were pleased to be rid of military rule. A graduate of Berkeley and Oxford, Bhutto tilted, at least slightly, toward Western democracy and away from a rigid interpretation of Islam.

One way Bhutto chose to reach out to the West was to make himself available to foreign correspondents. In preparing for my first visit to Pakistan, I requested an interview. It was granted promptly. He did not demand that I submit questions in advance, a standard practice among strongman rulers.

On being ushered into the prime minister's suite in Islamabad's contemporary Arabesque Secretariat, I was greeted not by a flunky but by Bhutto himself. He rose, extended his hand, and invited me to sit across from him at his desk. In his mid-forties, he was stocky, jowly, with full lips, hooded eyes, and receding gray hair. He was dressed smartly in a dark-blue, bespoke suit and Italianate silk tie. On a shelf behind him stood a bottle of Johnnie Walker Blue Label.

"Ice?" he inquired.

He poured the fine whiskey into two crystal glasses, and we sipped as the interview proceeded.

I found Bhutto to be quite charming, surprisingly candid when it suited him, and a charlatan when necessary. He recently had completed postwar negotiations with Mrs. Gandhi. The two pledged that from then on, they would settle their differences by peaceful means. That didn't work out, but Bhutto wanted me to believe he had gotten the better of Gandhi. He laced his fingers over his belly and smiled like a contented cat.

From then on, I met with him every few months. Most memorable was a helicopter tour in August 1973, after the Indus River had overflowed its banks and drowned villages across Sindh Province. For this outing, he presented himself to cheering crowds as a man of the people, dressed in a simple white cotton *kurta-pajama.* We made several stops, at which he offered condolences and promised quick government action. Then we flew to the Bhutto family estate at Larkana.

The helicopter whirled down onto an immense, grassy lawn. From my window, I spotted a white-clad man bolting from a grand, white mansion about two football fields away. He sprinted toward the helicopter as Bhutto stepped down. When the man was about fifteen feet from Bhutto, he dropped to his knees and speedily crawled the rest of the way. He pressed his forehead to the grass and, with his bare hands, wiped the mud from Bhutto's black leather chappals. If Bhutto noticed his vassal's presence, he showed no sign of it. More than anything else I saw during my years in the subcontinent, this display of abject servitude hammered home the immeasurable gap between classes.

And I saw plenty. For a story on Calcutta, I once jogged alongside a ricksha puller. I wore sneakers and carried nothing more than pen and notepad. He was barefoot and hauled a two-wheeled buggy loaded with a hefty memsahib, her two school-aged children, and a heap of bundles. The temperature was in the high nineties, with humidity and pollution to match. I dropped out after an hour. He, I assume, went on all day and into the night. He had no choice. His passengers paid him a few paise and no more mind than they would a horse.

On another Calcutta visit, a well-to-do couple took me to dinner at the Tollygunge Club, a faded but still-posh watering hole that the departing raj had abandoned. As we drove, their air-conditioned Ambassador was besieged by beggars. Many were barely elementary-school age. They tapped on the sealed windows, pointed toward their mouths, and whined forlornly, "Sahib, sahib."

"How can you stand this?" I asked.

The wife's brow furrowed as she turned toward me.

"Stand what?"

She and her husband truly did not see the beggars. They were nice people. The husband, an executive with a tea company, built factories in poor, rural areas and was known for paying local workers generously. The wife seemed solicitous. But, over a lifetime, they had developed a selective blindness as a means of coping with the horror around them.

Whether in India, Bangladesh, or Pakistan, the suffering and inequities I wrote about varied little. But government officials protested that my stories were biased against their country alone. A few days after I returned home from a two-week reporting trip to Pakistan, S. K. Singh summoned me to the Indian foreign ministry.

My articles, he groused, were one-sided.

"They make Bhutto look good and cast Mrs. Gandhi in a negative light."

I disagreed but also pointed out that Bhutto made himself available whenever I asked for an interview. It was natural, I conceded, that his views would make their way into my copy. Gandhi, however, had ignored all my interview requests. S. K. was a savvy operator. He sighed knowingly and rolled his eyes toward the ceiling. He promised to press the PM on my behalf.

As long as she remained in power, I never got an interview.

Figure 1 Cub Scout camper, with my parents, Goldie and Abe Simons, summer 1949.

Figure 4 AP Saigon colleagues at U.S. Army camp in Central Highlands, 1967. L–R, me, Peter Arnett, John Lengel, Rick Merron.

Figure 5 Catching a cyclo ride, Saigon, 1967.

Figure 6 Carol considers door-to-door salesman's wares outside our KL house, 1968.

Figure 7 Interviewing President Ferdinand E. Marcos in Malacañang Palace, 1969. He was looking down at me. Then, I realized his desk and chair were perched on an elevated platform.

**Figure 12 Carol (white hat) and Adam shopping at Beijing Department Store, 1989.**

Figure 13 I took this photo of the Tiananmen Square uprising hours before being caught up in the June 4, 1989, massacre.

# Chapter Eleven

# Excess Baggage

Near the end of March 1975, Phil Foisie telephoned me in the middle of the night, as was his custom, ignoring the nine-and-a-half-hour time difference between Washington and Delhi. His conversations typically began, "Lew, it's Phil." And stopped. It was a clever ploy, which found me at my most discombobulated and led me into making admissions and commitments I hadn't intended, while he sat back silently, presumably taking notes.

This time, though, he came straight to the point: David Greenway, now the *Post*'s Hong Kong–based correspondent, was covering the war in Cambodia and had requested a few weeks' break. Greenway's friend, David Cornwell, the famed British novelist pen-named John le Carré, had invited him to ski in Switzerland. I was to fill in while he enjoyed a well-deserved schuss in the Alps.

Thus began the most intensive four months of my reporting life. It would involve the Communist takeover of three countries, the assassination of the once-beloved leader of a fourth, and my expulsion from a fifth.

I flew from Delhi to Bangkok and, at the Cambodian embassy, paid a small bribe to have a journalist's visa stamped in my passport. Aboard Air Cambodge Flight 141 to Phnom Penh, I was seated next to a trim White man about my age. I had noticed on a previous visit that some government agencies still employed French consultants, and I took him for one.

*Mais non*, my seatmate bristled, then proclaimed in thickly accented English, *I am ze lovair of ze 'usband of ze Princess Bupphpa Devi.*

I was impressed. Buppha Devi, a renowned classical dancer, was a daughter of Prince Sihanouk, then exiled in Beijing. I had the unique opportunity of questioning an insider about life in Cambodia's enigmatic royal family. Alas, *ze lovair* brushed me off.

Some two dozen passengers were on the battered white-and-red Caravelle. Most were well-dressed Cambodians carrying cartons of duty-free Dunhill cigarettes and bottles of Black Label scotch. They were returning from the pleasures of the Thai capital to the frightening uncertainties of their war-ravaged homeland.

Had we been headed to Paris or the Côte d'Azur, the service on the brief flight might have made sense. Attendants in pale-green sarongs served a lunch of pâté in aspic; smoked fish; chilled, white asparagus spears; baguettes; cheese at room temperature; and nut-topped cake. To wash it down, bottomless Moët & Chandon. But we were flying into a war zone—a champagne flight to a doomed city.

Luncheon plates collected, the pilot came on the loudspeaker and told us to "prepare for a few bumpy moments."

The plane suddenly lurched into a steep dive directly above Phnom Penh's Pochentong Airport. Squawking, caged chickens stowed in the rear of the cabin skittered down the aisle as we corkscrewed to the runway. I learned afterward that the pilot had carried out the risky maneuver to dodge potential shelling by Khmer Rouge guerrillas. They had closed to within a few miles of Pochentong. Blackened, shattered hulks of planes destroyed in earlier barrages littered the airport, giving it the look of a child's playroom after a raucous tantrum.

I'd been going in and out of Cambodia for eight years and knew it was just a matter of time before it would fall to the Communists. But just how soon would come as a shock. Despite their having undergone four years of some of the most intensive US bombing in history, Khmer Rouge—Red Cambodian—guerrillas now held much of the country.

Greenway's fixer-interpreter-driver, Yun, picked me up in his leased white Mercedes, the vehicle of choice among Phnom Penh's resident press corps. Greenway had also left me a stringer arrangement with James Fenton, a brilliant and droll Englishman who, years later, became one of Britain's leading poets.

I was ready to roll.

We stopped at the once-grand Hotel Le Royal, its name now changed to Le Phnom. It was a colonial holdover, a nostalgic hostelry that correspondents like me relished for its romantic ambiance.

I left my luggage and we drove out of the city along the Mekong. "There is where the war is today," Yun told me as we looked toward the far bank. We parked and boarded a small, rickety ferry to Svay Chrum, a village on a small island bifurcating the river. A cyclo driver picked us up and pedaled to the other side. "There," Yun said as he pointed across the second branch.

"The Khmer Rouge are there now," the cyclo driver told us. "The government soldiers escaped and swam across to this side last night. Now they're in Phnom Penh."

Whether those troops would join the final defense of the city or melt into the countryside was beyond the cyclo driver's, Yun's, and my pay grade.

Back in my room late that night, I filled the claw-footed bathtub—water supply was unreliable. Then, by candlelight—electricity, too, was an occasional luxury—I wrote this:

"I can hear the crump-crump of rockets land somewhere in the city. The end is near. 'How much longer can it go on,' I asked a soldier. 'I don't know,' he answered sadly. 'I'm afraid if it continues and afraid if it stops.'"

The date on the story was March 27, 1975. Cambodia fell to the Khmer Rouge sixteen days later.

Two days after I wrote that story, Cambodia's president, General Lon Nol, fled to Indonesia, then on to the United States. He never saw his homeland again. His replacement, a retired general by the name of Saukham Khoy, begged Prince Sihanouk to return from China. The prince ignored him. Without Sihanouk working his magic one more time, re-stitching the ruptured seams that had held Cambodia together through the Vietnam War years, there was no hope.

The Khmer Rouge had fought their way so close to the city that Yun and I were able to tour the front lines by car in the morning, be back at the hotel in time for a poolside lunch with colleagues, and, that evening, write and file a story on what I'd seen. On one such day, after visiting the war, we stopped off at the PTT (Postes, Télégraphes et Téléphones) to see if there were any cables for me.

There was, a panicky one, from foreign editor Lescaze:

LEAVE PHNOM PENH IMMEDIATELY AND TAKE FENTON WITH YOU IF YOU CAN STOP REUTERS SAYS COMMUNIST TROOPS HAVE PENETRATED CITY AND THAI PREMIER SAYS IT HAS FALLEN STOP GOD BE WITH YOU STOP

The normally reliable British news agency and Thailand's highly regarded Prime Minister Kukrit Pramoj were justifiably alarmed. But, as Mark Twain said about reports of his own death, they had "grossly exaggerated" the timing. I messaged Washington and assured Lescaze that all was well.

At lunch, I shared Lescaze's cable with some colleagues and we had a good laugh. Except for James Fenton.

"If you *can*," he mulled. "*If* you can . . . ?! What the hell is that supposed to mean?"

In fact, Cambodia was well into its final throes. The death spasms had begun with the army. Dispirited soldiers were stripping off their uniforms and fleeing the battlefield in their underwear. Yun and I drove out of the city in hopes of finding some of the deserters. Just two miles from the hotel, we found a huddle of soldiers at a roadside marketplace, some of them boys of ten or twelve, hardly taller than the rifles they carried.

*Los Angeles Times* correspondent Jacques Leslie was in the midst of the group. I was surprised to see him. He was unhappy to see me. We were friends, both having worked in South Vietnam and now based in New Delhi, but I had just horned in on his exclusive. The soldiers were clustered around the grisly remains of a corpse, lying faceup on the dusty ground, disemboweled.

He was First Lieutenant Pen Samnang, their paymaster, and they claimed he had not paid them for months.

"He's been stealing our money," one told us.

They had shot him in the head, then excised his heart, liver, lungs, biceps, and calves. As Jacques and I looked on, a soldier placed the organs and flesh on a small wood fire. The smell was nauseating. When the meat appeared to be cooked, he cut it into bite-size chunks that he distributed among the men. They chewed and swallowed. Ritual cannibalism, I knew, was an ancient Cambodian tradition. This was the first time I had witnessed it.

"Consuming an enemy's body parts," the chef explained, "particularly the liver, will convey his strength to us."

A few days later, as I was walking along a shady street corner in central Phnom Penh, I heard shouting and then a shotgun blast. A uniformed soldier sprinted out of a bank and crumpled to the sidewalk, perhaps ten feet in front of me. A white cloth bag fell from his hand, and a neat brick of riels, the Cambodian currency, flopped out. A bank guard had blown off the back of the soldier's head. His brain spilled onto the pavement in a puddle of blood. I'd never seen a human brain before. It looked creamy, almost like a serving of scrambled eggs.

How does a normal person react to such horror? Would a normal person faint? Vomit? Scream? Run? What would a normal person do?

I took notes. And wrote the story. No longer was I normal.

I had developed an imaginary Gardol shield over my emotions. Colgate at that time was advertising that a wondrous new ingredient in its toothpaste provided transparent, impermeable protection against decay. By coating my mind with Gardol, I was able to see the horror around me while blocking it from my soul. The magic shield also helped me overcome my natural reserve and gather the requisite gall to ask audacious questions of people I normally wouldn't even approach.

I never tested whether the Gardol shield was bulletproof. But covering combat in Cambodia was considerably more dangerous than in Vietnam. Over the course of five years, thirty-seven journalists died or disappeared in Cambodia, while it took four times as long for twice as many to be killed in Vietnam. There, a correspondent could count on US troops to provide a fairly reliable reading of danger in the area. No Americans soldiers were known to have remained in Cambodia following a two-month incursion in 1970.

Cambodian army troops took a laissez-faire attitude toward foreign correspondents. On a foray to Ang Snuol, sixteen miles from Phnom Penh, Yun leaned out of the car widow and asked a soldier lounging on the roadside if we could continue safely. Casually, he waved us on. Minutes later, we came under fire. Yun threw the car into a wild U-turn and sped away. The unhelpful soldier was gone.

As the final days wound down, the Khmer Rouge continued to tighten their grip on the capital. Around-the-clock artillery attacks on Pochentong Airport interrupted deliveries of US food and ammunition, the city's lifeline. Denis Cameron, a former Hollywood photographer with a striking resemblance to Woody Allen, organized an extraordinary airlift of four hundred Cambodian orphans to Australia.

Cameron, who loved Cambodia deeply, did his best to minimize the gloom. He assembled a group of us for a banquet at a Chinese restaurant; bought a few kilos of marijuana at the central market, where it was cheap; and had the chef lace every dish, from peanuts to soup. (Chinese traditionally eat their soup last, to "fill the cracks.") By the end of the ten-course feast, which we consumed along with copious amounts of beer, most of us were flying high. I certainly was.

For a nightcap, half a dozen journalists, French, Brits, and Americans, went on to Madame Chantal's opium den. It was a first for me. I watched my colleagues and did as they did: entered a curtained cubicle, stripped and wrapped a checkered sarong around my waist, then lay on my side on a straw floor mat, head cradled on a little pillow. A small kerosene lamp burned nearby.

A skeletal man in shorts and singlet entered, crouched beside me and formed a pea-size ball of sticky, black opium paste on the tip of a long needle. He cooked it over the lamp and worked it into a pipe made of bamboo fitted with a tiny brass bowl. He tipped the loaded bowl to catch the lamp's flame. Once the drug was sizzling, he offered me the pipe. I sucked the smoke deep into my lungs and held it until I no longer could.

Repeat.

Again.

Even before I finished my third pipe—definitely an overdose for a novice—I was lost in dense haze. I have no idea how, but somehow I managed to drive the hired Mercedes back to Le Phnom and fell into bed. Throughout a hellish night, hallucinations and nightmares chased each other across my muddled mind. None was pleasant. Some were terrifying. When sunlight penetrated my eyelids, I staggered to the bathroom and threw up. My first experience with the pipe was my last.

While Cambodia was caving in on itself that April in 1975, Vietnam and Laos were following close behind. Screaming headlines across the front page of the *Post* tracked collapse upon collapse and forecast the impending birth of a red Indochina:

Communists Take Danang In Heavy Fighting

U.S. Evacuation, Communist Push Still Under Way

Camranh Bay, Nha Trang Fall In Drive South

Phnom Penh Defenses Broken

At about 6:00 a.m. on April 11, I was sipping tea and munching toast with marmalade at an oilcloth-covered table in Le Phnom's breezy breakfast room. A handful of other correspondents and I were listening over my Sony transistor to President Gerald Ford speaking live to a joint session of Congress. Filtered through the shortwave static, he sounded embarrassed. He was admitting American failure and abandonment.

"In Cambodia, the situation is tragic. . . . For the past three months, the beleaguered people of Phnom Penh have fought on, hoping against hope that the United States would not desert them, but instead provide the arms and ammunition they so badly needed. . . . I regret to say that, as of this evening, it may be soon too late."

It already was. The war-weary Congress had rejected Ford's appeal to continue funding Cambodia. Deserting this particular small, weak ally was merely the latest such instance in a long, loathsome pattern of US foreign policy. Forty-six years later, President Joe Biden would abandon Afghanistan. In between, America turned its back on the Kurds of Iran, Iraq, Syria, and Turkey no fewer than eight times.

Moments after the broadcast ended, with Ford wishing farewell and good luck to "the brave Khmer people"—he mispronounced it "kee-mer"—a civilian US embassy official strode into the breakfast room. He wore a holstered .45 caliber pistol on his hip, something I'd never seen on a diplomat.

"Embassy personnel will evacuate Phnom Penh early tomorrow morning," in what was being called Operation Eagle Pull, he told us. Correspondents were welcome to join them. Our Cambodian assistants and their immediate family members could come as well.

I knew this moment was coming. One way or another, all wars end. Still, I felt the diplomat's words strike like a physical blow, a punch to the gut. It left me breathless. When Yun showed up, I relayed the double-edged offer: He and his family could go to America; they must leave the only home they knew.

He, too, was stunned. What did I think he should do?

I recommended he discuss the matter with his wife and mother. He left and returned a few hours later.

"We've decided to stay," he said. "My mother is old and sick, and she doesn't think she could survive in a new country. Do you think this is the right thing?"

I considered for a moment before speaking.

"You've made the right decision," I replied.

I would come to deeply regret saying so. But at that moment, I felt reasonably confident. According to a droll adage, the Vietnamese plant rice, the

Khmer watch it grow, and the Lao listen to it; suggesting that the Khmer rank midway in passivity among the three Indochinese peoples. Cambodian and foreign experts I'd spoken with were anticipating a score-settling bloodbath in Vietnam, a tough but controlled outcome in Cambodia, and a relatively calm result in Laos. As it turned out, the forecasts for Vietnam and Cambodia were reversed. Only the Lao prediction was accurate.

Yun and I drove to the bank, the same one where the thieving soldier had his brain blown out. I withdrew the several hundred dollars remaining in the *Post*'s account, then changed it into riels on the black market. Returning to my room, I handed Yun the blocks of colorful bills. We embraced. I wished him well, and we bid each other goodbye.

Over the coming years, as I reported from Thailand on Cambodia's Killing Fields, I was haunted by memories of that day and my not encouraging Yun to leave.

On my final afternoon in Phnom Penh, I walked for hours through the streets on a combined sentimental journey and last-minute checkup. The city was encircled, as though by a giant boa constrictor squeezing out its life, yet people seemed oddly relaxed and unconcerned. While rockets exploded nearby, adults chatted on shophouse doorsteps while children played badminton without nets. Traffic was lighter than usual. Without US airlifts, the cost of gasoline had become prohibitive. Still, some families piled into their cars and drove off to visit friends and relatives. Restaurants were beginning to close in advance of the eight o'clock curfew. But anyone with enough riels to spend could find a meal late into the night. The government had ordered cinemas shuttered out of fear that they could be targeted by rocket attacks. The usual queues were gone but the theaters remained festooned with garish banners of bosomy women and heroic, armed men. Celebrations for the approaching lunar new year were canceled, but many residents ignored the strictures. I stopped into a little gold shop where, years earlier, I had bought Carol a bracelet, and spoke with the elderly Sino-Khmer owner. He responded to my obvious question with karmic fatalism. "What's the use of being afraid?" he asked. "I'll be careful and somehow I'll survive. The other side won't kill everyone. They don't want to destroy the city."

Ambassador John Gunther Dean hosted a farewell dinner at the American embassy for a group of correspondents that night. Dean, a Jewish refugee from Nazi Germany, had struggled futilely to convince another German-born Jew, Henry Kissinger, to encourage Prince Sihanouk to return home and form a coalition government with the Khmer Rouge. Kissinger, the quintessential realpolitik meister, refused to budge.

Dean was heartbroken and remained so for the rest of his life. Forty years later, he met in Paris with my old AP friend Denis Gray, who recounted what he said. "I failed. We'd accepted responsibility for Cambodia and then walked out without fulfilling our promise. That's the worst thing a country can do."

Dean didn't reveal his sorrow over that last supper, though. He was intent on depriving the guerrillas of the embassy's cellar of fine wines, and our glasses never ran dry. I can't recall what we ate, but the table was set with starched linen, silver, and crystal.

Earlier in the day, Dean had called on President Saukham Khoy, informing him officially that the United States was leaving him and his country to fend for themselves. I spoke with Khoy shortly afterward on the porch of his modest house.

"The United States led Cambodia into this war," he said bitterly, dabbing at his eyes with a white handkerchief. "But when the war became difficult, the United States pulled out."

Ford's speech had left him feeling "let down and frustrated," he said, but he clung to his last scrap of dignity, insisting that Cambodia never would surrender: *"Non. C'est impossible."* A day later, Khoy fled to Thailand on a US Marine Corps helicopter. He had kept his escape plan secret, not only from me but from his countrymen as well.

In contrast, Prince Sirik Matak, another influential figure who'd been instrumental in toppling Sihanouk, rejected the US evacuation offer.

"I have committed this mistake of believing in you, the Americans," he told Dean. The Khmer Rouge executed him a few days later.

In consigning Cambodia to the brutality ahead, the Ford administration was teaching the little Buddhist kingdom and the rest of the world the dubious value of an agreement with Washington: "Believe what we promise at your peril. In the end, it's America first."

Since 1789, the United States has broken more than five hundred signed agreements with international allies and Native American tribes.

At 7:00 a.m. on Saturday, another pistol-packing embassy official came to Le Phnom and announced that it was time to leave. White-uniformed room boys stood by silently in the airy hallways as we scurried in and out of our rooms. We were permitted one small bag each; everything else must be left behind. Photographers took their cameras. TV staffers shouldered their bulky gear. I took my typewriter, as did other reporters.

Dozens of us were bundled onto a large, open-bedded trailer truck and driven through empty streets. Approaching a traffic circle, I saw a hunched woman in a straw hat calmly sweeping the curb with a straw broom, as she did every morning. Just then, a late-model, red sports car, top down, entered the roundabout. The eyes of the driver, elbow propped casually on the doorframe, were hidden behind sunglasses. In the passenger seat, long black hair streaming, a young woman stared at the scores of foreigners sitting cross-legged atop a truck that normally might be hauling timber. The image of that privileged couple in their frivolous little car, the very antithesis of what was to come, is stamped indelibly in my memory.

We climbed down outside the padlocked embassy and crossed the street to a soccer field. A handful of American and European journalists had opted to stay behind. Syd Schanberg was one. He paced before the embassy gate looking tense, studying our faces. Like me, Syd was the father of two young daughters. And, like me, he had received instructions to leave.

Ben Bradlee had cabled the night before, ordering me that "under no circumstances" was I to stay. I replied, flippantly, in cablese:

DO NOTNOT WORRY STOP YOU UNUNPAY ME ENOUGH SIMONS

Syd rejected his orders. He told *New York Times* foreign editor James Greenfield that the story "represented five years of my life" and that he intended to see it through. As a short-term vacation replacement, I didn't share Syd's commitment. I did wonder, though, whether Bradlee—ferociously competitive with the *Times*—would have preferred that, despite his instructions, I also remain. Like military commanders covering their own behinds, editors often tell correspondents to stay safe in the midst of danger, knowing full well that if they did, they might miss out on a big story.

Syd's decision was influenced by an earlier disappointment. He had been enraged when his outstanding reporting on the Bangladesh war was passed over and the 1972 Pulitzer Prize went to Peter Khan, of the *Wall Street Journal*. Syd was determined not to miss out this time. He won the prize and the dramatic story of Schanberg and his loyal Khmer assistant, Dith Pran, was told in the 1984 Oscar-winning film, *The Killing Fields*.

Huge, green Sea Stallion helicopters settled noisily onto the soccer pitch, discharging marines in full combat rig. Taking up positions circling the field, they pointed their M-16s toward perplexed adults and excited schoolchildren scattered along the edge. As soon as we boarded, the craft lifted off and away, heading for the USS *Okinawa* and the USS *Hancock*, steaming in the Gulf of Siam. In all, the marines evacuated nearly six hundred Americans, Cambodians, and third-country nationals that climactic morning.

Rarely, if ever, had I been among a more despondent band of journalists. Wordless and sullen, we stared at our folded hands, at each other, down at the playing field and the astonished children gazing up at us. Most of us, I expect, were peering into our own minds:

How had it come to this? How had the mighty US military been cowed by a mob of poorly armed, illiterate Khmer peasants? What would become of those left behind—our interpreters, fixers, and drivers; the room-boys and waiters at the hotel; the cyclo drivers who delivered us to interviews; the PTT operators? What about our friends and colleagues who opted to stay? As would recur in Afghanistan in the summer of 2021, no one knew.

On board the *Okinawa*, I heard over the ship's radio Admiral Noel Gayler, the officer in overall command of the evacuation, speaking from his headquarters in Honolulu. The rescue mission, he said, "was very much in the American tradition where Americans look out for their own." Then, anticipating with evident dread what lay ahead, Gayler added, "Our hearts go out tonight to the Cambodians in Phnom Penh, who will have a very tough time."

Just how tough, neither he nor anyone else could have imagined. Minutes after the last chopper left, a Khmer Rouge shell struck the playing field, killing a child who'd been watching us fly away. It was a small sign of much worse to come.

I was standing with colleagues at the rail of the ship when the chopper ferrying Dean and other senior diplomats settled onto the deck. The ambassador was immaculately turned out in a dark suit, white shirt, striped tie, and matching pocket square. Beneath his left arm he carried a clear-plastic-wrapped bundle of three American flags, one of which had flown over the embassy until a few hours earlier.

"Good morning," he greeted us with deceptive cheeriness. "How are the press?"

My story on the evacuation, filed from the ship, was stripped across the top of the *Post*'s front page on April 13, 1975. The headline, Exit From Phnom Penh: Ditching The Excess Baggage, was an ironic expression of the unspeakable tragedy the United States had inflicted on Cambodia. Victorious Khmer Rouge soldiers met no resistance when they marched into the city four days later.

After spending the night aboard the *Okinawa* and disembarking in Thailand, I took a taxi up to Bangkok. Calls to friends and a hasty check of the morning's front pages made clear that Thais were terrified, with misguided reason. Conditioned by tales of toppling dominoes and anticipating the imminent collapse of Saigon (it happened seventeen days later), they were certain that North Vietnamese tanks would soon be rolling into the streets of their own thriving capital. What they failed to realize was that the Communists were thoroughly drained and that territorial expansion never was a part of their reunification plan.

I returned to Phnom Penh in 1989 to cover Cambodia's first free election, held under UN auspices. During my fourteen-year absence, the Communist regimes in Cambodia and Vietnam had turned on each other and fought a brief war that climaxed with a crushing victory by Vietnam and a decade-long occupation of Cambodia. This ended following drawn-out peace negotiations and Sihanouk's return home. Now, as I watched, the last Vietnamese soldiers departed and Cambodians went to the polls.

I was writing in my hotel room when I heard a soft knock and opened the door. A solidly built Cambodian with a touch of silver in his crew-cut hair was standing there. Confused, I stared for a long moment, unable to register what I saw. Could it be? Surely not. But, yes, it was. Yun! We clutched each other. We wept. And then we laughed.

"How?" was all I could manage. I expected an outpouring of unspeakable horrors.

"No, no," he said. "It is okay. I am okay. Wife and kids also okay."

His mother had died, of natural causes, at an advanced age. I pressed him for more, but he shook his head.

"I heard you were here, and I wanted to welcome you back to Cambodia," he said. "That is all." He left moments later.

I was baffled by Yun's having survived the eradication of the educated classes, particularly those who spoke French or English and—most unforgivable of sins—worked with Americans. His survival relieved my conscience. But, when I related the story of our reunion to a Cambodian journalist, he speculated that Yun might have been informing the Khmer Rouge of Greenway's and my activities.

I have no reason to believe that but, if it was so, he wouldn't have been the only local aide to have deceived sophisticated American journalists in Indochina. A Vietnamese Communist Party member by the name of Pham Xuan An had infiltrated first the Reuters and then the *Time* magazine bureaus in Saigon. He spoke English fluently, having graduated as a journalism major from a junior college in California. He quickly became a highly valued, masthead credited *Time* staffer and remained so through the end of the war.

An outed himself the day Saigon fell. He'd deceived such experienced correspondents as David Halberstam, Stan Karnow, Frank McCulloch, Bob Shaplen, and Neil Sheehan. Not to mention professional cynics like the CIA's Bill Colby and Lucien Conein, and Colonel Edward Lansdale, America's preeminent expert on irregular warfare. An snookered them all.

In 1985, a decade after the war ended, I had coffee with An in the pleasant, shady garden of his house in central Ho Chi Minh City, a reward from the grateful Communist government of reunified Vietnam. He'd also been granted the rank of general. We had met over coffee once before, in the early days of my AP assignment, when he'd invited me to Café Givral. This time, he told me he had been assembling a detailed file on me, as he had on numerous other correspondents. "I knew you far better than you knew me," he said.

The war in Cambodia had ended like a furious monsoon storm, with a shuddering clap of thunder. Khmer Rouge guerrillas dressed in black marched into Phnom Penh five days after the *Okinawa* and the *Hancock* sailed. The young guerrillas were trailed by crowds of residents, cheering but apprehensive, ignorant of the fate awaiting them.

They didn't have to wait long. A forty-five-year-old man by the name of Saloth Sar emerged from the shadows using the nom de guerre Pol Pot, which means "the original Cambodian." Under his leadership, the Maoist Khmer Rouge immediately replaced the expired government with an ominous group called "Angka," The Organization. Caustically, they renamed the country Democratic Kampuchea. Angka drove city dwellers into the countryside to work, often to death, as slave laborers. It reset time, making 1975 Year Zero, and commenced one of history's most ghastly mass murders.

South Vietnam collapsed two weeks later. On April 30, at 11:10 a.m., just four hours after the last Marine guards were helicoptered from the US embassy in what was for the moment still Saigon, North Vietnamese tanks plowed through the presidential palace gate. I was in Laos by then, covering its last days, and missed the grand finale of America's humiliation in Saigon.

South Vietnamese General Duong Van "Big" Minh, who'd taken on the impossible responsibilities of president just two days earlier, waited on the palace front steps and surrendered unconditionally to an NVA lieutenant in the lead tank. "The revolution is here," Minh acknowledged to the junior officer. "You are here."

The northerners raised their red flag over the palace and renamed the city in honor of Ho Chi Minh. More than 120,000 southerners began fleeing the country. An estimated 1,200 died in reeducation camps. As horrible as it was, the outcome was less extreme than Cambodia's.

Two down and one to go.

The war in Laos petered out gradually and with much less bloodletting. The diminutive country, once known as the "Kingdom of a Million Elephants," was the most backward of the three Indochinese states. It had been a late-comer to communism. Under France, a king reigned in a golden-domed palace in the royal city of Luang Prabang, while the French ruled from Vientiane. By the time the 1940s drew to an end, Pathet Lao, or Lao Nation, guerrillas were gaining control of the countryside.

The king and his royalist followers ceded military and civil control to the United States a decade later. The Americans, as always, everywhere, were in a hurry to get things done, to defeat communism and place Laos and the rest of Indochina in pro-US hands. But the Pathet Lao, who understood their people in ways the Americans and the French never could, patiently and methodically usurped full power.

On May Day 1975, having finished my reporting on the fall of Cambodia, I took the short air trip from Bangkok across the Mekong to Vientiane. My first stop was the Vietnamese embassy, where diplomats were celebrating the liberation of Saigon with hundreds of their overjoyed expatriate countrymen. Then I drove across town to the American embassy, the sole US mission still functioning in Indochina. It was wreathed in gloom.

During the height of the war, while based in Saigon, I had made several reporting trips to Laos. It was a beguiling place of pleasure and innocence.

During lunar eclipses, people fired rifles at the sky to frighten off the giant frog that was swallowing the moon.

For me and other correspondents, Vientiane's laid-back atmosphere was a respite. Alcohol, opium, and marijuana abounded, as did houses of ill repute. One establishment popular among Americans was the White Rose, a raucous bar-cum-brothel. Swaggering crew members of the CIA-owned-and-operated Air America frequented the place. These airmen-of-fortune were weighted down with bulky twenty-four-karat gold chain necklaces and bracelets with which, they said, they would buy their freedom if captured by bad guys.

The beer-swilling clientele, packed around small tables, hooted approval of naked Lao girls and women, who performed almost unimaginable acts involving fistfuls of cigarettes, ponies, and dogs on a brightly lit stage.

Then there was Madame Lulu's, a unique establishment located in a colonial-era villa on a sedate, tree-shaded street. The namesake proprietor, herself a relic of the French epoch, offered her customers European and Lao women she'd trained in the art of *bucco-génitales*, the *spécialité de la maison*.

Looking back, I'm struck by how inoffensive it all seemed to this onetime nice Jewish boy from New Jersey, by then a young husband and father of two little girls. No doubt I was influenced by the awareness that prostitution was widely accepted as one of the very few ways a peasant girl could work her way out of abject poverty. Once she'd earned sufficient money in the city, she could return to her village, build a house, marry, and raise a family, respectability intact, no questions asked.

Vientiane's few streets were so quiet and traffic-free that there was no need for the sole traffic light in town. Coated in dust, it seldom functioned, and no one paid attention when it did. Sullen, olive-uniformed Pathet Lao boy-soldiers lazed in the shade, Kalashnikovs slung over their scrawny shoulders. War seemed far away.

But that was an illusion. Between 1964 and 1973, US planes dropped an astounding 270 million bombs on the nation of two and a half million. That was more than America had dumped on all of its foes during World War II. Cluster-munitions, which the Americans endearingly called "bombies" and "bomblets," killed twenty-nine thousand Laotians and injured twenty-one thousand more. More than a third of the land was bombed.

A regular target was the Ho Chi Minh Trail, along which North Vietnamese troops trundled matériel southward. But the heaviest-hit area by far was the Plain of Jars, a two-thousand-year-old burial ground at the center of the country. Some military experts claim the plain became the most heavily bombed piece of land in the world.

The plain is renowned for the thousands of mysterious stone jars that litter its flat grassland. Archaeologists believe the vessels, some as tall as ten feet and weighing up to fourteen tons, played an important part in arcane funeral rites. US planes targeted the site because it was a critical NVA launching pad into South Vietnam.

As with the carpet-bombing of Cambodia, the air campaign over Laos was intended as an undercover mission. Secretary of State Kissinger labeled it the "Secret War." Targets were selected by American ambassadors in Vientiane, first the outspoken William H. Sullivan, then his successor, G. McMurtrie "Mac" Godley, a jut-jawed career diplomat who enjoyed being called "Field Marshal."

The US embassy compound was the ugliest foreign mission in Vientiane. The ambassadors called the shots from inside what was in fact a reinforced concrete bunker, its thick, windowless walls studded with dozens of air conditioners, each caged by steel bars. It made me think of TV weather forecasters, gazing at computer screens, telling viewers it was raining when a glance out a window would have shown the sun shining. The entire compound was wrapped in tall steel fencing and serviced by its own purified-water system and giant power generators.

Like a groping giant, the embassy was blind to the inhabitants of the country it was supposedly there to save from communism. If ever American foreign policy had broken loose of its moorings and lay in twisted, unrecognizable wreckage on the shoals of ignorance and wasted good intentions, it was in Laos.

The air campaign was not the only stealthy American activity in little Laos. In the cool, forested hills north of Vientiane, members of the CIA's ultra-elite, ultra-covert Special Activities Division—SAD—ran a surrogate army of ardently anti-Communist Hmong clansmen.

The Hmong, also known as Meo, an ethnic subset of southern Chinese who had migrated into Laos and Vietnam millennia earlier, were led by the charismatic General Vang Pao. They fought ferociously and were expert spies against the NVA and the Pathet Lao. As many as eighteen thousand Hmong were killed in 1968 to 1969 alone. Air America drops kept them supplied while SAD operatives guided their activities and made promises they rarely kept.

Years later, our next-door neighbor in Washington told me an extraordinary tale about himself: James Vinton Lawrence, scion of a wealthy Manhattan family with a history of adventuresome government service, turned out to have been the foremost SAD officer operating with the Hmong. Vint was an amiable fellow, with a mop of wavy, black hair and an infectious smile. A fluent Francophone, he'd become Vang Pao's confidant, working alongside him at Long Tieng, the Hmong headquarters, in north-central Laos. By the time we moved into the adjacent house, he'd quit the agency. A talented artist, he had become, of all things, a political caricaturist.

His four-year tour in Laos, from 1962 to 1966, coincided with the CIA's expanding its role from old-fashioned spying and dirty tricks to full-scale paramilitary field operations. When we realized that we'd both been in Laos around the same time, we marveled at the improbability. My writing appeared daily, in black and white, for all to see. Vint, by now recognized for his highly detailed monochrome drawings, described his deep-undercover work with the Hmong as "blacker than my blackest pictures." Now we were next-door neighbors and friends.

The war in Laos was over, for all practical purposes, before I reached Vientiane that May Day of 1975. And the United States was the big loser. Nowhere was this outcome clearer than at the expansive residential compound that housed staffers of the US Agency for International Development and their families.

Except for a tall chain-link fence surrounding it, the USAID compound looked like a middle-class, Florida subdivision that had been dropped from the sky and landed on the outskirts of Vientiane. More than five hundred American civilians lived there, in pastel-colored, ranch-style houses set on broad, palm-lined streets.

Perhaps the most poorly kept secret of the secret war was that USAID and CIA worked hand in hand in Laos. The aid agency provided cover for the spy agency and together they ran what amounted to a parallel government. USAID spent a then-stunning one billion dollars and left behind an impressive legacy of roads, schools, hospitals, and other valuable infrastructure. But its real mission was to support the right-wing, royalist element of the Laotion government, many of whose leaders grew rich on USAID contracts and bribes.

A few days after the guns fell silent in Vietnam and Cambodia, a Pathet Lao–inspired band of students broke into the residential compound and took two Marine security guards and a civilian hostage. The takeover became a big story.

On a break from hanging around outside the padlocked gate, waiting for a resolution, I dropped by the embassy. The ambassador had departed and deputy chief of mission Christopher A. Chapman was in charge. Like everyone else on the sharply depleted staff, he was gloomy.

"These are melancholy days for all of us," he told me.

That included top pro-American Lao officials, who began fleeing the country. I was in the bar of the Lane Xang Hotel one evening when a US embassy staffer bustled in with news of an imminent, crucial departure. I ran up the broad flight of stairs to my room and telephoned Defense Minister Sisouk na Champassak. A member of the royal family, he spoke English well, but he responded in mournful French when I asked if it was true that he was leaving.

"*Oui, c'est vrai*," he said. "*Tout est perdu.*" All was lost.

He hung up. I took a cyclo to the PTT and filed the story.

A week later, Chapman announced that the Pathet Lao had agreed to allow all five hundred compound residents to depart for Thailand. Unlike in Vietnam and Cambodia, diplomatic relations between Laos and the United States, though reduced, remained intact.

The social revolution shifted into high gear. The Pathet Lao imposed restrictions and limitations, one by one, on everyday life. Gambling was forbidden, a particular deprivation for Laotians, who were accustomed to playing games of chance at almost every opportunity, even during funerals. Brothels were shut. Western-style dancing was banned. Each reduction of freedom was, as Chapman told me, "another thin slice off the salami."

More than twice as many Laotians fled than died in the postwar revolution: Over seventeen years, as many as one hundred thousand anti-Communists, the majority of them Hmong, were killed in residual warfare against the Pathet Lao. Just over forty thousand, including members of the royal family, died in labor camps and under other harsh conditions. More than three hundred and sixty thousand—over ten percent of the population—escaped by swimming across the Mekong into Thailand.

The most publicized Mekong crossing was carried out by my friend and occasional stringer, John Everingham. A talented photographer, John had left home in Australia at age sixteen to see the world. When we met, he'd been living in Laos for a decade. With sun-bleached hair, a skimpy mustache and beard, he was a ringer for Johnny Depp. He spoke the singsong language well and shared his traditional stilt house near the bank of the Mekong with a bevy of young Lao women. After observing him one steamy afternoon, swathed in a sarong, lazing in a hammock strung in the shade beneath the house, the women giggling and fussing over him, Carol awarded him the title of Lord Jim.

As the Pathet Lao tightened their grip, they accused John of being a spy. They confiscated thousands of his priceless slides and kicked him out of the country. He returned ten months later. Equipped with scuba gear, he crawled along the muddy river-bottom from the Thai side, evading armed Pathet Lao boats patrolling the surface, rescued his terrified Lao girlfriend, who couldn't swim, by strapping her to his back and returning to Thailand. The remarkable story was memorialized in a 1983 TV film, *Love is Forever,* starring Michael Landon.

The Communists' incremental takeover of Laos reached fulfillment at the end of 1975, when the shadowy leader of the Lao Peoples' Revolutionary

## Chapter Twelve

# Stirring up Trouble in India

I had been away from Delhi for more than two months. My only communication with Carol had been a handful of terse cables that the foreign editor in Washington funneled between us. BEST REGARDS ON YOUR ANNIVERSARY SIGNED LESCAZE was her least favorite.

It was time to leave the now-defused war zone and return home.

During our decades abroad, Carol and I, like other expats, Foreign Service, and military couples, assured each other that extended absences and warm reunions kept our marriage fresh. That was true. But time apart also involved hardships, more so for the one left behind. As we readjusted our lives this time around, India fell into a new crisis of its own. It would change everything, for everyone, very much including us.

On June 12, 1974, the High Court in Prime Minister Gandhi's hometown, Allahabad, found her guilty of illegal campaign funding, including the use of military aircraft to shuttle party functionaries around the country, during her successful reelection bid four years earlier. The court ordered her to immediately abandon the prime minister's office and her seat in Parliament. It barred her from public office for six years.

This was stunning.

That she had been forced to testify before the court in a humbling public hearing, the first Indian prime minister to do so, was itself a shock. To put this in context, one year earlier, President Nixon opted to resign rather than face similar humiliation following the Watergate impeachment. Gandhi chose to slug it out.

Intense political pressure for and against her built instantly within her Congress Party machine, her cabinet, in parliament, and throughout the huge population. Opponents staged raucous street demonstrations, demanding Gandhi's ouster. For nearly two weeks, she rallied, addressing crowds of adoring supporters who gathered at a traffic roundabout near her tree-shaded official residence in New Delhi, at 7 Lok Kalyan Marg. She blamed her predicament on domestic political enemies and unidentified foreign governments, thinly veiled code for Pakistan and the United States.

"I will go on working for the development of the country in spite of obstacles created by certain people and foreign powers," she said.

In fact, beyond the campaign finance issue, Gandhi and her family were sloshing in corruption and scandal. The most damaging case involved her younger son, Sanjay Gandhi.

At twenty-five, Sanjay was short, slender, and boyish-looking save for a deeply receding hairline. His fair complexion, a widely admired characteristic of the Nehrus' Kashmiri Brahmin lineage, was set off by stylish, long, black sideburns and owlish, black-rimmed glasses. Appearances aside, he was hard as nails, what is known in Hindi as a *thuggee*.

Although he lacked financial means and appropriate training in business or technology, he had cooked up a scheme to build a Volkswagen-type people's car for India's newly emerging middle class. By illegally having 1,500 farmers dispossessed, he acquired, at bargain-basement prices, 297 acres of prime land just outside Delhi. Manufacturing was forbidden on the site because it was adjacent to a strategic Indian Air Force weapons depot. Through his mother, he arranged to have this essential information withheld from Parliament.

The name Sanjay chose for the planned car, apparently without irony, was Maruti, meaning "Son of the Wind God." In fact, his sole qualification for the undertaking was being the favored son of the political goddess, Indira.

Speaking out against Sanjay invited severe retribution. A close friend of mine, Bobbili George Verghese, the highly regarded editor of the independent *Hindustan Times*, was sacked for publishing articles and editorials exposing Sanjay's having extorted huge sums of so-called black money from wealthy, tax-evading businessmen to invest in Maruti dealerships.

The paper's owner, Krishna Kumar Birla, a member of one of India's two richest families, later confessed in a letter to George that powerful Congress Party officials had "suggested" he be fired.

Because of Sanjay's incompetence, it was nearly a decade before the first Maruti hit the road, and then, only through a merger with Japan's Suzuki.

During my three years in India, I had tried to interview Sanjay a dozen times, once ambushing him after waiting outside his office for more than an hour. He looked right through me.

"Mr. Gandhi does not approve of your writing," sniffed an aide walking beside him, "and he refuses to release any information to your *Washington Post*."

After the Allahabad court's ruling, Indira Gandhi applied the full force of her influence on Congress Party officials, demanding they help keep her in office. A handful stood up to threats that she would remove them from lucrative and powerful positions. But the party caved to her will and issued a blunt statement, declaring, "The leadership of Mrs. Gandhi is indispensable."

On June 18, I went out on a limb and wrote, "By completely ignoring the legal issue and stressing that India's fortunes and her own were one, Mrs. Gandhi indicated that she intends to suspend the nation's constitution."

Few of the Indians I knew believed it would come to that. They underestimated her. And they underestimated Sanjay and his hold over her.

Two days after my gloomy forecast was published, she delivered an impassioned appeal to a monsoon-drenched crowd in Delhi, calling on them and other supporters to disregard the court's order. The party had shuttled more than one hundred thousand people to the rally by truck, bus, and train. Their frenzied roars of "Indira Gandhi *zindabad*!"—wishing her a long life—shook the sodden air.

With Sanjay standing beside her on a brick-and-timber platform hurriedly erected for the occasion, she spoke into a bouquet of microphones, amplifying her little-girl voice.

"I don't want to talk about the judge or the judgment," she said, then adding with quiet menace, "I don't want to scare anyone."

In my article on that speech, I wrote that her defense minister had ordered the army to provide water tankers, other vehicles, and equipment to support the demonstration and that "soldiers in civilian clothes . . . be used at the rally."

That handful of words would soon have a major impact on me, my family, and the *Washington Post*.

I also reported that the order for military backup, which was illegal, had been withdrawn once word of it leaked. Having spoken to two field-grade army officers whom I knew well, I wrote, "According to a military source, tension is growing in the armed forces, which have a long and proud tradition of remaining out of politics. Resentment is said to be particularly sharp in the army, where officers are known to be annoyed over Mrs. Gandhi's refusal to resign."

That refusal forced India's Supreme Court once again to step into the breach. Supporting the Allahabad judgment, the chief justice barred Gandhi from voting in parliament. She ignored the order, just as she had the Allahabd judgment, insisting they did not undermine her position.

"There is a lot of talk about our government not being clean," she said, "but from our experience the situation was very much worse when [opposition] parties were forming governments."

Dismissing criticism of the way the Congress Party raised campaign money, she argued that all parties used the same methods. This was true. Making the point helped her hang on.

Still, her options were limited. In the end, she turned to Sanjay and his strong-arm tactics. Late Thursday night, June 26, Gandhi took the drastic step that I'd forecast in my reporting, the one Indians hoped she wouldn't and imagined she couldn't take. She put the constitution in cold storage and declared what became known as the Emergency.

Armed police burst into homes and dragged more than one hundred of her political enemies, including nearly every leader of the right-wing opposition, out of their beds. They seized at least forty members of Gandhi's own party, those who had demanded her resignation. She and Sanjay had drawn up the list the preceding afternoon.

In a brief address on All-India Radio, she made no mention of the arrests— which mounted within a few hours to more than three thousand, including a number of prominent Indian journalists. She attributed the emergency declaration to vague "internal disturbances."

The last straw had been a provocative speech by right-wing leader Jayaprakash Narayan to a cheering crowd of fifty thousand, calling for a broad-based campaign of civil disobedience. Narayan also appealed to the armed forces to disobey what he alleged were illegal orders. Gandhi accused Narayan of instigating a "widespread conspiracy and attempting to destroy democracy in the name of saving it."

Civil disobedience—satyagraha—was the tactic of nonviolent resistance to government authority used by Mahatma Gandhi with stunning effectiveness against Great Britain decades earlier. J.P., as Narayan was widely known, was a lifelong disciple of the mahatma. He had devoted himself during the years since independence to a nationwide drive against government corruption. Now seventy-three years old, it was he who brought the case against Mrs. Gandhi to the Allahabad High Court. She had him detained in a "rest home" outside New Delhi.

Gandhi imposed total censorship on all news media, domestic and foreign. Nothing could be published or broadcast without first being approved by the information ministry. To assure compliance, the government cut electric power to all Indian newspapers.

With my own time to file evaporating, I worked through the night, calling sources, including several wives of men who'd just been rousted from bed. Vina Mody, an American married to prominent opposition politician Piloo Mody, read me a note her husband had scribbled moments before he was led away:

"I heard the inevitable knock on the door. The fascist forces have overtaken the democratic process."

I finished writing the piece around 3:00 a.m. Knowing that the teletype operators at Reuters would not be permitted to send my copy to the *Post*, I decided to take a risk and level with the international telephone operator in

"He's never forgiven his mother for what he thinks she did to Feroze," the friend said. The Gandhis had married in 1942. He was a junior member of parliament, she a housewife. Seven years later, Indira left the couple's home with Sanjay and his older brother, Rajiv, and moved into the official residence of her father, Prime Minister Jawaharlal Nehru. Indira became her widower-father's hostess.

Feroze eventually joined them, but, as Indira's aunt Krishna Hutheesing wrote in *We Nehrus*, this was "not a good arrangement from a family point of view." Feroze felt "shut out" by his wife. He resented his "inferior status" and being mocked in public as "the nation's son-in-law." Tensions heightened further when Indira was elected to Parliament.

Feroze waked out and Sanjay's relationship with his mother deteriorated into alternating waves of love and hate. On the day that the Allahabad High Court found her guilty, she arrived back at the prime minister's residence—now hers—and Sanjay ran onto the lawn to greet her.

"He threw his arms around her and cried like a baby," an eyewitness told me. Yet, persistent rumors portrayed Sanjay as the dominant figure in the relationship.

Although I'd withheld the series while Carol and the girls remained in India, the authorities made their lives miserable anyway. They cut the phone line and blocked funds needed to pay my assistant and the household help. They refused to grant exit paperwork to Catherine, our Malaysian amah. And they posted an armed policeman on our street corner, taking down license plates. Many of our friends were frightened and stayed away.

On July 4th, isolated, frustrated, and increasingly scared, Carol scooped up the kids and drove to the US embassy, where Independence Day was being celebrated with hot dogs and burgers.

William Saxbe, Nixon's former attorney general, who'd recently replaced Pat Moynihan as ambassador, headed a receiving line in the foyer of Roosevelt House, the grand official residence. Farther down the line, Carol spotted the military attaché, dress tunic splashed with a fruit salad of ribbons, and his wife, an imposing woman of ample bosom.

"At that moment," she told me much later, "everything about that woman said 'America' to me." She fell upon the colonel's lady and dissolved into tears.

Saxbe ordered a press officer standing at his elbow to "get this woman out of here and make sure she receives the help she needs."

The next morning, an embassy officer escorted Carol and the kids to the airport. They swept past immigration and customs and were driven directly onto the tarmac to a waiting plane.

Decades later, I came across a cable sent to the State Department over Saxbe's name. It was one of thousands of secret US government documents released in Julian Assange's famous Wikileaks dump of 2010.

Dated June 30, 1975, the cable established the US government's official position on my expulsion. It recounted details of a meeting that day between a Foreign Ministry officer and the political counselor of the embassy and set out the official reaction to my ouster:

IF ASKED, EMBASSY PROPOSES TO TELL REPORTERS THAT THE EMBASSY HAS EXPRESSED ITS STRONG REGRET TO GOI [Government of India] AT SIMONS'S EXPULSION.

Sidestepping what must have been a tempting urge for ironic comment, the cable concluded:

WE HAVE JUST LEARNED THAT AN AMERICAN JOURNALIST (WITHOUT FILING) HAS ASKED A GOI PRESS AND INFORMATION BUREAU OFFICIAL TONIGHT WHETHER THE SIMONS EXPULSION STORY WOULD PASS CENSORSHIP. HE WAS TOLD THAT IT COULD NOT BECAUSE IT HAS NOT BEEN ANNOUNCED.

I met Carol and the girls at Hong Kong's Kai Tak Airport and we took a taxi to David Greenway's Midlevels flat, overlooking the island's magnificent Fragrant Harbor. David had been dispatched to Delhi to shut down the bureau, and his family accompanied him.

Carol was a wreck. My normally strong and composed wife, who'd been through war and riots, had succumbed to the pressures of irksome Indian bureaucrats. Normally enthusiastic and open to all challenges, she was worn out. A week or so after arriving, her neck locked and she was unable to turn her head. She wound up at Adventist Hospital, where she was stretched out on a traction machine. Slowly, Carol returned to being Carol.

Barely had she been discharged when news broke on August 15, 1975, that rebellious Bangladeshi soldiers had gunned down Sheikh Mujibur Rahman. Once again, I left her to fend for herself and the children in unfamiliar surroundings while I flew into turmoil, this time in Dacca.

Mujib, like so many before him, had succumbed to the temptations of elevating his already considerable power to absolute. Within three years of his triumphant return home, he had discarded parliamentary democracy; promoted himself from prime minister to president of the tottering, infant country; and seized unprecedented authority. Disappointed, then embittered, the public and the army turned murderously on him.

I took a taxi directly from Dacca Airport to 32 Dhanmondi, Mujib's home. At that point in my reporting career, I had covered a variety of killings and their aftermath, but never had I seen anything as ghastly as what I saw that day. The house was, literally, awash in blood—the entrance, the living room, a second-floor room, and several bathrooms were drenched. In Mujib's

According to Hitchens's account, Cherry was actively involved in the plotting.

After the murders, Mustaque was anointed president of Bangladesh. Mustaque then promoted Zia to army chief. Zia later staged his own coup and became the young nation's first military dictator.

Thus, in four tumultuous years, from 1971 to 1975, Bangladesh disintegrated from freedom's cause célèbre and was crumbling into the basket case that Kissinger acrimoniously had forecast if it broke from Pakistan.

Then, something utterly unimaginable happened.

Women left home.

Beginning as a trickle, a flood of younger women hired on in new factories that were making T-shirts and other cheap clothing for export to the United States and elsewhere.

Husbands, fathers, and brothers were outraged. Many responded with brutal assaults to what they perceived as an unacceptable challenge to their dominant position in their families. I interviewed girls and women who'd been hideously disfigured by male relatives throwing battery acid in their faces. Organizations were formed to help the victims. The women persisted.

Today, fifty years after their homeland's bloody birth, women at sewing machines account for over 80 percent of Bangladesh's exports. Individual incomes have surpassed those in India and Pakistan. Amazingly, economists now tout the country as a rising star. Not bad for a basket case.

In India, the seventies exploded into one of the more tumultuous decades in the modern history of the normally tumultuous nation. Having swapped her Bangladesh liberator's mantle for the iron glove of a tyrant, Indira Gandhi was tossed out of office in 1977. Voters reinstated her in 1980.

Then, in June 1984, she ordered an all-out military attack on a Sikh temple where an armed band of extremists had taken refuge. In retribution for the carnage, two Sikh members of Gandhi's army bodyguard—one of whom she had handpicked for the assignment—shot her to death on the lawn of her official residence.

Infuriated Hindus in turn massacred Sikhs, the men easily recognizable by their full beards and turbans. Police estimated as many as one thousand Sikhs were killed over four days.

No longer persona non grata in India, I flew from my base in Bangkok to Delhi. I attended the elaborate Hindu ceremony in which Gandhi's marigold-draped corpse was doused in clarified butter and set ablaze atop a massive sandalwood pyre. Her elder son, Rajiv, dressed in white, his face immobile, circled the fragrant flames the required seven times. Rajiv would succeed his slain mother as prime minister and, in 1991, he, too, would be assassinated.

Like raging metronomes, India and Bangladesh swung wildly between authoritarianism and assorted degrees of freedom.

*How little it took to destroy democracy*, I marveled. The Bangladesh part of the calculus was the more comprehensible of the two. Neither wing of Pakistan ever enjoyed more than a morsel of representative governance in its political diet. Dictatorship was the norm.

But India? India, which never hesitated to lecture the world whenever governments appeared to infringe the rights of citizens? All at once, this India differed not a whit from the banana republics it scorned.

How easy it had been. When Mrs. Gandhi had imposed the emergency, few younger Indians cursed and shook their fists. A few liberal intellectuals predicted it would all be over in a few months. (The Emergency, in fact, lasted from 1975 to 1977.) But most simply stood back and took the punishment Mrs. Gandhi imposed on their lives. Just as she took Sanjay's slaps.

Fear. It was all about fear. On the eve of Carol's departure from Delhi, a young couple we knew well ratcheted up their nerve and came to the house to express their regret and to wish her well. They had ignored a warning from the husband's parents that, "you'll have trouble if you go there." Moments after they arrived, the dead phone jangled back to life. Carol picked up the receiver. Silence. The couple left immediately.

Fear.

As Donald Trump would tell Bob Woodward decades later, "Real power is, I don't even want to use the word: Fear."

While young Donald was still dodging the draft and venereal diseases in Manhattan, Indira put the admonition in play. The better-off classes, those with paying jobs and pukka houses, knew they would suffer if they spoke out. So they didn't. The destitute, the basti dwellers, the Untouchables, risked little. But in Gandhi's India, they didn't matter.

## Chapter Thirteen

# Birth and Death in Bangkok

Thailand, where we were now living, was the kind of country that pre-Emergency, educated Indians mocked for lacking a democratic system. Yet, alone among southeast Asian nations—and India—it dodged the scourge of colonialism for centuries. By skillfully exercising the ancient wisdom of bending with the wind, like green bamboo, Thais accommodated the demands of the Japanese army in World War II and the Americans during Vietnam, while managing to retain control of their homeland.

The house we rented in Bangkok included a remnant of its former Japanese military occupants: a tatami-floored tearoom enclosed by sliding shoji screens. Imagining Emperor Hirohito's officers relaxing there, sipping sake and green *ocha*, we used it to entertain guests, much as we had in our Delhi conversation pit.

Our new home was a cozy, furnished cottage, less than half the size of our grand first Delhi residence. Carol and Catherine managed it handily. Our daughters loved being able to splash in the swimming pool of an apartment building on the property.

We settled into our new posting quickly and easily, making friends in the large foreign press corps and with the surprisingly large number of bilingual Thais. I rented an office two blocks away, at the English-language *Bangkok Post*. Carol found an editing job there, polishing the prose of Thai reporters.

Once Carol recovered from the trauma of her final days in India, the family relaxed. Thailand was familiar territory for me. I'd been in and out over the years and had a basic appreciation of its people and their ways. As a Westerner, a *farang*, acclimating to Thai society required minimal effort. Devout Buddhists, they were easygoing, with far fewer hang-ups than Hindus and Muslims. Among the first words my language tutor taught me were *sanuk*, to describe their fun-loving ways, and *mai pen rai,* to dismiss worry.

Women wore up-to-the-minute miniskirts and platform shoes; men gambled, drank, and whored with abandon. Commercial sex was big business. City streets were puddled with pink neon light from outlandishly designed soapy-massage parlors. The young women working in them were displayed by the dozens in glass showcases, pretending to flirt with customers, who selected them by numbers pinned to their skimpy outfits. Venereal diseases were rampant. AIDS was on the way.

Some Thais blamed American soldiers for corrupting them. There was something to this, but it wasn't the whole story. The GIs and their dollars were more than welcome. At the height of the Vietnam War, fifty thousand US military personnel were stationed at air bases and secret installations in Thailand. Many more flooded in on short R&R visits and were happily accommodated by local women.

Tragically, the four thousand Amerasian children left behind were stateless, rejected by both governments. Some GIs, though, married and returned home with Thai wives. Thai restaurants blossomed in America's strip malls.

My assignment had several key facets: Using Bangkok as a listening post; monitor the neighboring, newly Communist states of Indochina; travel to other countries of Southeast Asia; and, lastly, cover Thailand itself. Surprisingly, to me anyway, Americans seemed to have little interest in news from the country. I once received a telex from Phil Foisie, complaining that Thai names were "too confusing" for readers and that I should cut most of them out of my stories.

Events certainly warranted coverage, though. Take coups. Since 1932, when the army overthrew the king of what was then Siam and established a constitutional monarchy, Thailand has been battered by at least fifteen coups. Some were bloody, others little more than military or political bureaucratic shuffles.

Two deadly rebellions occurred during my three-year stint. Early in October 1976, the army joined forces with mobs of right-wing youths and, together, they massacred scores of leftist students at Bangkok's elite Thammasat University. The students, the cream of their generation, had been protesting for a week against the return of an exiled former military dictator, General Thanom Kittikachorn (one of those confusing names). Rightists, egged on by the military, were worried that the leftists would push Thailand in the same direction as Vietnam, Cambodia, and Laos.

Around 5:30 in the morning, on October 6, a frantic phone call from a student organization had me groggily clambering out of bed and driving to the university. Moments after I parked, hundreds of young vigilantes and soldiers armed with automatic weapons and artillery pieces stormed the leafy campus. Once again, I bore witness at close range to mass murder, inhuman brutality, and mutilated corpses. Even supposedly gentle Buddhists, I now realized, were capable of vicious behavior. My disgust with religion was now complete.

black. They were carrying rifles. They used very rough language and told us that we must leave the house immediately.

"My mother pleaded with them to let us to pack some things. They allowed us one suitcase each and my parents could bring their medicines. We were grateful for that. A truck with other people in the back pulled up and we were ordered to get on."

The truck drove along dirt roads for about two hours, said Rangsey, "into the countryside." Where, he didn't know. As a city boy, accustomed to soft living, he fared poorly at first.

"They forced me to work in the fields. My shoes quickly wore out and I was barefoot. My feet were always bleeding, cut and bruised over and over again, until they became toughened. When I fell down, they beat me with sticks. They did it to all of us."

One beating left him with a twisted leg and a permanent limp. With never enough to eat and dysentery a constant, Rangsey lost over thirty pounds. His parents were stricken with malaria and malnutrition. Within six months, both were dead.

Rangsey remained in captivity for four years, until 1979, when Vietnam invaded Cambodia. "The Khmer Rouge soldiers who controlled us went away to fight and, in the confusion, I escaped into Thailand." He applied for admission to the United States as a refugee. I don't know if he ever made it.

I had no doubt that Rangsey and others I interviewed, many of whom suffered far worse than he, were telling the truth as they knew it. But their field of vision was extremely narrow and short.

How representative of the entire country were these refugee accounts? I didn't know. In search of facts to support or counter the stories leaking out, I periodically visited the vast Khao I Dang camp the Thai government had set up near the frontier town of Sakaeo. I interviewed a handful of the seven thousand Cambodians who had managed to flee and now were housed in this settlement of raw-wood huts.

Mach Suan thought she was twenty-one or twenty-two when we met there. Bone-thin and sun-darkened, she wore a brown sarong and a gray T-shirt with a faded blue "Bulls" stamped on the front. We spoke through an interpreter.

She and her extended family—mother, father, grandparents, and her eight siblings—were forced out of Phnom Penh a week after Pol Pot's guerrillas swaggered in.

The family had lived in the city for as long as any of them could remember. They worked as tailors and seamstresses, carpenters and cooks. The youngest two were in elementary school.

Unlike Rangsey and his parents, they didn't get trucked out. Instead, they were herded, footsore and exhausted, for nearly a month into dense jungle, in the far north of the country. There, they were ordered to create rice paddies.

"They never told us how to do it and none of us knew anything about growing rice," Mach Suan told me. "We had to make our own tools, digging the ground with sticks."

Even before she and her family began their hopeless task, they were sapped by hunger. "I can't remember a time when my belly wasn't crying." By the time the Vietnamese invaded, only Mach Suan, an older brother, and a younger sister remained alive.

"I hope America will let us in," she said. "But, even if they don't, I will never return to my homeland. It is a land of death."

Today, having visited post–Khmer Rouge Cambodia several times and seen graphic evidence—mountains of skulls retrieved from the Killing Fields and meticulous records of unimaginably brutal torture and murder—I wouldn't think for a moment of arguing that the crimes against humanity weren't genocidal, as horrific as those of Hitler, Stalin, and Mao.

But I—we—didn't know it then, as it was happening. Barred from the country, my frustrated Cambodia-watching colleagues and I strained to weigh refugees' accounts against denials by the Khmer Rouge and the handful of Western leftists who defended them.

We were unable to answer with any degree of certainty even the most basic questions:

Were the Khmer Communists waging genocide against their own people? It was widely assumed that they were. But we didn't know.

How many Cambodians had they killed? Tens of thousands? Hundreds of thousands? A million? Two million? We heard and reported all these figures. But we didn't know.

What had the population of Cambodia been at the end of the war? Five million? Eight million? What was the population after the Khmer Rouge finished their gruesome work? What was the strength of the Khmer Rouge? Forty thousand? One hundred thousand? We didn't know.

By "we," I mean not only foreign correspondents but Thai journalists, military officials from numerous countries, American and other diplomats, academic experts—the "informed sources" to whom journalists turn when they cannot observe events themselves. All of us were speculating.

If none of us knew, why did the outside world assume the worst? Could it be, as the Khmer Rouge regime and its few foreign friends alleged, that Western news media and governments were guilty of distortion and wild fabrication?

Even the handful of outsiders who backed the regime possessed scant facts. Their arguments were based chiefly on their underlying belief that Western journalists and governments, Americans in particular, had a vested interest in putting the worst possible face on Democratic Kampuchea.

## Chapter Fourteen

# Knight Rider to the Rescue

Journalists are the playthings of events. Something happens somewhere, perhaps something about which you know nothing, and immediately takes over your life. You hit the ground running and, for days or weeks, sometimes much longer, you learn as you go. The unpredictability of what's around the next corner strains your nerves.

One way to regulate the stress is to establish a specialty. Covering a defined subject allows you to focus. Once I overcame my self-pity for being summoned back to the newsroom, I determined I would build on my overseas expertise. I would recover at least some of the independence and sense of self-worth I coveted.

It occurred to me that, like the abject human degradation I wrote about in Asia, poverty in the United States was seldom covered in depth, even more rarely at a deep, human level. I could see that filling the gap could be good for the *Post*, good for readers, and good for me. Unlike in Asia, where the poor almost always are the same people as the rich, in America—and most certainly in Washington, DC—poor usually meant Black. The mix of race and economics would make for explosive stories.

Poverty, I told Bradlee, would be my beat.

"Knock yourself out," was his unenthusiastic response.

I began wandering through some of the District of Columbia's most underserved public-housing projects, much as I'd picked my way through the wretched bastis of Bombay and the cardboard boxes of Jakarta. After my first few visits, I hired guides/interpreters to explain things to me and to translate a language I didn't understand any better than I had Maharashtran or Bahasa Indonesia. When I submitted the minimal cost in an expense account, Bradlee's curiosity was piqued.

"I'll be damned," he replied to my explanation. "Well, boss, you're the foreign correspondent."

In the end, working in my homeland much as I had as a foreign correspondent enabled me to produce some impactful stories. One resulted in a former wife of DC Mayor Marion Barry and four of her henchmen being imprisoned for stealing from the federal government and from some of the District's poorest Black residents. That series, which examined a Black self-help organization called Pride, Inc., was a Pulitzer finalist. Another led to a revolutionary, though short-lived, improvement in one of DC's most miserable public housing projects.

We'd been back in Washington about three years. Carol was comfortably at work as an associate editor at *Smithsonian* magazine. The children enjoyed living in the century-old Cleveland Park neighborhood, where they walked across the street from our roomy house to John Eaton Elementary School. Catherine looked after Adam, and attended a nearby Catholic church, where she also took classes to improve her English.

Everyone was happy.

Except me.

I was desperate to return overseas, yearning for the independence and freedom. The *Post* wasn't going to send me. Bradlee had chosen a new foreign editor and he had his own list of favorites to assign abroad. I wasn't on it.

I put out feelers. Jim Naughton, who was deputy managing editor of the *Philadelphia Inquirer*, told me the San Jose *Mercury News* was looking for a reporter with international experience to open a bureau in Tokyo. Both the "*Merc*" and the "*Inky*" were owned by Knight Ridder Newspapers, the second-largest chain in the country and respected for journalistic integrity.

Knight Ridder operated thirty-two papers, several of them substantial, including the *Detroit Free Press* and the *Miami Herald*. The *Inquirer* and the *Herald* each fielded a few foreign correspondents, and the *Mercury News* was about to enter the fray.

Catering to readers in Silicon Valley, where the semiconductor-fueled economy was booming, the *Merc* led the country in coverage of technology. Under the stewardship of Executive Editor Bob Ingle, the *Merc* was one of the first dailies to establish an online presence. *Time* magazine called it the most tech-savvy newspaper in the country.

The *Mercury News* also ranked near the top in advertising revenue. Annual earnings had reached $341 million, nearly a third of it from job listings. The classified-ad section was colossal: A reader needed as much muscle to hoist the bundle on a Sunday as for the *New York Times*.

Aside from its hefty weight, though, the *Merc* was not the *Times*. Sunday circulation was about 20 percent of the Gray Lady's and it certainly didn't plop each morning on the desks of the high and mighty in Manhattan and Washington. Nor did it compare with the *Post*, the *LA Times* or the *Wall Street Journal*. It was a second-tier newspaper. It was growing fat fast, but mainly because a boomtown was springing up around it.

I walked down a gray-carpeted hallway, feeling like I was traversing the last mile to the electric chair, and was seated in a tiny, windowless room at a desk with a thick booklet of questions on subjects I hadn't thought of for decades. Fighting off pangs of anxiety, I sweated through it. I didn't fail. At least no one told me I did. I half believe I must have flunked the math part, at least, and that Laurel and Hardy shredded those pages.

Tokyo was mine. I was sold. Carol was thrilled, the girls, not so much. Justine and Becca were on the verge of their teens and leaving their Washington friends was not in their plans. Grudgingly and gradually, though, they signed on. Adam, five, boasted to a kindergarten classmate that he was moving to Tokyo. "Oh yeah," the boy replied, "they speak Tokish there."

Most of my *Post* colleagues were shocked when I told them my news. And not in a good way. "The San Jose *Mercury News*? Why?"

Unexpectedly, a few seemed envious. "I wish I had the nerve," one quietly confessed over a congratulatory drink. "Good for you."

I recalled Howard Simons's counsel and knew that, whatever the others thought, the road less traveled was the way for me to go. We rushed to get the kids into school in time for the new term, enrolling the girls at ASIJ, the American School in Japan, and Adam at bilingual Nishimachi. We rented out our house in Cleveland Park. In a surprising and sad blow to us, Catherine said she would not go to Tokyo. Her greatest joy was caring for little children and ours had outgrown their need for her. We found her a job in DC with a young family, much like ours had been when she joined us fourteen years earlier in KL.

On the muggy September night before we left Washington, unable to sleep, I sat on our screened porch, finishing Ezra Vogel's seminal *Japan as Number One*. The Japanese economy in 1982 was a marvel. Japanese companies were flooding the United States with inexpensive, high-quality automobiles and electronics. They were snapping up US landmark properties like Pebble Beach and Rockefeller Center. Americans were jittery. Vogel argued that the chronic trade imbalance resulted from Japan's superior competitiveness. He suggested that studying Japanese behavior since the ignominious World War II defeat might help Americans overcome some of their own societal and economic shortcomings.

In fact, CEOs already were flocking to Tokyo, desperate to learn the secrets of their competitors, like just-in-time manufacturing. Numerous other distinctions, reflecting inbred social traits, did not translate, but the real secret was no secret at all:

Japanese are trained from infancy to consider the group first, with mutual-benefiting collectivism, while Americans are brought up to value individual wants and needs above others.

With Japan rising and the United States slipping, it seemed that forty years after the war, the winner and loser were trading places. That scenario turned out to be wrong. Japan never did become Number One. But the ground did not settle for more than another decade. I would be there to report on the ascent and decline of Japan, Inc.

Setting up news bureaus and homes was becoming old hat. That didn't make it easy, though, in a place that was incredibly expensive and over-crowded. Unable to speak or read Japanese, we were constantly reduced to asking, "Do you speak English," in shops and in the noodle-bowl of streets where we were always lost because addresses, instead of being in numerical order, were based on when the buildings were built.

We knew one person in Japan. Lillias Woods, an auburn-haired Irishwoman with a lilting brogue and a wicked sense of humor, had been a reporter at the *Bangkok Post* when we lived there. Now she was living in Tokyo, working at the *Japan Times*, and was about to marry her Japanese boyfriend.

Lillias was delighted to learn we were moving to Tokyo, and she offered to help us settle in. After we'd spent two weeks at the upscale Okura Hotel, she found us a *manshon* with two tiny, adjacent *apaatos.*

Finding a permanent place took more than a month. Typical Japanese apartments were too cramped and Western-style units on offer in the expat-dominated Azabu-Roppongi neighborhood—the so-called Gaijin Ghetto—were beyond our allowance, generous though it was. Besides, we wanted to live among Japanese, not foreigners.

Drawn by a floorplan posted in the window of a small real-estate agency and combining hand signals and muddled Japlish, we turned up a roomy flat in Minami Aoyama, a lively neighborhood of hip shops and restaurants; Buddhist temples; parks; gardens; and the famed Meiji Jingu, a Shinto shrine with its glorious, springtime River of Irises. The monthly rent was $12,000. Stunning as that was, it was less than many gaijin paid in the ghetto. Such a bargain!

The owner required me to deliver the full year's payment, in advance, in cash, to a nondescript office in a down-market Tokyo neighborhood. Each of the fourteen years we lived in the apartment, I made the same annual pil-grimage, carrying a briefcase of yen, but never meeting the owner or learning his name. My assistant speculated he was a "yakuza," one of Japan's famed, tattoo-covered, criminal gang members.

We were the only gaijin in the building. We hoped this would help us make Japanese friends and improve our language ability. It did neither. Carol and I studied with a tutor and eventually could manage our daily lives, as could Justine and Becca. Adam, benefiting from his bilingual school and his tender age, became the family interpreter, unwilling but available in times of need.

Our next-door neighbor, a stylish woman in her forties, avoided us like COVID-19. I sensed that she sometimes listened at her door for me to leave the shared hallway before she emerged. Occasionally and unavoidably, we did meet. Each time, I bowed and greeted her respectfully—*ohayo gozaimasu* or *konbanwa*—but never got more than the slightest nod in return.

At the start of what turned out to be our fourteenth and final year in Tokyo, I was elected president of the prestigious Foreign Correspondents Club of Japan. A few days later, the neighbor-lady and I came face-to-face while waiting for the apartment elevator. She bowed deeply and congratulated me effusively on my election—in flawless, Middle-Atlantic, American English. Bewildered, I asked her how she knew.

"Oh," she said, "I'm a member of the FCCJ. I lived in New York for years when my brother was a correspondent at the UN."

At the time I was club president, before foreign correspondents became an endangered species, nearly five hundred working journalists were members of the FCCJ, as were hundreds more corporate executives, Japanese and foreign. It was an important destination for anyone seeking exposure around the world. Among guest speakers that year was New York real-estate developer Donald J. Trump. He was on a swing through Asia to thank investors who'd bailed him out of his latest bankruptcies and to show off his new wife, Marla Maples.

Trump entertained us with a lively talk:

He claimed that Tokyo and Hong Kong investors were clamoring for him to build Trump Towers in their cities. (Never happened.)

He accused Japan of doing "one of the great tip-tap-taps [sic] of all time, keeping the ball rolling, giving absolutely nothing, and having the American idiots say, 'thank you.'" U.S. trade negotiators, he told us, were "morons."

A "top businessman," he said, would give Japan thirty days to meet American trade demands. Should it refuse, that person (guess who!) immediately would block the sale of all Japanese products in the United States. How such an impossibility could be accomplished Trump didn't say and my notes of that day indicate that no journalist, myself included, asked. Embarrassing.

At the head table, prior to his speech, Trump leaned toward me as we lunched on lamb chops and asked, "Do you normally eat this well here?" I replied truthfully, that, yes, we did. Only decades later, when I'd learned that he was even more full of himself than I'd gathered that day, did it dawn on me that he probably expected me to say something like, "Heavens no, sir, this is very special. In your honor."

Our neighbor's acknowledgment of my press-club election reflected the importance of brand names in Japanese culture. One may achieve professional distinction, perhaps amass a fortune, but nothing impresses more than a famous corporate name or where one went to college, say, thirty years earlier:

Harvard? *Ah so, desu ka*! *New York Times*? *Ichiban ii, desu yo*! *Associated Press*? *Daijobu desu.* But San Jose *Mercury News*? Ehhh?

While some semiconductor executives recognized the name, most Japanese drew a blank. Frustrated making unreturned phone calls, I came up with an idea. Instead of identifying myself solely with the San Jose paper, perhaps I could call myself the Knight Ridder correspondent. That way, I could say I represented thirty-two newspapers throughout the United States. The problem was that the chain was set up without a central news desk. Each paper handled its own correspondents, although their copy was made available to the group as well as to outside subscribers.

Bob Ingle flinched. His interest, after all, was in building the *Merc*'s identity in Japan, not that of the parent company. Eventually, though, he recognized what I was up against, and he acceded. Coincidentally, the corporation had just established the Tokyo branch of Knight Ridder Financial News, a Bloomberg wannabe. KRFN hired two dozen journalists and opened a substantial newsroom. I decamped from my small office in the Kyodo News agency building and we joined forces, raising the Knight Ridder flag over the Land of the Rising Sun.

My first assistant resigned to have a baby and I placed a help-wanted ad in several English-language dailies, seeking a replacement. Naoko Yamazaki, who had studied journalism at American University in Washington, responded. I snapped her up. She was a masterful reporter, researcher, fixer, interpreter and, for more than a decade, guided me through the fog of Japanese business, politics, and culture.

She made sure I followed the rules. For example, the regimen of the *meishi*, the business card. I must present and receive them respectfully, ceremoniously, with deep bows. I must take a proffered one in two hands and study it. I must never slip it into my pocket—a grave insult. I must insert it with care into a special card case. Naoko and I designed a folded card incorporating the Knight Ridder logo, Japanese on one side and English on the other. All thirty-two newspapers were listed within. The result was helpful, though not in the way I planned:

"Knight Rider," a make-believe American crime fighter who drove a talking muscle car, was popular among Japanese TV viewers at the time. They pronounced it *Naito Laida*. And so, willy-nilly, a "d" was dropped and I became the "Knight Rider" correspondent.

While I was acclimating to the rules for committing journalism in Japan, Carol was undergoing her own trials, like furnishing and equipping our new home while speaking no Japanese. Our bedrooms came with fragrant, grass-scented tatami, so we all slept on the floor and at least there was no need to buy beds. In September, Adam began half-day kindergarten at

relationship in the world, bar none," a misstep by either could have triggered all-out trade war.

American computer makers accused Japanese companies of stealing software and illegally copying hardware designs. In Detroit, angry auto-workers smashed Toyotas with sledgehammers. US beef and rice produc-ers were incensed at being shut out of Japan's lucrative markets, as were suppliers of timber and other construction materials. Citrus growers in Florida and California felt squeezed. Little commerce proceeded without angry disruptions.

Demonizing one's opponent like this is all too easy and, in the long run, unproductive. Americans, certainly, should have learned that from their numerous wars against numerous countries. But they didn't. Whether the fight is on the battlefield or the factory floor, understanding the other side requires effort and may seem counterintuitive. Every government and its army, every company and its boardroom, believes its cause is the only just one. Failing to recognize that about our enemies and competitors has led us into otherwise avoidable bloodshed as well as unnecessary economic duress.

I was granted the time to dig into this critical story. My job, as I saw it, was to help Americans fathom not only what they were up against but *why*. Leaving the daily grind of breaking news to the wire services, I was free to spend my time looking for offbeat stories and those of particular interest to the *Merc*'s readers—technology, computers, computer-chips, cars—looking for angles that others ignored.

I showed up at factories early in the morning, marveling as uniformed workers, on their own time, puffed through calisthenics and chanted company slogans. At futuristic plants, I ogled brilliant-yellow robots cranking out cars and trucks. Assembly-line workers mocked their American counterparts as slovenly and lazy. "I read that Americans don't buy cars made on Mondays because everyone knows the workers are hung over after the weekend," a car-painter at a Mitsubishi plant told me.

A mikan farmer in Shizuoka Prefecture, near Mt. Fuji, told me he worried that his government would buckle under Ronald Reagan's demands for Japan to import American citrus. "We shouldn't do that," he said. "We have our own oranges and they're much sweeter than yours."

While economic stories provided most grist for my mill, I was always looking for stories tucked into nooks and crannies, beyond the regular news flow, stories that might make a reader put down a morning coffee cup and mutter, "Well, I'll be damned!" Or, "Who knew?" What Ben Bradlee at the *Washington Post* referred to as "holy shit" stories.

I reported that entire families, drowning in unmanageable debt and dogged by loan sharks charging as much as 110 percent interest, were committing suicide. I wrote that in the land that gave the world the desktop calculator, the pocket calculator, and the wristwatch calculator, the preferred way to do sums was on the 2,400-year-old abacus.

In a nation of just 700,000 Christians out of a population of 117 million, mainly Shinto and Buddhist practitioners, *Kurisimasu* trees, cards, gifts, songs, street decorations, and parties were as ubiquitous as in the United States.

A piece on how the government-controlled tobacco monopoly promoted cigarette-smoking received an Overseas Press Club of America Award for Excellence.

To mark the fiftieth anniversary of the end of World War II, I traced the US island-hopping campaign across the Pacific—Guam, Saipan, Tarawa, Tinian, Peleliu, the Philippines, and Okinawa, all places that Japan's forces had occupied and which the Americans seized from them in bloody battles. On Iwo Jima, I climbed Mount Suribachi, where AP photographer Joe Rosenthal made the evocative picture of marines raising the American flag.

In Tokyo, I interviewed horrendously scarred, disfigured survivors of US fire-bombing. As many as 130,000 Japanese civilians had been burned alive in the deadliest man-made firestorms in the history of the world.

And, in Hiroshima and Nagasaki, where the two atomic bombs instantly vaporized well over two hundred thousand and tens of thousands more suffered slow, agonizing deaths over the years that followed, I asked survivors whether Japan should become a nuclear power. The answer, without exception, was a resounding *iie*—no!

Carol and I spent many more years living in Tokyo than anywhere else. I found the Japanese people endlessly fascinating and treasure my experiences among them. But the story never became my cup of green tea.

I preferred shirtsleeves to coat and tie and felt more comfortable and more welcomed by the poor and struggling people of developing nations than by the efficient, formal Japanese.

I preferred a triple-canopy jungle to a concrete one.

# Chapter Fifteen

# Filling the Dumpling

Ever since arriving in South Vietnam, in 1967, I dreamed of reporting from China, the cultural wellspring of Asia. I knew that without absorbing a measure of Chinese civilization, my understanding of the continent would remain wanting. Seventeen years had flown by, and I had gotten no closer to the mainland than Hong Kong, still a British colony.

Then I met Michael Browning. Some oversized, sweet-natured men are endearingly called "teddy bears." Michael was one of them. He stood six-and-a-half-feet tall with a barrel chest. Wary of his imposing bulk, he trod with the lightest of steps, almost like a *danseur en pointe*. He spoke with a residual Georgia drawl and his splendid writing was redolent with touches of the classics scholar he was.

Michael was the *Miami Herald* correspondent in Beijing. We began running into each other on major breaking stories around Asia. In November 1984, following the funeral of Indira Gandhi, murdered by two of her Sikh bodyguards, he and I and another correspondent shared a taxi to a Sikh village on the outskirts of Delhi.

After asking the driver to wait for us on the roadside, we threaded our way past compact, neatly arrayed houses, hoping to gauge how the Sikhs felt at this dangerous moment for adherents of their minority faith. The villagers we stopped to speak with were, understandably, ill at ease. We were imposing on them at a moment when they did not want to be questioned. Suddenly, a mob of howling men burst from behind some houses and attacked us. Our terrified driver hit the accelerator of his black and yellow Amby cab and took off. We were abandoned, outnumbered, surrounded, terrified and about to undergo a drubbing.

Several dozen fierce-looking men in long beards and brightly colored turbans pounded us with sticks and fists. The other reporter and I fought back as best we could while Michael, utilizing his overwhelming presence more than fisticuffs, forced the Sikhs to back away for a moment. We ran out of the village and kept going.

A mile or so down the road, we came to a small, one-room police station in a shady grove. We rushed in, spilling our story, displaying our scratches, lumps, and bruises, and demanded that the lone cop on duty go immediately to the village and arrest the miscreants. He stared at us for a moment as though we were loony, which, I suppose, we seemed at that moment, and went back to leafing through a glossy magazine of bosomy Bollywood starlets.

We flagged down a cab and returned to our hotels, modestly molested and fully defeated.

That night, Michael and I met for a beer. We rehashed our close call and then he came up with a novel idea: Wouldn't it be fun for the two of us to switch places? The seed planted, we went our own ways, he back to China and I to Japan. We continued to overlap, in Manila, Seoul, Hong Kong, and each time, the subject of a swap came up. Both our wives were intrigued, and we kept the idea afloat.

Finally, we broached the plan to our editors. We'd both been at our posts for half-a-dozen years and suggested that our newspapers as well as we would benefit from a change of scene. "Surely," we argued, "readers would appreciate a fresh take." Surprisingly, the editors agreed. The plan was that for the next two years, Michael would be based in Tokyo and I in Beijing.

China. At last. I would round out my Asia circle.

On New Year's Day, 1989, the Browning and Simons families shared a dim sum lunch in a Hong Kong restaurant. We exchanged advice and keys and left for our new homes.

The "sleeping giant" of Napoleon's seventeenth-century nightmare was at long last stirring, though not yet fully awake, and I anticipated a semi-sabbatical. I would study Mandarin. I'd travel—the Great Wall, of course; the Forbidden City; the Terracotta Army; the Silk Road and the Islamic Far West; cosmopolitan Shanghai; isolated Tibet. . . . I would write long, vivid features about all the fascinating people I'd meet, their cultures, their food. I'd add the long-missing stuffing to my hollow *bao*—my Chinese dumpling.

The apartment we inherited from the Brownings was toasty when we unlocked the door. The Foreign Ministry, which controlled the Qijiyuan residential compound, made sure the foreign correspondents and diplomats living there got ample steam heat. Ordinary Chinese shivered, huddled around stoves burning coal dust that poisoned air and lungs.

Justine and Becca were at college in the States, and Carol, Adam, and I had plenty of space. The apartment seemed to have been modeled on a utilitarian Soviet design, with high ceilings and tall windows. From the front, we overlooked a broad, busy boulevard and from the rear a dirt courtyard and children's playground. My two-room office was in an adjacent building, steps away.

fills the whole city. The truth is more mundane. Despite the horrors, life goes on. People get up in the morning and wash their faces. They eat. They shop. They talk to their neighbors. Children play."

Late in the afternoon, she called for the third time and said that things had quieted down, and she and Adam were leaving for the hotel. They kept to the backstreet *hutongs*, the narrow alleys and lanes lined with single-story, gray, mud-brick courtyard houses that were the tranquil remnants of Old Peking. When they heard shooting, they ducked into doorways.

I met them midway. They brought me underwear and socks, a fresh shirt, toothbrush, aspirin, a bottle of scotch, and a tripod and camera with a telephoto lens. The desk clerk had been ordered not to allow foreign journalists to rent rooms with a view of Tiananmen. I snagged one by paying a usurious $300 a night. I had insisted on a room with a clear, close view of the square. On the balcony, I mounted the tripod and camera, which I aimed at a long line of tanks. The three of us crouched, like spies, behind a waist-high wall and watched.

Adam, who was twelve at the time, wrote later what he saw:

"I've never witnessed machine-gun fire before. It seemed to me that the army was doing an awful lot of shooting and you had to admire all those people who kept coming out into the streets after bursts of fire. I guess it was dangerous, so it seemed better to be together with Mom and Dad."

Once we were settled into our overpriced room, Carol's thoughts turned to Audrey's bicycle. My magnanimous wife, who has been known to put others' interests before her—and my—own, insisted I retrieve it. By now, the square was an armed camp, swarming with thousands of PLA troops.

At dawn, I slipped out of the hotel; scaled a tall, spear-tipped steel fence; ducked behind three burned-out buses slewed across Chang'an Jie; and took possession of the little bike. Knees akimbo, I began pedaling back toward the hotel. In a heart-thudding moment, I heard chanting from the square. Soldiers were going through morning calisthenics. Abandoning my last shred of common sense, I turned toward the noise. A figure emerged from the morning haze a few feet ahead of me. Helmet pulled low, rifle across his chest, he was running in place. He pretended not to see the crazy foreigner on the bicycle and I pretended not to see him.

During the predawn assault, soldiers had dragged protestors from the square, forced them into a nearby shopping street and shot them. I visited Youdian Hospital, where bloody corpses were stacked in a hallway. A doctor told me that he calculated the death count from ten hospitals at five hundred.

"This is vicious behavior," he whispered in lightly accented English. "My government has gone insane."

Outsiders have never determined how many were killed in and around Tiananmen. Britain's ambassador to China reported ten thousand. My best guess is about seven hundred. Soldiers were among them. Wherever I went, on foot or bicycle, I encountered dead, beaten, and bleeding civilians, and someone would plead, "Tell the world! This is the Chinese Communist Party! This is what China does to its own people! Tell everyone!"

Back at the hotel, around noon, I was writing my contribution to the day's story when Adam shouted for me to come to the balcony. I rushed out as he snapped his version of the photo that would become the icon of the Tiananmen massacre. A lone man, in dark trousers and light-colored shirt, bundles in both hands, walked almost nonchalantly into the road and stopped directly in front of a column of eighteen tanks.

The mechanical giants halted. For perhaps three minutes, the man played cat-and-mouse with the lead tank, dodging left and right when the machine attempted to maneuver around him. He clambered lithely onto the turret and seemed to shout to the soldiers inside. Carol was screaming, uncontrollably, "Get back! Get back!" I stopped breathing.

Machine guns rattled sporadically in the background. The crowd was stunned, deathly silent. At last, someone emerged from the sidelines and pulled the man away. As far as I know, he was never correctly identified, never seen or heard from again.

I snatched the phone and called Michael, dictating something about "the bravest man in the world." Adam wrote about it this way:

"It was one of those things you only read about or see on TV. You admire the guy so much. It was an unbelievable thing that he did, and I'll never forget it."

He retold the story a few years later, in his college application.

We returned to our apartment the next day and called Florida, assuring our mothers that we were safe. Both subscribed to the *Miami Herald.* "I'm not worried, dear," my mother said. "I know how the news always exaggerates." I pretended to be affronted: "Mother, those are my stories you're reading!"

The following morning, Michael and I were in the office, in the building next to our apartment, mulling what that day's story would be, when we were interrupted by a tinny voice amplified over a bullhorn. Miss Lu interpreted: "Do not throw stones. We are your friends. We are the People's Liberation Army. The People's Liberation Army loves the people."

And then, I know no better way to put it, all hell broke loose.

Carol and Adam were back in the apartment. Her notes read, "I watch from the window. Suddenly, the chants are drowned out by machine-gun fire and I hear and feel bullets hitting the brick walls of our apartment. Adam is playing Nintendo with two Japanese children from downstairs. I find one of them, a six-year-old, at the window ledge, grab him, and carry him into the room on the other side of the apartment. I hear glass shattering and all I can think of is the usual, "What's going on here? Why one minute, 'We love the people,' and the next minute, shooting?"

I still have no reasonable answer to Carol's question. But to put the moment in perspective, Beijing—all China, really–was teetering at the edge of pandemonium. A terrifying rumor was racing through the hutongs, the universities, among the intelligentsia, and among correspondents.

Two opposing armies, one from Beijing and one from another part of the country, were facing off. China was about to explode into civil war, into "White Terror." *Báisè Kǒngbù* is a state of social frenzy so extreme that its very mention fills Chinese with dread. It occurred for the first time in 1927, in Shanghai, when nationalist leader Jiang Kai Shek ordered his forces to murder thousands of members of the Chinese Communist Party. Initially called the "Shanghai Massacre," White Terror became a turning point in the Chinese revolution, unleashing a years-long, nationwide purge of Communists. Now, the rumors went, it was about to strike again.

It didn't. Troops cleared the square, scrubbed blood from the paving stones, and the city settled into quiet tension.

With Beijing under martial law, Jim Lilley, the new US ambassador and a thirty-year CIA veteran, ordered all embassy dependents to evacuate. Two charter flights were arriving, and Carol and Adam, like other correspondents' families, were invited to join the flight to the United States. My editor encouraged them to go. We decided that they'd stay.

Many American families bailed out, causing the American School to shut down. Carol and I approached the headmaster of the Japanese school and asked if he would permit Adam to enroll. Sucking his teeth noisily in contemplation, he responded that such a thing never had been done before. A gaijin kid! The headmaster doubted that our fair-haired boy's Japanese was good enough. Test him, we urged.

He did and Adam passed.

For the remainder of the school year, he was the lone—and often lonely—non-Japanese. Treated initially as a curiosity, then largely shunned, he found the experience frustrating. He began complaining of morning stomachaches.

On his first report card, his teacher wrote, "Adam has many opinions, which he freely expresses." This was not meant as a compliment. Then came the moment that changed everything for our boy. His school's basketball team, in its season-ending game, was tied with a rival (whose nationality I have forgotten). A teammate passed the ball to Adam, by several inches the tallest player on the court. He shot. And scored. And won the game. The Japanese parents and students in the bleachers—led by Carol and me—leapt to their feet, cheering wildly. Adam's teammates were thrilled. They high-fived and pounded him on the back. He was a hero. He was accepted.

We wondered if foreign correspondents would be expelled from China, but the government held back. Ousting journalists would further alienate Western governments, many of which had responded to the massacre with unbridled outrage. President George H. W. Bush, vacationing at Kennebunkport, Maine, had issued a lackluster response. While he "deplored" the use of armed force against peaceful demonstrators, he had "hope that China will rapidly return to political and economic reform so that this relationship, so important to both our peoples, can continue its growth."

Then Deng appeared on TV, so stern, so harsh and unyielding, praising his troops for "their sacrifice" while utterly ignoring the suffering of the civilian population, that I realized Bush was daydreaming. Or, perhaps, he was treading lightly for personal reasons. He had been the first US ambassador to China and retained numerous high-level contacts. Several of his family members conducted lucrative business there.

"China has fallen into a deep, black pit and it may be many years before the light shines on this country again," I wrote. But I got it wrong. Deng and his successors recouped the support of pragmatic Chinese by elevating economic development to such a massive scale that previously deprived people could now dramatically improve their living conditions. Deng was adopting the teachings I'd learned about two decades before, the same ones Chinese technocrats had brought home from Singapore's Lee Kuan Yew: An authoritarian regime that delivers sufficient wages, food, and consumer goods to its people can command their loyalty for many years.

Modified versions of Lee's advice have worked in other Asian states, explained by what British political analyst Hans Kundnani at the peak of the COVID-19 epidemic termed "authoritarian residue." Residual or not, autocracy offers leaders the advantage of producing results in a hurry, free of opinion, debate, and voting. And, not only in China and other parts of Asia, but in the United States and elsewhere in Europe as well, rising numbers of citizens seem willing to pay the price.

# Chapter Sixteen

# The Other Chinese

Calm returned to Beijing, and with it, Michael Browning. No longer could he bear to ignore the China story, which the Tiananmen Massacre had driven onto the world's front pages. He felt compelled to come back. I was reluctant to leave, but I understood how he felt, and we agreed to cut short our exchange.

Once we got back to Tokyo, the American Chamber of Commerce in Japan, the ACCJ, hired Carol as its director of publications, a plum, fulltime position. Gone was the hectic bicycling among her freelance jobs then racing home to start dinner before taking off her coat. Now, over relaxed meals of Asian-American dishes of her interpretation, we exchanged our latest intelligence on Japan-US relations. Our apartment was quiet. Both girls were still away at college and Adam was in his first year of high school, returning home well into the evening. When we noticed that he reeked of cigarette smoke, we quickly established that he'd become a mah-jongg parlor habitue'. He proudly showed us the yen he won. This was remarkable for a fourteen-year-old gaijin. But we were not particularly pleased with his becoming so comfortable in Japan that he'd be unable to function elsewhere, a familiar pattern among long-term expat kids. In any case, he became bored being an "only child" in our household and, after a year, shipped out to a boarding school in the States.

We found on our return from China that Japan, yesterday's unchallenged Asian giant, was being hammered by a stunning economic reversal. The nineties were booming almost everywhere across Asia. Economists and political scientists forecast a "Pacific Century." Like most observers, I had anticipated that Japan would lead the parade. But it was not to be.

Japan's soaring economy went the way of most bubbles. It burst and two decades would be lost before it recovered, though never reaching its former, giddy heights. The world was shocked, I as much as anyone. A handful of international experts for years had warned of the dangers inherent in Japan's excessively interdependent *keiretsu*, conglomerates of cross-shareholding manufacturers, supply-chain partners, distributors, and financiers. But the naysayers were ignored.

Tipped over by evaporating wealth, a snaking lineup of made-in-Japan dominoes scattered and fell. Hardest hit when the overheated air went out of real estate, banks, stocks, automobiles, electronics, and other manufacturing were those who'd given most.

*Sararimen,* the loyal foot soldiers of postwar Japan, who committed body and soul to a single employer in return for a stable salary and lifetime security, were devastated. These were men branded with the company trademark. At their weddings, their bosses were the guests of honor, seated at the center of the head table. The first time I wandered through Aoyama Bochi, the elegant, cherry blossom–shaded cemetery near our apartment, I was astonished to see employment records chiseled into tombstones.

In 1989, when we left Tokyo for Beijing, salarymen were honored, mythic, ten-foot giants, pumped up with nationalist, corporate, and personal pride. One year later, many were limp, deflated, pathetic figures, slouching their days away on park benches, dark-suited and necktied, too humiliated to admit to their wives and children that they'd been sacked.

The underclasses—the modest numbers who had scraped by on menial labor and part-time jobs during the fat years—were degraded even further. As the highest real-estate prices in the world plummeted and work evaporated, some were reduced to living on the streets. Cardboard cartons, like those I'd visited in Jakarta years before, became their shelters; threadbare shoes neatly aligned alongside.

The well-off took some hits, too. A friend once had shown me around the exclusive Mitsukoshi department store in Ginza, saying she was happy to pay inflated prices because "I enjoy the salesgirls bowing and handing me the beautifully wrapped packages." Now, she admitted ruefully, she searched for bargains.

In an attempt to untangle this knotty string of events, I roamed from Tokyo to Sapporo; Yamaguchi to Osaka; Chibu to Niigata. Everywhere I went, I found worry and despair caused by the unwanted change.

As the economy shattered, the country's cozy political arrangement broke apart, too. The Liberal Democratic Party (LDP), which in fact was distinctly conservative and authoritarian, lost a general election for the first time since 1955. The LDP's greatest legacy had been a postwar social contract binding politicians, elite bureaucrats, major companies, and workers in a multifaceted community, all for the greater good. This public/private cooperative had rebuilt the shattered nation in record time. Now, at the very moment Japan was poised to surpass the United States for world economic dominance, order and confidence crumpled into confusion and doubt. In the next decade, from

1990 to 2000, eight prime ministers shuffled in and out of office, unable to devise a strategy to lead the nation out of the doldrums.

And, as politics wobbled, so did social norms. Women struck out on their own. During my early years in Japan, the "Office Lady" (OL) was a standard fixture in every private-sector and government establishment. Submissive, dowdy in blue skirt, matching vest, and white blouse, the OL bowed, ran errands, and prepared tea for the men. She was expected, required really, to resign once she married. By the mid-nineties, however, as my assignment was drawing down, women were moving on to desk jobs, even, on occasion, to executive positions. Good for them. Not so good for men. As more women entered or rose in the workforce, more men were let go. Divorce, though low by international standards, rocketed as women rejected the burdens and boredom of marriage, in which they played a second-class, overworked role. Among middle-aged couples, the divorce rate shot up 300 percent in a decade. Younger women, no longer embarrassed to be single at twenty-five, were saying thanks but no thanks—kekkou desu—to proposals. Weddings hit their lowest level since the end of World War II. Government figures revealed that the number of fifty-year-olds who had never married doubled for women to 10.6 percent and quadrupled for men to 20.1 percent. Births plummeted to an unprecedented nadir of 1.4 children for each Japanese woman, leaving Japan ranked 185 out of the world's 195 countries. The population was shrinking, growing older faster than anywhere else in the world. The Japanese even created a word, Kōreikashaka, for the phenomenon. The number of people aged sixty-five and older nearly quadrupled. More Japanese were dying than being born. More adult diapers were sold than baby nappies.

Production muscle atrophied as more Japanese retired than entered the workforce. Unlike most other advanced countries, homogeneous Japan always had barred the door to immigrants. Not until 2020 did the government begin granting decade-long work visas to foreigners. What the new influx will mean over the long term is unclear, but it at least buys Japan time to work on its problems as the world order shifts profoundly toward China.

Having spent my first two post-China years thrashing through Japan's economic tsunami, I began rethinking an idea that had collected dust in a rear compartment of my mind since Journalism-School. My first class reporting project, self-assigned, was on men who'd recently fled China for New York's Chinatown and were living and working in wretched conditions in *Meiguo, the Beautiful Country.*

These men were a tiny part of a huge, worldwide community of so-called Overseas Chinese. In addition to the mainland's 1.5 billion people, 56 million ethnic Chinese live beyond its borders, the vast majority in Southeast Asian countries. Together, these Overseas Chinese, or OC, outnumber the populations of two hundred of the world's nations. I'd long been curious about them, many stunningly wealthy and powerful in their adopted homelands. My interest was rekindled by our year in their motherland.

Post-Tiananmen China picked up speed as it sailed out of the doldrums, and I speculated that the immense diaspora would play a major role in its future. Concurrently, powered by rapid industrialization, the four "Asian Tigers"—Hong Kong, Singapore, Taiwan, and South Korea—leapfrogged quickly from Third World to developing and then to the realm of high-income. All but South Korea had large OC populations.

The Tigers' stunning success opened the way to less dramatic, but still remarkable, advances by the four "Tiger Cub" economies—Indonesia, Malaysia, Thailand, and Vietnam. Even the Philippines, its whiplashed people sorely disappointed by Cory Aquino's failure to make their dreams come true, benefited to a degree. All were home to numerous ethnic Chinese.

The Overseas Chinese are not a homogeneous monolith, but diverse, with widespread linguistic and geographic origins. Now China was reaching out to them systematically, in a well-coordinated campaign. The central government in Beijing as well as the provincial towns from which the OC had emigrated were calling. The effort, based on intra-Chinese understanding, was proving extremely successful. Yet, outsiders were paying little or no attention.

Once I recognized the scope of the story, I asked to have Michael Zielenziger, an aggressive and motivated *Mercury News* reporter with a deep interest in Asia, join me. "Z" and I traveled separately for months over thousands of miles through Southeast Asia, China, and a number of US cities, interviewing scores of ethnic Chinese. What we learned amazed us. The loosely linked but worldwide network of expatriates was forging a powerful economic alliance with China. The reunited family was on track to eclipse American and Japanese influence across Asia. This was big news.

How and why it was happening had a multi-layered explanation. Overseas Chinese, whose ancestors for centuries had flooded into Southeast Asia in search of opportunity, long sought to buy acceptance and to demonstrate loyalty to their adopted homelands by investing locally. As a result, despite their being distinct minorities, their family-owned banks and mercantile companies controlled the economies of Indonesia, Malaysia, Thailand, and the Philippines. In Hong Kong, Taiwan, and Singapore, their power was nearly absolute, not only economically but politically as well.

Despite their efforts to fit in, though, ambitious and hardworking OC were envied, resented, and feared as a fifth column by native Southeast Asians. The indigenous populations attacked them in frequent, violent outbursts. Once China became Communist and Indochina followed, Southeast Asians worried anew that their ethnic Chinese neighbors would turn against their adopted countries and reestablish primary loyalty to the motherland.

The feared treachery didn't happen. Still, China was calling, and OC were picking up the phone. Americans and other Westerners were blissfully ignorant of the development. Z and I set out to educate our readers. Greater China—mainlanders plus outlanders—was becoming the leading force in the dawning Pacific Century.

The result was a four-day series that the *Mercury News* headlined, "Enter the Dragon," a spin-off of Bruce Lee's 1973 martial arts movie hit.

In the series, which was a 1994 Pulitzer Prize runner-up, we wrote that the Overseas Chinese were capitalizing on their *guanxi*, connections, and responding positively to China's appeals based primarily on promises of financial rewards and, secondarily, on ethnic loyalty. They were investing eight of every ten dollars streaming into the mainland.

Tellingly, the flood began shortly after the Tiananmen Massacre. While Westerners panicked and ran, Overseas Chinese rushed in, fathoming Chinese thinking in ways other outsiders didn't. They intended to help modernize China's economy. They believed that crushing budding democracy in Beijing could be manipulated to hasten market reform, not slow it down. They were right.

In China's coastal enclaves, where many overseas families had roots, provincial organizers launched local investment drives to attract those who'd emigrated and become tycoons abroad. The expats opened their wallets and were repaid handsomely. Some of their money was invested openly while much was passed under the table.

Few elsewhere seemed to know or, if they did know, they didn't care. Washington and Tokyo paid very little attention to the Overseas Chinese, whose quiet networks moved more aggressively and effectively than any government's. US Undersecretary of Commerce Jeffrey Garten was a rare exception. He got it. An old Asia hand who previously had worked for an Overseas Chinese–owned shipping firm in Hong Kong, Garten told Z, "We have to pay attention to the Overseas Chinese as an economic network, a commercial network, and as a very important new and growing phenomenon in the world economy. A better understanding of Overseas Chinese and a more strategic approach to developing closer ties with them is absolutely critical."

In some Asian countries, old, nagging fears of Chinese expansionism reignited as Beijing began spending increasing amounts of its OC-sourced income on building up its military. Economist Kenichi Ohmae told me that as Japan continued to suffer economic stagnation, it was growing concerned that China would pull the Overseas Chinese—and, with them, their countries of residence—"back into its sphere of influence."

In Manila, Philippines Secretary of the Interior Rafael Alunan conceded that, "We're not just concerned, we're awed. China will clearly be the major player in Asia in a decade or so, and we see the Overseas Chinese as part and parcel of the whole package."

In Bangkok, Choedchu Sophonpanich, a member of the family who owns Bangkok Bank, the largest financial institution in Southeast Asia, and whom I'd known for many years, explained the duality. Beyond financial profit, he said, Overseas Chinese also were motivated by cultural ties.

"To most of us," he said as we slurped a noodle lunch in his favorite Chinese restaurant on bustling Silom Road, "China is just a good place to make quick profits. But it is a special place, too, because of culture, language—roots, I guess you'd say." His bank had opened its first China branch in the port city of Shantou.

"Why there?" I asked.

"Because it's where my grandfather came from to Bangkok in the late nineteenth century."

Much as diasporic Jews, whatever their politics, *kvell* over Israel's achievements or Boston Irish raise a *slainte* when Republic of Ireland XI win an important match, ethnic Chinese, no matter what they may think of the Communist leadership, take *xǐyuèin* in the successes of the motherland. Washington Sy Cip, a Manila-based Chinese-American, who owned the largest accounting firm in Southeast Asia, put it to me this way, "It's not that we're loyal to China, but we take a certain pride in China's accomplishments as stories keep coming out on how China's economy will surpass the United States' in twenty years or so."

Overall, our reporting proved perceptive. With a 2021 GDP of $14.3 trillion, China's wealth today is second only to the US $21.4 trillion. Japan, so recently in second place, fell to a distant third, at $5 trillion.

But Z and I missed the boat on a critical point. We anticipated that as mainlanders grew wealthier and better educated, under the influence of their expatriate cousins they would demand, and receive, a more democratic nation. Former Secretary of State James Baker shared our optimism. China's economic reforms, he wrote enthusiastically, "would in the long run lead to political liberalization, the surest way to ensure human rights for all." Z and I added that closer ties among the world's ethnic Chinese would make a positive contribution to that lofty goal.

Baker was wrong and so were we. China continues to abuse human rights advocates. Police raid their homes and offices, arrest them, subject family members to surveillance, harassment, and detention, and restrict freedom of movement. Once wide-open Hong Kong is being buried beneath Beijing's increasingly oppressive domination. Buddhist Tibetans as well as Muslim Uyghur, Kazakh, and other minorities endure surveillance, indoctrination, and imprisonment in a vast gulag. Despite the influx of dollars from OC citizens of democratic societies into its capitalist-lite marketplace, China remains repressive. The Overseas Chinese largely ignore the issue.

At the same time, the Communist government has elevated living standards to a level I wouldn't have believed possible during my stay in China three decades ago. Urban housing, shops, and restaurants compare favorably with those anywhere in the West, as do health care and education.

But the human rights we so optimistically anticipated? Millions of Chinese are too busy hunting for parking spaces for their new cars and admiring their new outfits in the mirrors of their new apartments to worry about what they don't have.

## Chapter Seventeen

# Time to Go

By 1996 our three children were living in the United States, Justine and Becca working and Adam at college. As much as we still loved our lives in Asia, we'd also come to realize how much we had deprived ourselves and our own parents and we didn't want to continue the separation over another generation. Both of our fathers had died while we were abroad, and our mothers were in their eighties and nineties.

It was time to return home.

As we rode down the elevator of our Tokyo apartment building for the last time in fourteen years, we held each other and Carol shed a few tears. And that was that.

*Time* magazine had offered me a position in Washington, covering the State Department. I took it. But not before Editor-in-Chief Norman Pearlstein warned me about the perils of switching from a daily paper to a weekly newsmagazine.

"It's not for everyone," Pearlstein cautioned during a chat in his vast, Persian-carpeted suite in Manhattan's Time & Life building. I reminded him that, only a few years earlier, he'd been a correspondent in Asia for the *Wall Street Journal*.

"As I said," Pearlstein reiterated without further comment, "it's not for everyone."

He was right. Both *Time* and State were poor fits for me. I'd known for years that *Time*'s group journalism didn't appeal to me, but I failed to think it through to its logical conclusion—that I'd be unlikely to deliver the kind of reporting the magazine required. I was far too accustomed to flying solo to find happiness as a member of the flock in a newsroom—any flock, any newsroom.

As for the beat, having spent decades observing US foreign policy at work in the field, I had reasoned that Foggy Bottom would be a logical next stop. Wrong again. My interest as a foreign correspondent focused on how policy affected the lives of real people, not how it was organized and the sausage made.

The headquarters of the State Department, the Truman Building, is a huge granite block, shot through like Swiss cheese with a bewildering catacomb of blank hallways. As in my aimless ramble through Calcutta's Writers' Building, I spent my days shuffling from one bureaucrat's office to another's, seeking to extract fine-grained policy points they'd rather I didn't know. I wrote files that an editor in New York meshed with other reporters' files and massaged into a finished story for the magazine.

After a miserable year, I left. For the first time in my adult life, I was unemployed. I began suffering crippling panic attacks and seeing a therapist. It was clear that my only option was to go off on my own, as a freelancer. Emphasis on the free. From friends who were independent journalists, I knew that this life could be difficult—long periods without work, trifling pay, no health insurance or other benefits. Fortunately, Carol had just become managing editor of *AARP* magazine and was able to fill the voids. We owned our house. The kids were settled. There was no pressing reason for me not to take the risky step.

T. D. Allman graciously introduced me to Oliver Payne, an editor at *National Geographic*. It turned out to be a long-lasting gift. I would work happily with Ollie for the next fifteen years. Over lunch, he and Editor-in-Chief Bill Allen offered me an investigative feature assignment that would take me back to my old stomping grounds.

Indonesia was on fire.

The two explained that what they had in mind would not be a standard *Geographic* place piece. It had all the essential ingredients of a great news story: In addition to gross ecological mismanagement, there was corruption, greed, politics, opportunism.

My kind of story.

Millions of peasant farmers, following the ages-old slash-and-burn agriculture system, were setting fields and forests ablaze. The practice leaves a rich layer of ash that helps fertilize future crops. Contained, the fires are productive. But industrial producers of palm oil had taken over. The agribusiness moguls clear-cut the life-giving rainforest before torching the landscape and then carpeting it with nutrient-sapping monocrop plantations. The vast scope of their operations had raised a pall of smoke so dense and widespread that seventy-five million people in eight nations, a territory larger than all of Europe, were choking on the fumes, growing sick and dying.

Of course, this being Indonesia, corrupt politicians, from President Suharto and his family on down, were raking in huge payoffs by selling land rights to the plantation operators, most of them Overseas Chinese from Indonesia and neighboring Malaysia.

Like so many other general-interest magazines, the *Geographic*, with its famous yellow-framed cover, was groping for survival as its readership aged and shrank. "Old Yeller" needed change, a new direction. There were just so many times it could run pieces on the latest broken vase or tarnished necklace uncovered in King Tut's tomb. Allen was ready to try harder news stories and the Indonesian fires, a worldwide environmental disaster, seemed an ideal place to begin.

The assignment came with an unexpected advantage. As a *Geographic* writer, I discovered, I was less threatening to interviewees than I'd been as a newspaper reporter. Many of the people I met recalled reading stories as children about elephants or ancient Rome and ogling photographs of bare-breasted "native" women. They were happy to talk.

"Ah, yes, *National Geographic*. That's how I learned English!"

There were other benefits as well at a time when most news organizations were tightening their belts: plenty of time, no-holds-barred travel, a generous expense account and one of the highest pay scales in print journalism. I couldn't ask for anything better.

In the late summer of 1997, photographer Michael Yamashita and I flew to the Indonesian province of South Kalimantan, on the island of Borneo. Mike was a star in the *Geographic*'s galaxy of world-class photojournalists. He also happened to be a volunteer fireman in Chester Township, his New Jersey hometown. A perfect fit for this story.

We stepped off the plane on a brutally hot, soggy day into an environmental nightmare. What passed for air was a throat-burning, eye-smarting stew of toxic gases and floating ash that coated buildings gray and made it impossible for us to breathe normally and see beyond a few yards.

Our first stop was a hardware store, where we bought heavy-duty industrial respirators. We hired an interpreter and a driver with a four-wheel-drive vehicle and headed south toward the inferno. There were no hotels and very few houses. We knocked on the door of an isolated house and the kindly homeowner, taking pity on the crazy *orang asing* going to, instead of away from, a life-threatening hazard, invited us to spend the night.

By the next afternoon, we were well into a landscape straight from Hell. For as far as I could see in the murk, the rolling land was baked crisp and dusted with white ash, like an immense, sugar-flecked, chocolate sheet cake. Tendrils of smoke curled from the peaty earth into a chrome-yellow sky. Charred and shattered tree trunks pierced the horizon here and there, lonely sentinels watching over what only days before had been dense, green rainforest.

Freshly cut dirt roads slashed the terrain like raw, red scars and the stillness of the scorching afternoon was broken by gear-gnashing trucks, whipping up veils of dust. The vehicles were hauling colossal tree trunks to the nearby Java Sea coast. From there, teak and other prime hardwoods would sail to construction-crazed China. Lesser-quality trees would be peeled into plywood.

We came across a small, balding, bare-chested, and bare-footed man. He wore a pair of shorts so thoroughly patched that determining the original material was impossible. He was squatting on his haunches in a scorched field, planting bright-green cassava seedlings behind his home, a crude box he'd nailed together from rough, raw timber. In a few days he, his wife, and their three children would poke shallow holes elsewhere in the still-warm soil and drop in rice seed.

His name was Abdur Rani. In this grotesque landscape, I saw only death and destruction. But Abdur saw opportunity, a new cycle, life itself. Fire was a regular marker on life's clock to Abdur, a member of one of Kalimantan's half dozen Dyak tribes. He counted his age, forty-one, by the annual fires his parents and then he had set since his birth.

He seemed to thrive on smoke. As if there wasn't more than enough enveloping us, he sucked deeply on a yellowish *kretek*, the Indonesian cigarette blended from tobacco and fragrant cloves. As *kreteks* burn, the cloves snap and crackle, releasing a spicy scent I enjoyed whenever I visited the country. To me, they were redolent of the romantic East. The smoke was sweet on the tongue but harsh on the lungs, just as the fires were on the Earth's lungs.

Abdur was oblivious.

"Fire is good," he said through our interpreter, who kneaded Abdur's Dayak dialect into standard Indonesian, for his own comprehension, then into English, for ours. "Burning this land means we'll have enough food to fill our bellies for the year. Fire means a better life for us. More fire means more clear land, and more clear land means more planting and more food."

And more palm oil for the world.

Which means more soap, more bread, pastries, cereal, peanut butter, chocolate bars, salad dressings and margarine, more shampoo, cosmetics, cleaning products, and biodiesel.

Which in turn means even more destruction of the rain forests, more erosion, leaching, soil compaction, decreased soil fertility, diminished natural plant regeneration, interruption of hydrological cycles, water salinization, waterlogging, flooding, and drought.

The unprecedented intensity and extent of the 1997 fires—The World Wildlife Fund called it "a planetary disaster"—were set in play by drought the previous year, Indonesia's most severe in half a century. The drought resulted from a monsoon that had been stunted by an extreme El Niño. This periodic warming of Pacific Ocean waters reverses global weather patterns, substituting dry seasons for rainy, calm for storms, heat for cold. Abdur hadn't heard of El Niño. He did know, though, that the delayed monsoon gave him longer, better conditions for burning.

Indonesia's government blamed peasants like Abdur for the horrific disaster raging through the archipelago and across all of Southeast Asia. But that muddled the truth. Only large-scale industrialists had the capacity to spread that much deadly pollution through that much territory and to denude the rain forest so quickly.

I knew from earlier reporting in Indonesia that the most powerful of these colossal land-concession holders was a droopy-eyed, mustachioed fellow by the name of Mohamad "Bob" Hasan. The son of an Overseas Chinese tobacco trader, Hasan, like many OCs seeking to assure their future in Indonesia, had converted to Islam and adopted a Muslim name. More importantly for his well-being, he ingratiated himself with Suharto and became the president's weekly golfing partner. During the current fire crisis, he was acting as Suharto's spinmeister.

Mike and I called on Hasan at his palatial Jakarta home. Wearing an egg-yolk-yellow silk shirt, black trousers, no socks, and soft black Italian loafers, he received us in an air-conditioned living room the size of a basketball court. He was a charmer, well suited for the task with which I presented him: rationalizing the fires and denying his own and his golf buddy's complicity.

His own landholdings, he told us, comprised a mere two million acres (twice the size of Rhode Island). Environmentalists assured me that the figure was but a fraction of Hasan's holdings. He skipped nimbly into an impressive recitation of the laws limiting forest-exploitation, followed by a brazen fairy tale of his own creation, "Because of my friendship with the president, Indonesia has become one of the world's leaders in reforestation."

The residual smoke in my lungs helped me force a cough to disguise what otherwise would have been a laugh. Mike and I knew this was a sick joke. We had tracked the fires for a month, covering twelve hundred miles on foot, by car, truck, boat, ferry, and chartered plane. We wore our rubber masks whenever possible, but there were times when the heat made it intolerable. Our faces streamed with sweat that blended with the thick dust to slather us in a muddy red paste.

A doctor I had interviewed in Pangkalanbuun, in central Kalimantan, said the official air pollution index in this town of two hundred thousand people was the equivalent of each of them smoking between four and eight packs of *kreteks* a day. Some leader in reforestation!

Shortly after I returned home, my head began to feel like it had been stuffed with cotton. My hearing was muffled, as though I was submerged in a swimming pool. I grew dizzy and fell down the stairs, breaking an ankle. A doctor guessed that pollution had affected the inner ear. After two months, my symptoms cleared up and my ankle healed.

As I finished writing, a different kind of crisis swept across Indonesia, more troublesome to Suharto's survival than the forest fires. Indonesia, like other Asian Tigers at the time, was unable to absorb all the investment money pouring in. The economy collapsed. The rupiah dropped like a stone, losing 80 percent of its value. Overnight, food, fuel, and other basics became unaffordable. The public panicked and rioting swept Jakarta.

After thirty-two years in office, Suharto was forced to resign.

Although the *Geographic* edition that would carry my story was already at the printer, Bill Allen took the extraordinary and expensive step of ordering it held so I could update the piece with the dramatic news. Shrewd and manipulative to the end, Suharto managed to avoid trial by having himself certified mentally incapable. He died ten years later, at age eighty-six, in disgrace.

Readers responded to the fire story with positive letters. I took on more assignments, many based on my own proposals. One such story stirred interest well beyond the *Geographic*'s normal sphere. Published in November 2002, it opened with this:

A month or so before Christmas, three people, most likely male, walked into a crowded shopping mall in Oklahoma City. Dressed as maintenance workers and carrying plant sprayers, they strolled among the holiday shoppers, tending to the potted plants that decorated the gaily lit corridors. A short time later, their work complete, the three walked to mall exits and vanished into the night. At that moment two other teams were doing the same thing at malls in Atlanta and Philadelphia.

At 7 p.m. On December 9, the President of the United States met secretly with his National Security Council—which included the national security advisor, the secretary of defense, and the chairman of the joint chiefs of staff. The President stunned them with his opening remarks: "The Centers for Disease Control (CDC) has confirmed that at least one case of smallpox—and maybe as many as 20—have occurred among civilians in Oklahoma City. . . . Presumably, this disease has been deliberately introduced and [is] the result of a bioterrorist attack on the United States."

As the President spoke, a laboratory in Oklahoma confirmed 20 cases of smallpox and said it suspected 14 more. Nine other cases were reported in Atlanta and seven in Philadelphia. Federal and state authorities immediately swung into action, and within 24 hours FBI agents were combing the streets of Oklahoma City. At the White House, the deputy secretary of health and human services confirmed that the only two known sources of smallpox were at the CDC's heavily guarded repository in Atlanta and the Vector laboratory outside Novosibirsk, Russia.

Intelligence revealed that a former Vector scientist, an expert in smallpox, had left Russia and was believed to be in Iraq. By the next week, tens of thousands of Americans showing symptoms, or imagining them, were overwhelming hospital emergency rooms. Television news repeatedly ran footage of a tearful mother, toddler in arms, pleading for vaccine as a policeman shoved her back into the crowd.

Meanwhile, chaos swamped those who were trying to manage the crisis. Congress and state legislatures, the FBI and CIA, fire and police departments, the Defense Department and National Guard, public health agencies and private physicians—all lost valuable time and energy in the confusion over procedures and turf.

By December 15, officials had confirmed 2,000 cases in 15 states, with more in Canada, Mexico, and Britain. The death toll had hit 300. A week later there were 16,000 cases in half the states in the country, and a thousand people had died—200 from reactions to vaccine. Cities were paralyzed as millions tried to flee the epidemic. Vaccine supplies were now exhausted, and violence was rampant in the streets. Health authorities projected that by February there would be three million cases of smallpox in the United States. One million Americans would be dead, with no end in sight.

GAME OVER!

The doomsday scenario was, in fact, a game. It was played in June 2001— three months before the 9/11 attacks in New York and at the Pentagon— around a table at Andrews Air Force Base in Maryland.

Former Senator Sam Nunn assumed the role of president, with other prominent figures playing cabinet members, military leaders, heads of federal agencies, state officials, and journalists. The point of the exercise, code-named "Dark Winter," was to see how prepared the United States was to deal with a biological weapons attack.

So how did it go? Who won and who lost? Soon after the exercise, Nunn testified before Congress, the real one, about the failures Dark Winter had exposed. America was critically short of vaccine, Nunn warned. It had not trained top officials, planned a coordinated response, built an adequate public health infrastructure, educated the public or the media, practiced the few plans that were in place, or ranked bioterror as a high national priority.

Although there are obvious differences, the parallels between Dark Winter and the COVID-19 pandemic, two decades later, are striking. Early in the COVID-19 crisis, President Trump accused China of cooking up the virus at a lab in Wuhan, planning to use it as a weapon.

Trump never proved the claim, but he may have been right. China, like the United States, Russia, and very likely a number of other countries, has experimented with biological, chemical, and nuclear weapons for years. Together, they are known as weapons of mass destruction (WMD).

A few months before Nunn and his associates played Dark Winter, *Geographic* photographer Lynn Johnson and I had set out to research a story on the threats humanity faced from WMD. I had proposed the idea to Ollie Payne with little more to go on than gut feeling.

Lynn and I roamed some of the world's darkest and most chilling corners, in Russia, Kazakhstan, Ukraine, Iran, Japan, and the United States. At the time—late winter, 2000—ordinary people barely paid attention to WMD, hardly aware they existed.

Then came 9/11 and the realization that almost anything could be made into a WMD. The airplane assaults on the World Trade Center and the Pentagon were quickly followed by the discovery of anthrax spores in letters mailed to politicians and media figures.

The sobering lessons of Dark Winter jumped to the top of government agendas around the world. Officials scrambled to prepare for, and prevent, the next attack. That came after our story.

In all the places we visited, we searched out those who'd already suffered from one kind of WMD attack or another: nuclear, chemical, and biological. Some of what we saw and heard was unbearable: freakish human fetuses preserved in jars of formaldehyde in Kazakhstan, cancer-riddled Mormon men and women in Utah, two middle-aged brothers with the minds of infants living with their aged mother in an isolated village on the Russian steppe.

In Iran, Sasan Safavian, gaunt and fragile, spoke to me with excruciating difficulty, his words choked off by a racking cough that forced claws of pain deep into his chest. Seated on the floor, propped upright by a cushion against the wall of his Tehran apartment, he held a bony hand to the sunlight filtering through a curtained window to shield his sensitive eyes. He'd lost forty pounds in eighteen months.

Safavian said he began dying in 1983 when, as a sixteen-year-old ambulance volunteer, he was caught in two poison-gas attacks unleashed against Iran by Iraqi dictator Saddam Hussein. "Frogs and birds were lying dead all over the ground," he said. "My throat was bleeding, and blood-filled blisters appeared all over my body. . . . We had no gas masks, and we hadn't been trained. We didn't believe one Muslim country could use chemical weapons against other Muslims."

In Sverdlovsk, Russia, eighty-year-old Olga Vyatkina leaned heavily on a cane, staring at the snowbanked gravestone where she had buried her only child, Alexander, when he was twenty-seven. He was one of sixty-eight known victims of the world's worst outbreak of inhalational anthrax.

The words were playground-childish but, repeated endlessly by him and his backers, they stuck.

But, for reporters to have injected so-called "balance" into reporting on Trump's irresponsibility and disrespect for the nation would have been professionally and morally reprehensible. This raises a profound question: How should a reporter cover a president who lies compulsively?

The answer, I believe, is obvious: Record the lies and report them. Let them do the talking. In Trump's case, there was so much false material that the journalist's thumb on the balance scale was overkill. The reporter, as TV's dour Sergeant Joe Friday used to remind us, had no need to embellish. "Just the facts, Ma'am."

The best stories tell themselves. Pete Carey, Katherine Ellison, and I didn't destroy Ferdinand Marcos. The facts did. A journalist's gratuitous assessment is a turnoff for those readers locked onto one side of an issue and is unnecessary for those on the opposing side. Staying above the fray is today, perhaps more than ever before, the sine qua non of the journalist's job.

As the first rough draft of history, often written under pressure and on deadline, journalism may be expected to be riddled with errors. It is remarkable they are as few as they are. Indeed, a reasoned case may be made that the so-called first draft of history, reported by an intimate observer and printed before the cake goes into the oven, may be closer to the truth than before it is baked and served years later in books.

History books, with the original news sources relegated to footnotes, introduce previously unknown information and undoubtedly provide fuller, more thought-through accounts and analyses. But they are of necessity accounts viewed through the kaleidoscope of time, twisted and turned to accentuate winners and diminish losers.

"History is written by the victors," is a quote often attributed to Winston Churchill, who wrote and made a lot of history. Or, twisted a turn or two more by Harvard English Professor Louis Menand, "History is not facts, but the meaning of facts."

As with the existential tree falling in the existential forest with no one to see or hear it, a good historian, like a good detective, can reconstruct a reasonable version of what happened without being there. But, how true will it be? How close will it be to the facts at the moment they played out? What we call truth years after the fact often is little more than the most persuasive retelling of history.

Perhaps it is as Robert Caro, that superb author of classic biographies and gatherer of facts, wrote, "While I am aware that there is no truth, no objective truth, no single truth, no truth simple or unsimple, either; no verity, eternal or otherwise; no truth about anything, there are facts, objective facts, discernible and verifiable. And the more facts you accumulate, the closer you come to whatever truth there is."

But what about when journalists colorize black-and-white facts in order to support their own beliefs and prejudices? What about those journalists who, perhaps genuinely and for good reason alarmed, infuse their reporting with their valid concerns? While providing the journalists with gratifying release, such writing serves less to inform than to convince—to influence. That's the historian's turf and the columnist's. It is not the reporter's duty or prerogative.

By telling readers and viewers not simply that a president did something or other, said this or that, but speculating about his mood at the time, guessing his motivation, and assessing the outcome, journalists are moving beyond their clear-cut mandate and playing an unlicensed role.

Now that I am no longer an active journalist, I feel free to say and write the things I never would have. I have no doubt that Trump was America's arsonist-in-chief. He poured the gasoline and tossed the matches. His disdain for facts, honesty, democracy, and the Constitution led to millions of Americans falling ill and dying of COVID-19. He relentlessly attacked the press, in Soviet- and Nazi-era rhetoric, as "fake news" and "the enemy of the people." He mesmerized his followers into believing that the media, not he, were responsible for the medical and financial suffering they experienced during his administration.

The most successful purveyors of disinformation are those who abandon all pretense of truth. Not bothering with petty falsehoods, they concentrate on the outrageous Big Lie.

Thus, the Nazis accused Jews of ritually drinking the blood of Christian children. Vladimir Putin claimed that the government of Ukrainian President Volodymyr Zelensky—a Jew—was infiltrated by Nazis. Donald Trump's insistent "stop the steal" campaign lacks all evidence.

I witnessed and reported on similar bogus crusades in China, North Korea, Iran, Indonesia, India, the Philippines, and other countries. Baseless lies tend to work because they lend an aura of legitimate authority to the incipient beliefs and hatreds of those at whom they are aimed. In dictatorships like Hitler's Third Reich and Putin's Russia, the press publishes what it's ordered to.

Today's America, with Trump out of office but vilifying journalists as never before, is quickly closing the gap. If American leaders continue to molest us, threaten us, intimidate us, diminish us, our country will be well on its way to tyranny in a very short time. Stalin did it in the Soviet Union and Putin is doing it in Russia; Hitler in Germany; Mao and now Xi in China; Indira Gandhi and currently Modi in India; the Kims in North Korea; Saddam in Iraq; the mullahs in Iran; Pol Pot in Cambodia; the Assads in Syria; and Marcos in the Philippines, where it happened again under Duterte and likely will continue under Marcos' son, Bongbong.. And more, many more. Americans—those politicians and the citizens who vote for them—who unjustly smear journalists might ask survivors of those despots for their views. They didn't think it could happen there, either. Until it did.

There are good reasons why journalists are among a dictator's first targets: A free press serves the governed, not the government. A free press means an informed people. A free press means a free country.

As a defender of freedom, the journalist deserves no less regard than the soldier, the police officer, the firefighter, and other first responders. Those in uniform and those in elected office vow to protect their fellow Americans "from all enemies, foreign and domestic." Those of us in the press swear no oath. But we commit to reveal to our fellow citizens as much truth, as many facts, as we can gather, whether they like what we report or find it offensive.

Our role is not to protect the nation's leaders from the people, but to protect the people from their leaders. We commit neither to please nor to offend.

We are there, whether it's a war zone; a crime scene; a protest march; a flood; a forest fire; a late-night meeting of the zoning commission, the school board, or a White House news conference. We risk our lives, our health, our marriages because you, the reader or viewer, can't or choose not to.

We ask the questions that citizen-readers can't or choose not to, whether the person we ask them of considers them friendly or hostile. We're looking for facts, not friends. You may agree or disagree, like or dislike what we report to you. But we represent you. We live next door to you, our kids go to the same schools as yours, we shop in the same stores, and want the same safety, security, and opportunity for our families.

We are you.

Everingham, John, 174
"Exit from Phnom Penh" *(Washington Post)*, 168

Faas, Horst, 60–61, 135
Faas, Ursula, 61
Fabian Socialism, 146
"fake news," 250
FCCJ. *See* Foreign Correspondents Club of Japan
Federation of Malay, 110–11
Feldman, Edward, 87–88
Fenton, James, 160
*A Few Good Men,* 248
Fleisher, Goldie (nee Simons), 39
Foisie, Jack, 80, 121
Foisie, Phil, 121–22, 127, 129, 141
forced sterilizations, in India, 183–84
Ford, Gerald, 164, 166
*Foreign Affairs,* 118–19, 248
Foreign Correspondents Club of Japan (FCCJ), 209
foreign press correspondents: Associated Press and, 50; in Bangkok, 117; censorship during World War II of, 56; censorship of, 56; complaints about, 55–56; goal and purpose of, xv–xvi; hierarchy for, 66; Joint US Public Affairs Office and, 70. *See also* free press
France, Vietnam's independence from, 89
Frankel, Irving, 39
Freedom Fighters (Mukti Bahini), in Bangladesh, 126, 134–35
free press, freedom through, xvi
Fromm, Joe, 133
Fulbright, J. William, 120
Fuller, Keith, 53–54

Gaddafi, Muammar, 154
Gallagher, Wes, 53–54, 56–57, 62
Galman, Rolando, 2, 11–13
Gandhi, Feroze, 184–85

Gandhi, Indira, 146–57, 215, 250; assassination of, 189; censorship under, 180; Congress Party and, 150, 177–80; as dictator, 181–82; economic crises for, 151; The Emergency and, 183–84, 189; forced sterilizations under, 183–84; Gandhi, Sanjay, assault by, 184; Indo-Pak War and, 127; "Iron Lady of India," 150; marriage of, 184–85; Nixon and, 124–25; political corruption allegations against, 177–82; public protests against, 177; purchase of U.S. wheat, 150; re-election of, 189; removal from Prime Minister office, 177–80; *Washington Post* reporting on, 179, 181–82
Gandhi, Mahatma, 146
Gandhi, Rajiv, 185; assassination of, 189
Gandhi, Sanjay, 177–79; forced sterilizations under, 183–84; Gandhi, Indira, assault against, 184; as *thuggee,* 178
Garten, Jeffrey, 233
Gayler, Noel, 168
General Zia. *See* Rahman, Ziaur
genocide, in Bangladesh, 126
Gerth, Jeff, 6
Giap. *See* Vo Nguyen Giap
Godley, G. McMurtrie, 172
Gomez, Brian, 98–99
Gorbachev, Mikhail, 220
gossip. *See chismis*
Graham, Don, 63
Graham, Katherine, 63
Gray, Denis, 166
Great Britain: Indian independence from, 146; Partitioning of Pakistan and, 122–27. *See also* colonialism
"Great Leap Forward," in China, 196
Great War. *See* World War I
Green Berets, 77–78
Greenfield, James, 167
Greenway, David, 81, 159, 186
Griffin, Chrissie, 188

Griffin, G. B., 187–88
Gucco, Jesus, 10
Gulf of Tonkin, 127
Gypsies. *See* Romani peoples

Habib, Philip, 30–31, 34
Halberstam, David, 118, 169
*Hancock* (warship), 167–69
Harrison, George, 126
Hasan, Mohamad (Bob), 241
"hawking," in Singapore, 111–12
al-Hazmi, Nawaf, 107
Heath, Ted, 138
Herrera, Manuel, 23
Hersh, Seymour, 18
"Hidden Billions" (San Jose *Mercury News*), 20–21
Hindus: ethnic conflict with Muslims, 122–27; in Pakistan, 122–27
Hitchens, Christopher, 188
Hmong, 172, 174
Ho Chi Minh, 89–90
Ho Chi Minh City, Vietnam, 69. *See also* Saigon
Ho Chi Minh Trail, 85, 171
Hong Kong, 159
hotels, as correspondent meeting spots. *See specific cities*
Hoyt, Palmer, 51
Hue, Vietnam, 79–80; Marine Corps in, 84; Perfume River, 80; *La Rue Sans Joie,* 80. *See also* Tet Offensive
Huet, Henri, 62
human rights violations: in Bangladesh, 138; in China, 234–35
Hun Sen, 202
Hussein, Saddam, 244, 246, 250
Hutheesing, Khrishna, 185
Hu Yaobang, 218–19

Independent Association for Diplomatic Studies and Training, 71
India, 177–87, 189–90; All-India Radio, 153, 180; civil disobedience in, 180; Congress Party in, 150, 177–80; Dalai Lama in, 145; as dictatorship, 183; droughts in, 148–49; economic crises in, 151; economic relations with U.S., 147; The Emergency in, 183–84, 190; expulsion from, xv, 186–87; food crisis in, 147; forced sterilizations in, 183–84; Himalayan border conflict with China, 153; independence from Great Britain, 146; Indo-Pak War and, 127, 135–37, 141; in Non-Aligned Movement, 114; nuclear testing in, 153–54; Partitioning of Pakistan from, 122–27; poverty in, 148–49; Reuters in, 180; "Smiling Buddha" operation, 153–54; Soviet Union and, 124; state bureaucracy in, 132; Supreme Court in, 179; *Washington Post* correspondents in, 181. *See also* Calcutta; Gandhi, Indira; New Delhi
"India, Free 25 Years, Enjoys Stability Amid Poverty" *(Washington Post),* 146
Indochina: Communism in, 175, 193–94; French colonialism in, 59. *See also* Cambodia; Laos; Vietnam
Indonesia, 238–46; Berkeley Mafia in, 102–3; democracy in, 102; ethnic Chinese in, 102; geography of, 99; Malay in, 102; Malaysia and, 95; military violence against civilians in, 102; Muslim population in, 99; in Non-Aligned Movement, 114; poverty in, 99–100, 102
Indo-Pak War: Gandhi, Indira, and, 127; Khan, Tikka, and, 136–37; length of, 127; rape and sexual assault during, 135–36; U.S. public interest in, 141
Ingle, Bob, 18, 204–6, 210
Iran, 155, 164, 201
Iraq, 70, 164, 201, 246
"Iron Lady of India," 150
Islamabad, Pakistan, 155

Jackson, Harris, 247

Jakarta, Indonesia: emigration to, 101; *The Year of Living Dangerously,* 102

January 6th attacks, on U.S. Capitol, 24

Japan, 207–14; collectivism in, 207; declining birth rates in, 231; economic growth of, 207, 229–30; "Education Mother" in, 212; Foreign Correspondents Club of Japan, 209; individualism in, 207, 211–12; Liberal Democratic Party in, 230–31; in Malaysia, 110; Rape of Nanjing, 217; Reagan, Ronald, and, 213; return to, 229–30; salarymen in, 230; in Singapore, 110; social conformity as culture of, 212; social norms in, 231; trade imbalance with U.S., 212–13; Trump in, 209

*Japan as Number One* (Vogel), 207

*Japan Times,* 208

Jewish communities: New York University and, 45–46; in Paterson, New Jersey, 38–40, 43–44. *See also* anti-Semitism

Jiang Kai Shek, 227

John Paul II (Pope), 4

Johnson, Lyndon, 56; decision to not seek re-election, 93–94; Lee Kuan Yew and, 113; Vietnam War and, 93–94

Joint US Public Affairs Office (JUSPAO), 70

journalism: under authoritarian leaders, 250; bottom-up, 100–101; in Manila, 30; opinion in U.S., 140; political change influenced by, xvi–xvii; public role of, 247–51; public trust in, xvi; social change influenced by, xvi–xvii; top-down, 100–101. *See also* foreign press correspondents; free press

Juliano-Agrava, Corazon (Rosie), 11–14, 23

JUSPAO. *See* Joint US Public Affairs Office

Kanga, J. G., 149

Kapunan, Eduardo (Red), 29

Kapunan, Linda, 29

Karnow, Stanley, 6, 169

Kaul, Triloki Nath, 181

Kazer, Audrey, 223

KBL Party, in Philippines, 25

Kehler, Randy, 119

Kennedy, Jackie, 9

Kennedy, Ted, 125

Kerry, John, 29

Khan, Abdul Qadeer, 154

Khan, Peter, 167

Khan, Tikka, 136–37

Khe Sanh, Vietnam: Charlie Med (U.S. field hospital), 87; Marine Corps in, 85–86, 90–91; North Vietnamese Army in, xv, 85–86; siege of, 84–89; Tet Offensive and, xv; U.S. military failures in, 88–89; Viet Cong in, xv; Vo Nguyen Giap and, 85–86, 91

Khmer Rouge, in Cambodia, 160–63, 196–201; death count under, 198; in *Washington Post,* 199–200

Khomeini, Ayatollah, 154

Khoy, Saukham, 161, 166

Killing Fields, of Cambodia, 165, 198

*The Killing Fields,* 167

King, Martin Luther, Jr., assassination of, 92

Kissinger, Henry, 118, 188; Bangladesh and, 138; Blood Telegram, 125–26; Lee Kuan Yew and, 115; Mao Zedong and, 125; Prince Sihanouk and, 115; "Secret War" of, 172, 201; Yahya Khan and, 125

Kittakachorn, Thanom, 192

Knight-Ridder Company, 203–14; correspondent team created by, 27; Pulitzer Prizes won by, 36. *See also* San Jose *Mercury News; specific newspapers*

Kopff, Gary, 259

Koro Syndrome, 103

Krim, Jonathan, 17–18, 27, 36

Kuala Lumpur, Malaysia, 95–96; Associated Press in, 98; civil unrest in, 104–5; colonial Brit population in, 98; cosmopolitanism of, 98–99; criminal laws in, 104; Sharia law in, 108
Kundnani, Hans, 228
Kurds, 164
Kushner, Jared, 23

labor strikes, Brotherhood of Railway Signalmen, 52
"Land of Smiles," 193
Landon, Michael, 174
Lansdale, Edward, 169
Laos: CIA in, 173; Communism in, 175, 193–94; Communist takeover of, 175; cultural revolution in, 174; Hmong in, 172, 174; Ho Chi Minh Trail, 85; People's Revolutionary Party, 175; USAID in, 173; war in, 170, 172–75
Larouche, Lyndon, 118
Laurent, Michael, 135
Laurie, Jim, 2
Lawrence, James Vinton, 172–73
Laxalt, Paul, 23–24, 34–35
Lazaro, Manuel, 14
Lazarus, Emma, 43
le Carré, John, 159
Lee Hsien Loong, 115
Lee Kuan Yew, 109–16, 228; Asian values for, 115; attempted bribes by CIA, 112–13; as benevolent dictator, 116; Chinese government policies influenced by, 115; criminal laws under, 112; Johnson and, 113; Kissinger and, 115; People's Action Party and, 112–13; as puritanically incorruptible, 109
Leith, Brian, 259
Lenderking, Bill, 71–72
Leonard, Sugar Ray, 44
Lescaze, Lee, 127
Leslie, Jacques, 161–62, 182

Liberal Democratic Party, in Japan, 230–31
*Life,* 145
Lifschultz, Larry, 187–88
Lilley, Jim, 227
Lindenauer, Margie, 50
Long, Gia, 80
Lon Nol, 161
Lord, Bette Bao, 222
Lord, Winston, 221–22
*Los Angeles Times,* 56, 80, 121, 161–62, 201–2
*Love is Forever,* 174
Luce, Clare Booth, 117
Luce, Henry, 117
Lugar, Richard, 27–30

MacArthur, Douglas, 5
Magsaysay, Ramon, 8
Mahathir bin Mohamad, Tun, 106–7; anti-Semitism of, 107
Malacañang Palace, 4; Marcos, Ferdinand, sequestration in, 33
Malay (ethnic group): in Indonesia, 102; in Malaysia, 107
*The Malay Dilemma* (Mahathir bin Mohamad), 106–7
Malaysia, 95–108; *amok,* 103–4; Arabs in, 107; brain drain from, 106; as British colony, 110; emigration from, 106; ethnic Chinese in, 96; ethnic conflict in, 95–96; in Federation of Malay, 110; historical development of, 96; independence for, 95; Indonesia and, 95; Japanese invasion and occupation of, 110; Johore State royal family in, 96; Koro Syndrome in, 103; Malay in, 107, 110; Muslims in, 108; Penang, 103; race riots in, 110; Reuters in, 97; Singapore expelled from, 110–11; socioeconomic reforms in, 106–7; *Straits Times,* 96–97; strategic location of, 110; terrorist cells in,

107; traditional dress in, 108. *See also* Kuala Lumpur
Man, Lathi, 182
Manafort, Paul, 24
Mangold, Tom, 67
Manila, Philippines, 1–36; Baclaran Church, 29; calls for civil disobedience in, 30; *chismis* in, 16–17, 20, 22; as City of Man, 4–5; Coconut Palace in, 4; Cultural Center of the Philippines, 4–5; Malacañang Palace, 4, 33; military during contested presidential election, 31–33; municipal building projects in, 4–5; poverty in, 4; press corps in, 30; public riots in, 1; urban blight in, 4; voting crowds for presidential election in, 26–27. *See also* Marcos, Ferdinand
*Manila Times,* 8
Mansfield, Mike, 212
Mantle, Mickey, 44
Mao Zedong, 7, 196, 219, 250; Cultural Revolution under, 254; Kissinger and, 125; Nixon and, 125
Marcos, Bongbong, 25, 36
Marcos, Ferdinand E., 1–36, 249, 250; Aquino, Benigno, Jr., as political rival, 2; Aquino, Corazon, as political rival, 9–10; Aquino family relationship with, 3–4; assassination commission created by, 11–14; calls for resignation of, 29; Chua and, 5–6; concession to election loss, 34; dollar salting and, 17; early family life, 5–6; election campaign for, 25–31; election to presidency, 6; fake military record, 6; financial corruption of, 4; health issues for, 12; marriage to Imelda, 7–8; martial law under, 6; national military as personal bodyguard for, 15; political assassinations of Aquino, Benigno, under, 1–3; political exile in U.S., 35; political opposition to,

6; public demonstrations against, 10–11; public exaggerations by, 27; public response to assassination commission, 14; Reagan, Ronald, and political support of, 6, 10, 23–25, 28, 30, 34; Reform the Armed Forces Movement and, 14–15
Marcos, Imelda, 4, 11, 24–25; Aquino, Benigno, Jr., and, 8; Bernstein, Joseph, and, 18–20, 22; Bernstein, Ralph, and, 18–20, 22; Cultural Center of the Philippines and, 4–5; financial corruption of, 4; marriage to Ferdinand, 7–8; *Mercury News* stories on, 16–21; municipal building projects by, 4–5; political power of, 6–7; real estate holdings for, 16–20
Marine Corps, U.S., 82; in Hue, 84; in Khe Sanh, 85–86, 90–91; Reserve Troops, 46–48
Marshall Plan, 118
martial law: in Cambodia, 165; under Ferdinand Marcos, 6
*Marty* (Chayefsky), 39
Matak, Sirik (Prince), 166
Matthews, Jay, 201–2
Matthews, Linda, 201–2
McCoy, Alfred W., 6
McCulloch, Frank, 169
McGovern, George, 196
McNamara, Robert, 118, 120
Mehta, Ved, 184
Menand, Louis, 249
*Mercury News. See* San Jose *Mercury News*
Mesa, Amulfo de, 2–3
*Miami Herald,* 27, 51, 204, 215, 226
*Midnight Massacre in Dacca* (Dasgupta), 187
al-Mihdhar, Khalid, 107
Miller, Judith, 246
Minh, Duong Van "Big," 170
Modi, Narendra, 183, 250
Mody, Piloo, 180
Mody, Vin, 180

Mondale, Walter, 26
Monet, Claude, 21
money laundering: dollar salting,
    17; through offshore holding
    companies, 21
Mother Teresa, 137
Moynihan, Liz, 152
Moynihan, Pat, 152, 185
Mujib. *See* Rahman, Sheikh Mujibur
Mukti Bahini. *See* Freedom Fighters
*Murder of a Gentle Land* (Barron and
    Paul), 199
Murrow, Edward R., 117–18
Muslims: Baharis, 135; in Bangladesh,
    126, 135; ethnic conflict with
    Hindus, 122–27; in Indonesia, 99; in
    Malaysia, 108; in Pakistan, 122–27;
    Sunni Muslims, 126
Mustaque Ahmed, Khondaker, 187
My Lai Massacre, 18

Naraya, Jayaprakash, 180
*National Geographic,* 90, 238–46, 253
NATO. *See* North Atlantic Treaty
    Organization
Naughton, Jim, 204–5
NBC News, 56
Nehru, Jawarharlal, 153, 185; Fabian
    Socialist philosophy of, 146. *See also*
    Gandhi, Indira
Neufeld, Peter, 183
New Delhi, India, 129–30, 141–57;
    Ashoka Hotel, 131, 182; bribing of
    officials by journalists, 144; "Delhi
    Belly," 152; physical response to
    environment, 143, 152; *Washington
    Post* bureau in, 141, 144
"New Order," in Cambodia, 196
New Society Movement, 25
*Newsweek,* 49–50, 199
*New Yorker,* 184
*New York Times,* 6, 22, 48, 71,
    84, 167, 246
*New York Times Sunday Magazine,* 199
New York University, 45–46

Ngo Dinh Diem, 7
Ngo Dinh Nhu (Madame), 7
Nicholson, Jack, 248
9/11 attacks, 107, 243–44
Ninoy. *See* Aquino, Benigno, Jr.
Nitisastro, Widjojo, 102–3
Nixon, Richard: Bangladesh and, 138;
    China and, 125–26; Gandhi, Indira,
    and, 124–25; India and, 124–25;
    Mao Zedong and, 125; resignation
    of, 177; Sime and, 44
Noguchi, Isamu, 53
Non-Aligned Movement, 114
Norgaard, Noland ("Boots"), 52
North Atlantic Treaty Organization
    (NATO), 118
North Vietnam, Reunification Day, 69
North Vietnamese Army (NVA), 62–63,
    76; in Khe Sanh, xv, 85–86; murder
    of civilians by, 82
Novak, Robert, 25–26
Nunn, Sam, 243
NVA. *See* North Vietnamese Army

Office of Strategic Services (OSS), 89
Ohmae, Kenichi, 233
*Okinawa* (warship), 167–69
one-worldism, 118
Ongpin, Jaime, 27
Operation Eagle Pull, 164
Ople, Blas, 22
Orendain, Joan, 15, 30
Ortega, Carmen, 7
OSS. *See* Office of Strategic Services
Overseas Chinese, 231–35; indigenous
    attacks against, 232–33
Overseas Press Club of America Award
    for Excellence, 214

Pachundkar, Baban, 148–49
Pahlavi, Shah Reza, 17, 154
Pakistan: Awami League, 123; Awed
    Bengalis in, 123–24; Bhutto in, 134,
    138, 154, 155–57; during Cold War,
    124; ethnic conflicts and violence in,

122–27; Hindus in, 122–27; Indo-
Pak War and, 127, 135–37, 141;
Mujib in, 123–24; Muslims in, 122–
27; Partitioning of, 122–27; rape and
sexual assault as element of official
policies in, 136; Urdu language in,
123; as U.S. ally, 124
Pamaran, Manuel, 23
*Paris Match,* 199
Partitioning, of Pakistan, 122–27
Paterson, New Jersey, 37–44; Jewish
community in, 38–40, 43–44;
Romani peoples in, 38; social
interactions with non-Jews, 41
*Paterson Evening News,* 42
Paul, Anthony, 199
Payne, Oliver, 238, 244
Pearlstein, Norman, 237
Pelletreau, Nancy, 129–30
Penang, Malaysia, 103
Pencayte, John, 67
*Pentagon Papers,* 119–21
People Power, in Philippines, 5, 32
People's Action Party, in
Singapore, 112–13
People's Liberation Army, in China,
221–22, 226
People's Revolutionary Party,
in Laos, 175
Pham Xuan An, 169
*Philadelphia Inquirer,* 27, 84, 204
Philippines: *barong tagalog* in, 14;
Bataan Peninsula, 28; colonial
history of, 6; Communist
Hukbalahap in, 4; Communist New
People's Army in, 3; dollar salting
in, 17; economic collapse in, 4; KBL
Party in, 25; mixed public response
to U.S. intervention, 5; New Society
Movement in, 25; People Power
in, 5, 32; poverty in, 4; presidential
election in, 26–28; Reform the
Armed Forces Movement in, 14–15,
30–32; Roman Catholic Church in,
31; Sandiganbayan Court in, 22–23;

*Separate Report of the Chairman,*
14; *utang na loob* in, 21. *See also*
Manila; Marcos, Ferdinand
Phnom Penh, Cambodia, 160–64;
evacuation of, 164; Operation
Eagle Pull in, 164; Le Royal
Hotel, 131, 160
Phomvihane, Kaison, 175
Plain of Jars, bombing of, 171–72
political assassinations. *See*
assassinations
Pol Pot. *See* Sar, Saloth
Ponchaud, François, 199
poverty: in India, 148–49; in Indonesia,
99–100, 102; in Philippines, 4; in
Vietnam, 100
Powell, Colin, 246
Pramoj, Kukrit, 161
Pran, Dith, 167
Pratt, Harold, 118
presidential elections, in Philippines,
26–28; military response during,
31–33; voter fraud during, 28;
voter intimidation during, 28; voter
suppression during, 28
*Providence Journal,* 48
Pulitzer Prize, for journalism: for
Arnett, P., 61; for Associated Press
correspondents, 62; Knight-Ridder
Company and, 36; for *Philadelphia
Inquirer,* 84; San Jose *Mercury News*
and, 1, 36; *Wall Street Journal,* 167
Putin, Vladimir, 250

Qiang Qiang, 7

race riots: in Malaysia, 110; in
Singapore, 110. *See also* ethnic
conflicts and violence
Rahman, Sheikh Mujibur (Mujib),
155, 186–87; assassination of, 187;
as Father of the Country, 123–24;
political assassinations of family
members, 187; release from prison,
134; return to Bangladesh, 138–40

Rahman, Tunku Abdul, 96–97, 106, 110–11
Rahman, Ziaur (General Zia), 187
RAM. *See* Reform the Armed Forces Movement
Ramos, Fidel (Eddie), 14–15, 23, 30–32, 36
Rangoon, Myanmar, 131
Rangsey, 196–97
Rani, Abdur, 240–41
rape and sexual assault, 135–38; during Indo-Pak War, 135–36; as official policies in Pakistan, 136
Rape of Nanjing, 217
Razak, Tun Abdul, 106
*Reader's Digest,* 54, 199
Reagan, Nancy, 34
Reagan, Ronald: Japan and, 213; Mondale and, 26; political support for Ferdinand Marcos, 6, 10, 23–25, 28, 30, 32
Reform the Armed Forces Movement (RAM), 14–15, 30
Reuters, 55, 169; in India, 180; in Malaysia, 97
riots. *See* civil unrest
ritual cannibalism, in Cambodia, 162
Roberts, Gene, 84
Robertson, Pat, 118
*Rocky Mountain News,* 52
Roman Catholic Church, in Philippines, 31
Romani peoples, 38
Rosenthal, Joe, 214
La Rue Sans Joie (The Street Without Joy), in Hue, Vietnam, 80
Rutgers University, 45

Safavian, Sasan, 244
Saigon, Vietnam: Associated Press offices in, 60–61, 79–80; Caravelle Hotel, 60; CBS News offices in, 60; Continental Hotel, 131; fall of, 69; French colonial influences in, 59;

North Vietnam attacks in, 79. *See also specific people; specific topics*
salarymen, in Japan, 230
Salim, Emil, 102–3
Samnang, Pen, 162
Samphan, Khieu, 199
Sandiganbayan Court, in Philippines, 22–23
San Jose *Mercury News:* assassination of Benigno Aquino and, 10, 17–18; Ceppos and, 1, 18, 205–6; copyrighting of news story, 13–14; "Enter the Dragon," 233; global reputation of, 25; "Hidden Billions," 20–21; Ingle and, 18, 204–6, 210; journalistic reputation of, 204–5; Krim and, 17–18, 27, 36; local Filipino response to, 18; Pulitzer Prizes, 1, 36; real estate holdings for Imelda Marcos, 16–21
Santos, Dante G., 12–14
Sar, Saloth (Pol Pot), 170, 196. *See also* Khmer Rouge
Saunders, Harold, 187
Saxbe, William, 185
Schanberg, Syd, 167
Schurz, Carl, 88
"Secret War," in Cambodia, Kissinger and, 172, 201
Seiderman, Carol (nee Simons): at *AARP,* 238; American Chamber of Commerce in Japan and, 229; in Bangkok, 191; in China, 216, 224–25, 227; at Columbia University, 49; at *Denver Post,* 51–52; health scare, 255; in Japan, 207, 210–11; in Kuala Lumpur, 95, 104, 108; in New Delhi, 142–43, 151, 182; in Saigon, 79; at *The 21st Century,* 54; in Washington D. C., 204, 237–38
*Separate Report of the Chairman,* 14
Seton, Adolph (Al), 48–49
sexual assault. *See* rape and sexual assault

"Shanghai Massacre." *See*
"White Terror"
Shankar, Ravi, 126
Shaplen, Bob, 169
Sharia law, in Kuala Lumpur, 108
Sheehan, Neil, 169
Sherman, William Tecumseh, 93
Siddiqui, Kadir "Tiger," 135
Sihanouk (Prince), 159, 165
Sime, David, 43–44
Simons, Abe, 39
Simons, Adam, 204, 207, 212, 216,
224–25, 227
Simons, Becca, 151, 216
Simons, Howard, 205
Simons, Justine, 96, 216, 256
Simons, Louis, 39
Sin, Jaime (Cardinal), 31–32
Sinclair, Upton, 18
Singapore: Asian values in, 115;
Associated Press in, 116; civil unrest
in, 106; criminal laws in, 111–12;
democracy in, 115; economic growth
in, 111; expulsion from Federation
of Malay, 110–11; expulsion from
Malaysia, 110–11; "hawking" in,
111–12; Japanese occupation of, 110;
in Non-Aligned Movement, 114;
People's Action Party in, 112–13;
race riots in, 110. *See also* Lee Kuan
Yew; Malaysia
Singh, S. K., 157
Sison, Maria Luisa, 28
Sisters of Charity, 137
"Smiling Buddha" operation, in
India, 153–54
*Smithsonian,* 204
Solarz, Stephen, 21–22, 36, 188
Sonnenfeldt, Helmut, 118
Sophonpanich, Choedchu, 234
South Korea, 232
Soviet Union: China and, 90; India
and, 124; weaponry during
Vietnam War, 77
*Sports Illustrated,* 44

*St. Louis* (warship), 48
Stockwin, Harvey, 105
Stone, Roger, 24
*Straits Times,* 96–97
The Street Without Joy. *See* La
Rue Sans Joie
Suan, Mach, 197–98
Suharto, 241–42; as dictator, 99;
political corruption of, 102;
wife of, 7
Sullivan, Bill, 17
Sullivan, William H., 172
Sun Kening, 221
Sunni Muslims, in Bangladesh, 126–27
Sun Tzu, 90
Swinton, Stan, 117
Syria, 164

Taiwan, 232
Tan, Abby, 10, 15, 23, 35
Tan Boo Thien, 99
Tarbell, Ida, 18
Tet Offensive: Khe Sanh and, xv;
military policy influenced by, 84;
tactical post-analysis of, 83–84
Thailand: CIA in, 194; colonial history
in, 191; cultural festivals in, 193;
as "Land of Smiles," 193; political
history of, 192; rebellions in, 192–
93. *See also* Bangkok
*This Week With David Brinkley,* 24
Tibet: China's treatment of, 145. *See
also* Dalai Lama
"Tie a Yellow Ribbon Round the Ole
Oak Tree," 9
Tien, 7
Tienanmen Square Massacre, 218–28;
Deng Xiaopeng and, 219, 228;
military response to, 223–25; role
of students in, 219; U.S. response
to, 227–28
Tiger Cub economies, 232. *See
also* Malaysia; Philippines;
Thailand; Vietnam
*Time,* 30, 81, 169, 199, 204, 237

top-down journalism, 100–101
*The Trial of Henry Kissinger*
    (Hitchens), 188
Truman, Harry, 119–20
Truman, Preston, 245
Trump, Donald, 19, 24, 50, 248; The
    Big Lie and, 250; in Japan, 209;
    Modi comparisons to, 183; opinion
    journalism and, 140; on power,
    190; public exaggerations by, 27;
    treatment of journalists by, 250
Tuckman, Bob, 58–59, 62
*Tufts Daily,* 49
*The Tunnels of Cu Chi,* 67
Turkey, 164
Twain, Mark, 161
*The 21st Century,* 54
Twining, Charles, 199–200

Ulevich, Neal, 193
United Press International (UPI), 55
United States (U.S.): Aquino, Corazon,
    in, 9; "Dark Winter" scenario
    exercise, 243–44; history of failed
    international agreements with, 166;
    India and, 147; January 6th attacks
    in, 24; Marcos, Ferdinand, in, 35;
    as nation in decline, 248; opinion
    journalism in, 140; Pakistan and,
    124; in Philippines, 5; Philippines
    as colony of, 6; public trust in
    journalism in, xvi; Special Forces
    during Vietnam War, 78; Tienanmen
    Square Massacre and, 227–28; trade
    imbalance with Japan, 212–13;
    weaponry during Vietnam War,
    77–78. *See also* Air Force; Central
    Intelligence Agency; Marine Corps;
    *specific wars*
UPI. *See* United Press International
Urdu language, in Pakistan, 123
U.S. *See* United States
USAID, in Laos, 173
*U.S. News and World Report,*
    132–33, 220

Ut, Nick, 62
*utang na loob* (blood debt
    obligation), 21

*Vanity Fair,* 223
Van Pao, 172–73
VC. *See* Viet Cong
Ver, Fabian, 11, 13–15, 18, 30, 36
Verghese, Bobbili George, 178
Viet Cong (VC), 62–63; in Khe Sanh,
    xv; murder of civilians by, 82;
    tunnels of, 67–69
Vietnam: Arnett, P., in, 75; black market
    economy in, 65; cemeteries in,
    72–73; Chinese incursion in, 202;
    Chinese influences in, 89; collapse
    of, 170–73; Communism in, 193–94;
    financial corruption in, 65; first
    arrival in, 58; Gulf of Tonkin, 127;
    Hmong in, 172; Ia Drang Valley, 76;
    independence from France, 89; Plain
    of Jars bombing in, 171–72; poverty
    in, 100. *See also* Ho Chi Minh City;
    Khe Sanh; Saigon; Vietnam War
Vietnam War: Agent Orange chemical
    attacks, 89; Bangkok during, 192;
    Ban Me Thuot, 75–76, 78–79;
    casualty counts, 70; censorship
    of foreign press correspondents
    during, 57; Danang, 80; Dien Bien
    Phu, 85–86; Dong Ha combat
    base, 72–73; Ho Chi Minh Trail,
    85, 171; Hue, 79–80, 84; Johnson
    administration and, 93–94; Joint
    US Public Affairs Office during,
    70; military hawks' response to,
    120; My Lai Massacre, 18; social
    conflicts over, 92–93; U.S. Air
    Force in, 86; U.S. Marine Corps
    in, 82, 84–86; U.S. Special Forces,
    78; Vietnamization of, 93–94; war
    correspondents embedded with
    troops during, 71; weaponry during,
    77; Westmoreland and, 56, 62–65.
    *See also* Army of the Republic

of Vietnam; North Vietnamese
Army; Viet Cong
*Village Voice,* 22
Villegas, Bernardo, 17
Vogel, Ezra, 207
Vo Nguyen Giap (Giap), 85–86, 91
Vyatkina, Olga, 244

*Wall Street Journal,* 167, 237
Washington, D.C., 203–4, 237–38
*Washington Post,* 15, 22–23, 56, 63,
120, 220; in Bangkok, Thailand,
closing of bureau in, 201; Bradlee
and, 167, 181, 201, 213; bribing
of officials by, 144; "Exit from
Phnom Penh," 168; expulsion of
correspondents from India, 186–87;
foreign coverage desk at, 121; on
Gandhi, Indira, political corruption
allegations against, 179–82; "India,
Free 25 Years, Enjoys Stability Amid
Poverty," 146; in India, 181; Khmer
Rouge reporting by, 199–200; in
New Delhi, 141, 144
*Water-Lily Pond* (Monet), 21
weaponry, during Vietnam War: from
Soviet Union, 77; from U.S., 77–78
Weapons of Mass Destruction
(WMD), 244–46
Webb, Kate, 75
*We Nehrus* (Hutheesing), 185
Westmoreland, William, 56, 62–65, 85
Wheeler, John, 86
White, Ed, 78–79

*White House Years* (Kissinger), 188
"White Terror" (Shanghai Massacre), in
China, 227
Wikileaks, 185
Wilson, Woodrow, 39
wire services, 55. *See also* Associated
Press; Reuters
WMD. *See* Weapons of Mass
Destruction
Woods, Lillias, 208
Woodward, Bob, 120, 190
World War I (Great War), 39
World War II (WW II): Bataan Death
March, 28; censorship of foreign
correspondents during, 56; Ho Chi
Minh, 89–90; Marshall Plan after,
118; Office of Strategic Services
during, 89
World Wildlife Fund, 240
WW II. *See* World War II

Xi Jinping, 250

Yabut, Nemesio, 19
Yahya Khan, Agha Muhammad, 124–25
Yamashita, Michael, 239
Yamazaki, Naoko, 210
*The Year of Living Dangerously,* 102
Yong, Catherine Leong Sow, 97
Young, Kenneth, 118

Zelensky, Volodymyr, 250
Zielenziger, Michael, 232, 256
Zimmerman, Paul, 50

# About the Author

**Pulitzer Prize winner Lewis M. Simons** began his career as a foreign correspondent in 1967, at the height of the Vietnam War. He saw the war through to the end, covering the fall of the neighboring states of Cambodia and Laos.

Since then, he has reported on some of the most far-reaching developments in politics, economics, civil unrest, and social conditions throughout much of the world. His beat spanned India, Pakistan, Afghanistan and Bangladesh; Iraq and Iran; China; Japan; North Korea and South Korea; as well as the former Soviet Union. He was a staff correspondent for The Associated Press, the *Washington Post*, Knight Ridder Newspapers, and *Time* and wrote major stories for *National Geographic*.

In 1986 Simons and two colleagues at the San Jose *Mercury News* won the Pulitzer Prize for International Reporting for exposing the billions the Marcos family looted from the Philippines. "Your series made history," wrote the late US Representative Stephen Solarz. Columbia University cited the articles as among the fifty best in fifty years. Simons was also a two-time Pulitzer finalist, and has received numerous other journalism awards, including the George Polk and the University of Missouri's Investigative Reporters and Editors. He was the Edward R. Murrow Fellow of the Council on Foreign Relations.

Simons's op-ed and analytical articles have been published in the *New York Times*, the *Washington Post*, *Foreign Affairs*, *Atlantic*, and *Smithsonian* magazines. His work has also appeared in *USA Today*, where he is a member of the Board of Contributors, and in online media, including the *Huffington Post*, the *Daily Beast*, *Daily Kos*, Yaleglobal.com, and *Columbia Journalism Review*. He has been on ABC, NBC, MSNBC, CNN, BBC, and CBC.

He is the author of *Worth Dying For: A Pulitzer Prize Winner's Account of the Philippine Revolution,* coauthor with Senator Christopher S. Bond of *The Next Front: Southeast Asia and the Road to Global Peace with Islam*, and a contributing author of half a dozen books on war and international affairs.

Simons served in the Marine Corps Reserve. He is married to fellow journalist Carol Simons. They have three adult children and reside in Washington, DC.

CPSIA information can be obtained
at www.ICGtesting.com
Printed in the USA
BVHW041319150922
646976BV00001B/1

9 781538 173169